Fixing
the Planet

An Overview for
Optimists and Activists

Michael Norton

Praise for Planet

'We are standing on the edge of an industrial in energy, in transport, in food and farming and within society itself, that one hundred years from now they will describe this moment as a liberation ... This book is a powerful introduction to the way things were and the way things can be. Keep it by your bed.'

Tim Smit, founder of The Eden Project

'This book gives you all the information anyone could want about the state of the world and how to save it. Michael Norton's gripping read, filled with a wealth of facts, will arm you in any discussion, teenagers and adult alike who want to make the case for rescuing the planet. This will give you hope for what can still be done, if we all act now.'

Polly Toynbee, *Guardian*

'A fantastic panorama of how to right the wrongs of the world, packed full of examples of everyday people taking action and making change every day. If you ever doubted you could make a difference – read this and you'll know you can!'

Dawn Austwick, former CEO, National Lottery Community Fund

'Humankind's body politic is being ravaged by an advanced form of necrotising fasciitis called "profit maximising neoliberalism". But the antibodies we need to see off this wasting disease are getting stronger by the day – as *Fixing the Planet* so eloquently makes clear.'

Jonathon Porritt, co-founder Forum for the Future

'A wonderfully accessible encyclopaedia of facts, examples and inspirations that can serve as an antidote to the fatalism that is perhaps our biggest risk today.'

Geoff Mulgan, Professor of Collective Intelligence, Public Policy and Social Innovation, University College London

'This is BRILLIANT!'

Sharla-Jaye Duncan, founder The Intrapreneurs Club

1 3 5 7 9 10 8 6 4 2

First published in 2022 by September Publishing

Copyright © Centre for Innovation in Voluntary Action
(charity number 1122095) 2022

Designed by Emily Sear

Printed in Denmark on paper from responsibly managed,
sustainable sources by Nørhaven

ISBN 9781914613111

September Publishing
septemberpublishing.org

Forces of destruction

Resources for good?

The kind of hope I often think about …

'**Either we have hope within us, or we don't … [hope] is an orientation of the spirit … it transcends the world … it is anchored somewhere beyond its horizons … it is not the same as joy that things are going well, or a willingness to invest in enterprises that are obviously headed for early success; but rather an ability to work for something because it is good, and not just because it stands a chance to succeed.'**

– Václav Havel, playwright and first president of the post-communist Czech Republic, speaking in 1990

I started writing this book in March 2020, during the first week of the Covid-19 lockdown in the UK. It was a really good time to reflect on the state of our planet. The global economy was shuddering towards a huge recession. Our streets had almost emptied, our skies were aeroplane-free. The air was fresher and in our cities we could hear the birds singing. The price of oil had collapsed and for the first time carbon emissions had fallen (temporarily) below what is needed to keep within the 1.5°C target for limiting global warming.

Has the Covid-19 pandemic given us pause for thought? Do we really want to go back to where we were when it's over? Or might we find ways of creating a cleaner, greener and much better world, for ourselves and for everybody else on the planet?

Today there are 7.8 billion of us, more than 1,500 times what the population was 7,000 years ago. We have not just spread around the planet but, with our brains and creativity, we have come to dominate the world for our own benefit, hunting and killing wild animals to extinction, turning the natural environment into farmland for growing the animals and the crops that we need to feed ourselves. We have moved from being hunter-gatherers to urban dwellers living in settlements, then in towns, then in cities and now in megacities. We developed the technologies for doing all of this more effectively first with iron and coal, and now using nuclear and solar power and many emerging technologies, which together give us the ability to mould the world to meet our human needs. We are now in an age that people are calling 'the Anthropocene' – a new geological epoch in which humans are having a significant impact on the Earth and its ecosystems.

The Anthropocene could be the era in which humans are able to create 'the best of all possible worlds'. But instead, we might be heading towards 'the uninhabitable Earth' – which is the title of a 2019 bestselling book by David Wallace-Wells.

We have all the resources that we need to make a better world. We have lots and lots of ideas for doing things better. There are new technologies we can mobilise. There is the prospect of abundant energy using ever-cheaper renewable sources. We can come together through social networks and meet together remotely using Zoom conferencing, rather than spending so much time travelling on gridlocked roads and in public transport bursting at the seams. We can enhance our human capacity using artificial intelligence, machine learning, robotics and nanotechnologies. We were able to splash out trillions on mitigating the Covid-19 pandemic; the money was found because it was seen as an emergency. We developed vaccines in superfast time because we needed to protect ourselves. We know that we have all the financial resources, all the creativity and all the energy to be able to solve the world's problems. But we will only be able to do this if we can find ways of deploying these better.

In this book, I want to show many of the ways in which things are being done badly. Inequality is increasing, which sustains poverty and makes the world poorer for all of us. Disease can spread around the world at terrific speed, as we are now seeing. We can conquer disease, but only by acting together. We are wasting far too much of our resources on war and terror, and we are locking far too many people up, some of them completely innocent. We abuse our bodies through the food we eat and the substances we ingest. And we are trashing the planet with our waste and our CO_2 emissions.

I will try to describe these and other problems in simple terms and provide a miscellany of facts drawn from a variety of sources – not all are up to date and some are hard to measure. But it does not matter if they are a few per cent out this way or that way, as they indicate the scale of the problem and the urgency for doing something. Many of the 40 chapters start with a map or a table illustrating an issue covered in the chapter, showing which countries are doing the worst and sometimes also those that are doing the best – whether it is drug-taking or population growth or nuclear weapons.

I also include stories of hope, of people who are trying to address a big problem with their own big idea. Most of them are 'ordinary people', not unicorn start-ups with tens of millions of Silicon Valley venture capital behind them and expectations of making huge profits. Many are people I have come across in my work, whom I know and respect. I want to show that we can all make a difference – each and every one of us – with our ideas and our creativity, plus of course the energy to get off our backsides and actually do something. You may think that the difference you can make is tiny compared with the scale of the problem. But what you do will make a difference, and if millions of others also do something it will multiply into real change. By doing something, you might also inspire others and you will show governments and business that it is also an issue that they should care about. The more of us who act, even on a small scale, the more likely it will be that a better world is within our grasp.

We should be optimistic about our future and our children's future. Rather than rushing headlong towards climate catastrophe, we should be looking to a future with birdsong rather than a 'Silent Spring'. There should be 'No Going Back', no going back to the complacency and carelessness of the pre-Covid-19 world, but we should emerge differently through what we have learned from the pandemic and living in lockdown.

Can we put a halt to global warming or even reverse the process? Can we find solutions that will make our lives more sustainable and the future of our life on this planet more secure? Can we create a world in which we all work together to make life better for all of us? Do we have the collective will and cohesion to do this? Do we have enough time? These are some of the big questions that this book will explore.

Michael Norton
London, March 2022

Amy says ...

I am Amy Bray, the 19-year-old founder of conservation charity
Another Way. As a teenager, I dedicated my life to marine
conservation and tackling climate change. Throughout my last
years at school, I skipped a couple of afternoons a week to go
into other schools in Cumbria and beyond to talk about the impact
of plastic pollution on our health and on marine life and what we,
as young people, can do to tackle this. For example, I have been
single-use-plastic free for the past four years. I am also vegan, I
don't take flights and I only buy second-hand clothes. Another
Way has planted 12,000 trees, runs two zero-waste shops and
inspires people to live more sustainably. So often, I hear people
saying 'What can we really do as individuals?', or 'How can our
actions make any difference when companies and governments
are responsible for so much?'

The thing is, tackling the climate and ecological crisis – and
indeed the health crisis, inequality and poverty, and so many
more issues – is going to require all of us to do something,
whether through changing our diet, joining a local campaign to
add our voice or being mindful of how our every action impacts
the environment. I might think that young people shouldn't be
expected to fix the future when adults are in power. But blame
and anger are not going to solve anything. If we can turn our fear
and fury into action, then this can pave the way towards a better
future for all who live on our beautiful planet Earth.

Amy Bray, founder of Another Way

Ayrton says …

As Michael's book makes clear, there are lots of problems that
we need to solve. Some, such as climate change, are so vast and
complex that they seem beyond the scope of any one person to
make a serious impact. But, as the many examples in this book
show, it's astonishing what people can really achieve when we
put our minds to doing something. I have been campaigning on a
wide range of issues since I was nine, including homelessness,
factory farming, food and water security, conflict minerals and
cyberbullying. I am now 18 and I have learned that it really is
possible to make a difference.

I believe that the greatest lever for change lies within ourselves. For
example, if I see greed at the heart of a problem I care about, I will
try to become more generous; where lack of empathy is the key
factor, I will try to be as compassionate as I can. Never believe
anyone who tells you that you can't make a difference – I have
seen again and again that even quite small actions can have an
impact. I have also directly seen the power of youth and how the
passion and the energy that we bring can be transformative. Each
of us is much more powerful than we might believe and together
we are a force to be reckoned with.

Ayrton Cable, activist

Our warming world

01

Global warming hotspots:

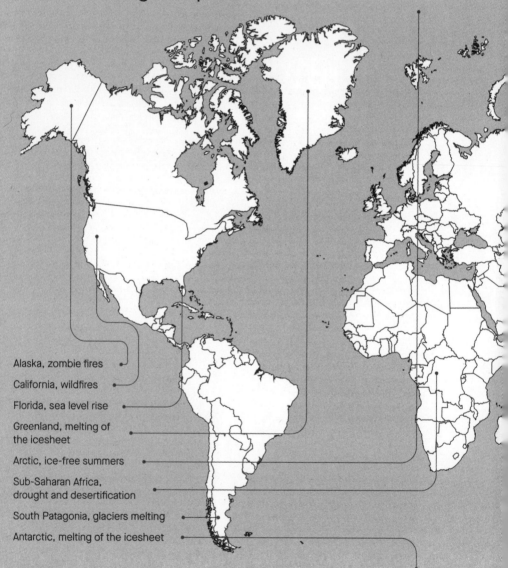

Alaska, zombie fires

California, wildfires

Florida, sea level rise

Greenland, melting of
the icesheet

Arctic, ice-free summers

Sub-Saharan Africa,
drought and desertification

South Patagonia, glaciers melting

Antarctic, melting of the icesheet

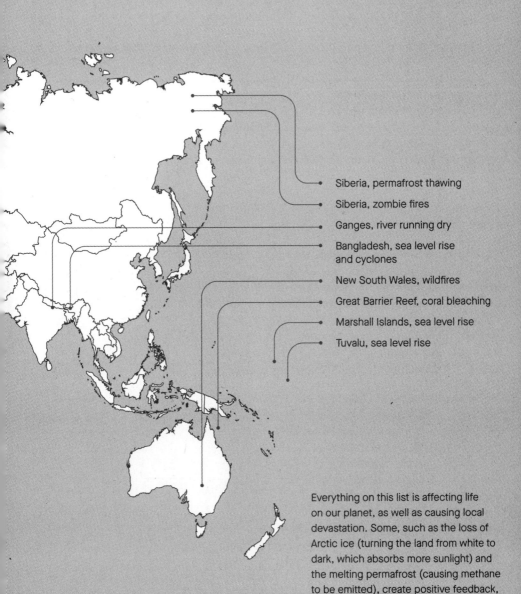

Siberia, permafrost thawing

Siberia, zombie fires

Ganges, river running dry

Bangladesh, sea level rise
and cyclones

New South Wales, wildfires

Great Barrier Reef, coral bleaching

Marshall Islands, sea level rise

Tuvalu, sea level rise

Everything on this list is affecting life
on our planet, as well as causing local
devastation. Some, such as the loss of
Arctic ice (turning the land from white to
dark, which absorbs more sunlight) and
the melting permafrost (causing methane
to be emitted), create positive feedback,
which accelerates global warming.

Think about global warming

Since the beginning of time, the Earth has been warmed by sunlight shining through the insulating blanket of the atmosphere, which is made up of carbon dioxide, water vapour, ozone, methane and nitrous oxide. This traps heat on the Earth, creating what is called the Greenhouse Effect. This keeps the climate stable enough to sustain life. Without this, the Earth would become too cold for life.

Since the Industrial Revolution, burning fossil fuels has increased greenhouse gas emissions. These gases trap more and more heat that would otherwise escape into space. The planet's temperature has risen and continues to rise. The world could become too hot for human existence. Scientists estimate that humans can manage a maximum temperature of 43°C in 50 per cent humidity and 51°C in a dry climate. The number of extreme hot weather events in the world is rising. During the ten years from 1980 to 1989, there were 1,080 high temperature incidents with recorded temperatures of 50°C or above. From 2010 to 2019, there were 2,510 such incidents. These were mostly in the Middle East and the Gulf. In 2021, a Kuwaiti city recorded 53.5°C, which is a world record. Also in 2021, Sicily recorded a temperature of 48.8°C, a European record, and North American records were broken with 49.5°C in British Columbia and 50.5°C in Washington State.

We have known about the Greenhouse Effect for quite a long time. In 1859, Irish scientist John Tyndall published a series of studies suggesting how greenhouse gases including CO_2 were trapping heat in the Earth's atmosphere. We continued to burn coal. Oil then became the dominant carbon-based fuel and we burned lots of that. Despite all the rhetoric, resolutions and policy statements, we continue raising CO_2 levels in the Earth's atmosphere. The Scripps Institution in San Diego tracks levels of CO_2 in the atmosphere on a daily basis.

⌔ 2050, the worst-case scenario

It's 2050. As the remaining New York church bells welcome in the New Year, people are taking time to reflect on how things have changed over their lifetimes. With a global temperature 3°C higher than at the turn of the century, the world is now a very different place.

Millions of people have already fled from the low-lying Pacific islands of Tuvalu, Kiribati and the Marshall Islands because of an 80cm rise in sea levels. The Marshalls were the first to go and their former residents are now living destitute in Indonesia – only Kiribati and Tuvalu residents were allowed to move to New Zealand.

In Europe, the Alps finally lost their snow and ice. Only the biggest glaciers remain; the skiing industry collapsed 20 years ago. The Himalayas have also lost about a third of their remaining ice cap, and last year the Ganges River ran dry for the first time. Panic swept through India and Bangladesh, and, in the biggest migration in human history, nearly 300 million people are currently moving towards Europe.

Polar bears are now a fading memory – the last one was seen in the far north of Canada in the late 2020s. All of the Arctic Ocean is now ice-free in the summer except for two or three large ice floes. Chinstrap and Emperor penguins have disappeared from the Antarctic but these extinctions are dwarfed by what is currently going on in Amazonia. Over three-quarters of what was once tropical forest has now been devastated by fire and in the ashes the desert is spreading.

♧ 2050, the best-case scenario

New Year's Eve 2049 is being celebrated around the world with more than the usual pleasure. It's the biggest party since the start of the millennium. This isn't just an accident of numbers, but because 2050 was the deadline set by the United Nations for the global economy to switch away from burning fossil fuels. And to the surprise of everyone, especially the cynics, the target has been met – but only just in time.

The real breakthrough was the 2025 International Climate Treaty. Under this treaty, the populations of countries declared uninhabitable by the UN were offered residence in Europe and North America because of these countries' role in causing global warming – reversing decades of harsh immigration policies designed to keep environmental refugees out of the rich countries.

The USA, Europe and Australia had to buy carbon permits from the poorer countries. So well-populated but low-oil-consuming countries like India and Brazil suddenly found that they had a massive budget surplus. This money was enough to pay off the debt of less developed countries and kick-start solar- and wind-power projects across the developing world.

It will still be touch and go for several decades. But what has surprised people most is the fact that humanity was able to rise to its biggest ever challenge.

(Adapted loosely from outtherenews.org, May 2001)

Climate change deniers

The urgency of the need to do something has been affected by the narrative put out by climate change deniers, variously denying that it exists, that its impact (if it does exist) will not be that great and that anyway, it is not man-made. The Intergovernmental Panel on Climate Change (IPCC) was established as far back as 1988 to assess climate change based on the latest science. Experts from around the world synthesise the most recent developments in climate science, adaptation, vulnerability and mitigation, and report regularly.

In August 2021, the IPCC stated for the first time that it was indisputable that human activity was causing global warming, saying that, 'Recent changes in the climate are widespread, rapid and intensifying, and impacts are affecting every region on Earth including the oceans. Many weather and climate extremes such as heatwaves, heavy rainfall, droughts and tropical cyclones have become more frequent and severe.' If we continue to pump more and more CO_2 into the atmosphere, things will only get worse.

We should consider Pascal's wager. Pascal was a seventeenth-century philosopher and mathematician. He argued that a rational person should live and act as though God exists. If God does not exist, there would be only a finite loss (renouncing some pleasures and luxuries in life), whereas there would be infinite gains if God does exist (being in heaven), avoiding infinite losses (an eternity in hell). The same is the case for global warming. Spend now on mitigating the problem just in case (whether you are a believer or a sceptic), rather than continuing to face an existential risk.

The scientific community overwhelmingly endorses the urgency of doing something.

The scientific community overwhelmingly endorses the urgency of doing something. But their views are questioned by climate change deniers and sceptics who question the need to do anything. These are some of the more influential:

Myron Ebell, Director of Global Warming and International Environmental Policy at the Competitive Enterprise Institute and Chair of the Cooler Heads Coalition, which focuses on 'dispelling the myths of global warming'. He developed the Trump presidency's approach to climate change.

Jim Inhofe (Republican Senator for Oklahoma), Chairman of the Senate Committee on Environment and Public Works (2003–2007 and 2015–17): 'Man-made global warming is the greatest hoax ever perpetrated on the American people.'

Nigel Lawson, Founder, Global Warming Policy Foundation: 'The IPCC's consistent refusal to entertain any dissent, however well researched, which challenges its assumptions is profoundly unscientific.'

Bjorn Lomborg, President, Copenhagen Consensus Center, author of *The Skeptical Environmentalist*: 'We need to solve climate change, but we also need to make sure that the cure isn't more painful than the disease.'

Steve Milloy, founder of JunkScience.com. He describes 'junk science' as 'faulty scientific data and analysis used to advance special and, often, hidden agendas' and has offered a prize of $500,000 to anyone who can 'prove in a scientific manner that humans are causing harmful global warming'.

Marc Morano runs ClimateDepot.com, set up by the Committee for a Constructive Tomorrow, and has authored a report listing hundreds of scientists whose work questions whether global warming is caused by human activity.

Fred Singer, scientist (died 2020): 'Climate change is a natural phenomenon ... since 1979, our best measurements show that the climate has been cooling just slightly.'

Roy Spencer, meteorologist: 'The Earth is not that sensitive to how much CO_2 we put into the atmosphere. I think we need to consider the possibility that more CO_2 is better than less.'

Climate change denial mostly comes from the USA. More than 90 per cent of papers sceptical on climate change originate from right-wing think tanks. In the 2016 primaries, every Republican presidential candidate questioned or denied climate change. But what is almost as bad as a climate change denier is a climate change believer who sits and does nothing. As Edmund Burke is reported to have said,

'The only thing necessary for the triumph of evil is for good men to do nothing.'

Dying to tell people

Many people have been prepared to take extreme action to highlight the dangers of climate change. This is possibly the most poignant example. On 13 April 2018, David Buckel, a prominent gay rights lawyer and environmental activist, poured gasoline over himself, lit it and burned himself to death in Prospect Park, Brooklyn, New York, in an attempt to raise awareness of the dangers of climate change and its existential threat to humanity.

David had emailed media outlets with a statement decrying humanity's passivity in the face of pollution and global warming. He was found dead by passers-by. A note left by his body said: 'I just killed myself by fire as a protest suicide.' He hoped his death would be seen as 'honourable' and that it 'might serve others'. In a world that was burning fossil fuel to climate destruction, he noted, 'Most humans on the planet now breathe air made unhealthy by fossil fuels and many die early deaths as a result – my early death by fossil fuel reflects what we are doing to ourselves.'

A crime against humanity

Polly Higgins was a British barrister. She led the campaign for 'ecocide' to be recognised as a 'crime against humanity'. Ecocide is 'the extensive damage to, destruction of or loss of ecosystem(s) of a given territory, whether by human agency or by other causes, to such an extent that peaceful enjoyment by the inhabitants of that territory has been or will be severely diminished'. This concept had emerged from the Vietnam War, when the USA sprayed 80 million litres of Agent Orange and other herbicides over the Vietnamese countryside in order to expose and more easily kill Vietcong fighters.

Polly sold her house and gave up a high-paying job to dedicate herself to creating a law that would make governments and businesses criminally liable for the damage they do to ecosystems. In 2010, she published a book, *Eradicating Ecocide*, which set out her case. She proposed an ecocide law to the United Nations and also as an amendment to the Statute of Rome, which was the treaty that established the International Criminal Court.

In 2011, she inspired a mock trial at the UK's Supreme Court. She continued campaigning until her death from cancer in 2019 aged just 50. Such a law could be a powerful tool for climate campaigners and environmental activists.

Ecocide is a new word. Our language continues to evolve as life evolves. Words such as 'upcycling' and 'greenwashing' are now in common use. What words will we need for a climate-challenged future? Invent a new word and submit it to be included in the AimHi Earth Future Dictionary at aimhi.earth/challenges.

A future for young people

'Eco-anxiety' or 'ecostential dread' is a fear about our future on our planet which is affecting more and more young people. In 2021, the Climate Psychology Alliance released a report based on interviews with 10,000 young people in Australia, Brazil, Finland, France, India, Nigeria, Philippines, Portugal, the UK and the USA which showed that 60 per cent of young people aged 16–25 were worried or extremely worried about climate change and 40 per cent fearful of having children.

60% of young people aged 16–25 are worried or <u>extremely</u> <u>worried</u> about climate change

But young people all over the world are doing something. The best known is Greta Thunberg, who, in August 2018, as a 15-year-old Swedish schoolgirl, took Fridays off school and sat outside the Swedish Parliament with a simple message that read: 'School Strike for the Climate'. This resonated around the world, inspiring the Fridays for Future movement, which has mobilised millions. But it is not just Greta; there are many others. Here are three:

Juliana versus United States: In 2015, 21 young people aged between 8 and 19 supported by Earth Guardians and Our Children's Trust filed a suit in Oregon against the US government asserting that government actions in encouraging and permitting the combustion of fossil fuels were violating the young generation's rights to life, liberty and property. The case wound its way through the US legal system with victories and setbacks along the way, but in 2020 the case was dismissed on the grounds that the plaintiffs lacked standing to sue. An appeal against this decision was denied in 2021.

Clover Hogan: In 2019, the 19-year-old Australian founded Force of Nature to try to turn eco-anxiety into action: 'We need to challenge the stories that keep us feeling powerless and each take responsibility for protecting the planet for generations to come.'

Amy Bray: Also in 2019, this 16-year-old from the UK founded Another Way to encourage more sustainable living: 'We believe in the power of ten; if one person spreads a message to ten people on one day, and the next day those ten people told ten more each, then in only ten days, the whole world hears the message. If all seven billion of us made one difference, imagine how many problems could be solved.'

A different future is possible

We must act: 'We are in a life or death situation of our own making. We must act now.' Extinction Rebellion is a global movement which uses non-violent civil disobedience including shutting down city centres, occupation of roads and bridges, hunger strikes and mass arrests to compel government action on climate change, biodiversity loss and other environmental catastrophes. It was founded by Roger Hallam, Gail Bradbrook and others, and has now spread around the world.

We can do it: *Drawdown: The Most Comprehensive Plan Ever Proposed To Reverse Global Warming* is a book edited by Paul Hawken for Project Drawdown. 'Drawdown' is the point at which the amount of greenhouse gases stops increasing and begins to decline. To achieve this, Hawken's book proposes 80 solutions in 7 categories: buildings and cities; energy; food and agriculture; land use including forests and peatland; materials and recycling; transport; education of women and girls. All are feasible and affordable. Hawken's next book was *Regeneration: Ending the Climate Crisis in One Generation*, published in 2021. This sets out a concrete plan for avoiding or sequestering over 1,600 gigatonnes of CO_2, which is enough to meet the IPCC targets for both 2030 and 2050. His 27 solutions include such things as growing azolla fern and reinstating tidal saltmarshes. Forest restoration and better forest management is the most important, as this will contribute around one-quarter of what is needed. The solutions ultimately come down to the key principles: 'cut emissions, protect and restore ecosystems, address equity, and create life. One might call it a regeneration revolution.' There is hope!

DO THIS:

Sign up to the Climate Prediction Project, a distributed computing project where your computer is linked up with thousands of others around the world to run climate models which attempt to answer questions about how climate change is affecting our world.

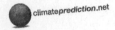

READ THESE:

Six Degrees: Our Future on a Hotter Planet (2007) and *Our Final Warning* (2021), both by Mark Lynas – wake-up calls on what life will be like if global warming isn't controlled.

Our
carbon
footprint

02

↳

Top carbon emitters amongst the major countries

Figures in tonnes of CO_2 per annum per capita:

Saudi Arabia 18.48

Kazakhstan 17.60

Australia 16.92

United States 16.56

Canada 15.32

South Korea 12.89

Russia 11.74

Japan 9.13

Germany 9.12

Poland 9.08

Iran 8.82

South Africa 8.12

China 7.05

UK 5.62

Italy 5.56

Turkey 5.21

These are the figures for countries with larger populations compiled by the Union of Concerned Scientists for 2018; they are for fuel combustion only. Selected other larger countries: France, 5.19; Brazil, 2.19; Indonesia, 2.30; India, 1.96.

Some key facts about global warming

↑ 1.1%

The global average temperature has increased by around 1.1°C since pre-industrial times. The 2015 Paris Agreement under the United Nations Framework Convention on Climate Change (UNFCCC) aimed to limit this rise to 1.5°C if at all possible.

↑ 0.2 metres

Sea level rise is driven by expansion of the volume of water as the ocean warms, the melting of glaciers all over the world, and the melting of the Greenland and Antarctic ice sheets. If global warming results in a 2°C temperature rise, then 70 per cent of the world's coastlines will be facing a sea level rise of 0.2m from present levels.

↓ 80–93%

To meet the Paris target, hefty cuts in CO_2 emissions will be needed. Emissions in industrialised countries will need to drop by 80–93 per cent by 2050. In lower-income countries, the reduction will need to be at least 25 per cent.

CO_2 concentration in the atmosphere in July 2021 was 417ppm – the highest level in over 800,000 years – and is continuing to increase. You can track the latest figures at co2.earth.

🌡 2.6–2.7°C

The world is not on track to limit warming to 1.5°C. The best estimate is that if all present commitments by governments are met, the expected warming will be in the range of 2.6–2.7°C.

36 billion tonnes

Globally, 2 billion tonnes of CO_2 were emitted in 1900; we are now emitting over 36 billion tonnes per year and each year emissions are increasing (although there was a temporary fall off in 2020–21 due to the Covid-19 pandemic).

China is the world's largest CO_2 emitter –
accounting for around 28 per cent of global
emissions – followed by the USA at 15 per
cent; the European Union (including the UK) at
10 per cent; India at 7 per cent; and Russia at
5 per cent.

The USA has 3 per cent of the world's
population and has contributed 25 per cent of
cumulative global CO_2 emissions.

Asia is the region with by far the highest
emissions, accounting for 53 per cent of the
global total, but it is home to 60 per cent of
the world's population. Note that this region
also exports a large quantity of goods to
Europe, North America and the rest of the
world, with CO_2 emissions 'embedded' in these
exported products.

To take into account the large amount of
CO_2 embedded in traded goods, it is more
relevant to calculate emission levels based
on consumption rather than production and
the figures need to be adjusted for this. For
example, China exports 14 per cent of its
emissions and the USA imports 7.7 per cent.
The exports and imports of any country
should be subtracted or added to calculate its
consumption emissions.

There are large inequalities in CO_2 emissions.
The world's poorest countries have contributed
less than 1 per cent of cumulative emissions
and are the most vulnerable to consequences
of climate change.

Check out more facts and explanations
on global warming at Our World in Data
(ourworldindata.org). The UNFCCC maintains a
registry for Nationally Determined Contributions
and organises the Conferences of the Parties
(COPs), held annually to bring the international
community together for discussion,
negotiation, decision and hopefully action.

COP26, held in Glasgow in 2021, was generally
seen as a last chance for the world to set in
place policies that will effectively address
global warming. Most countries committed
themselves to achieving net zero emissions
by 2055 or 2060. These commitments will be
reviewed and efforts made to strengthen them
at COP27, to be held at Sharm El-Sheikh in
2022. Although this represents some progress,
the general consensus is that a great deal more
still needs to be done. We also need to see
behind the rhetoric to ensure that the pledges
made by governments are translated into
effective action, such that the targets pledged
are at least achieved. The difficulties are best
illustrated by the last-minute intervention by
India and China at COP26 to agree to the
'phasing down' of coal burning rather than its
'phasing out'.

Calculating your carbon footprint

Every aspect of our daily lives has a carbon consequence. What we eat, what we buy, how we travel to work and for leisure, the temperature of our homes (in winter with central heating and in summer with air conditioning), how we entertain ourselves ... everything we do adds to the amount of CO_2 entering the Earth's atmosphere. The global average for 2017 was 4.8 tonnes for each person on the planet. But if you are living in a rich country, you will probably be emitting far more than this; in a poorer country, much less. Before doing anything else, you should measure your carbon footprint at carbonfootprint.com.

Major contributors to our emissions

CO_2 is responsible for 64 per cent of man-made global warming. Other contributors include methane, at 17 per cent, and nitrous oxide, at 6 per cent. These are the main sectors for generating CO_2:

The energy sector	35 per cent
Agriculture and forestry	24 per cent
Industry	21 per cent
Transport	14 per cent
Homes (heating and cooking)	6 per cent

When we think about the contributors to global warming, our first thoughts will usually be driving cars, flying, power stations and deforestation. But there are some surprises:

Meat-eating: Globally, the livestock industry produces more greenhouse gas emissions (including methane) than all cars, planes, trains and ships combined. The worst offenders are red meat (beef and lamb, pork to a lesser extent), but poultry and dairy are also significant contributors. A kilogram of beef protein has the equivalent CO_2 emissions of a passenger flying from London to New York and back. As people are getting richer and the population continues to grow, more people are eating more meat. There will need to be a significant change in our diets if the world is to meet global emissions targets. New technologies for food production will help. For example, growing 'lab meat' in factories rather than rearing and killing animals, or products like Impossible Burgers, which are made from vegetable ingredients but engineered to taste like meat.

Having more children: Every child that comes into the world will have its own carbon footprint and be generating CO_2 throughout its life, and many of these children will go on to create their own children for the next generation, and these in turn their own children. As the world's population has increased, this has inevitably led to a major increase in greenhouse gas emissions. Some societies and communities value large families. But the world's population level will be a critical factor in achieving climate change targets. Having one fewer child could be your most significant contribution towards addressing global warming.

Data: The electricity consumed by cloud computing globally has more than tripled between 2007 and 2020. It has become a major contributor to rising energy use. Every time you upload a photo or stream a film, energy is required to operate the huge servers which make this possible, as well as to power your devices. Moving from traditional cameras to digital cameras may have reduced the use of chemicals and paper but photographing everything and then uploading and sharing all these photos and videos consumes energy.

Bitcoin mining (also other crypto-currencies): This is a way of turning large amounts of energy into cash. In recent years, it has been extremely profitable. The mining process involves machines racing to solve complex maths and using these calculations to keep the network secure and create more currency. China was the largest country for crypto-currency mining but banned it in 2021 as an illegal financial activity and because of the strain that it was putting on the grid. The largest mining operations are now in the USA and Kazakhstan, with substantial operations in countries such as Russia and North Korea.

Pets: All over the world, people like to keep pets. In the USA alone, there are more than 163 million dogs and cats, which are together consuming around 19 per cent of the calories that humans do, which is equivalent to 62 million more Americans. The greenhouse gas emissions of all US pets is equivalent to over 13 million cars. In their ground-breaking book *Time to Eat the Dog? The Real Guide to Sustainable Living*, Robert and Brenda Vale examined the impact of pets on global warming and their 'carbon pawprint'. Their advice is that a small vegetarian pet, such as a rabbit, is better in many ways than a larger, meat-eating animal. From the point of view of carbon emissions, a goldfish that can live in a bowl (rather than a heated, constantly filtered aquarium) would be better still. Best is not to have a pet. Could you help look after other people's instead? In the UK, look at borrowmydoggy.com and the Cinnamon Trust for canines needing occasional or short-term companions.

Fashion: This accounts for as much as 4 per cent of the UK's CO_2 emissions. An average person buys 18 kilograms of clothes each year, around 87 per cent of which will end up in landfill or incineration. This is an area where everybody can easily make a difference – buy less, buy second-hand, pass your old clothing on to others, repair damaged clothing, wash less frequently (as it shortens the life of the fabric as well as using energy). Fashion has become faster and we need to slow it down.

How are things going to change?

These will be the three main contributors to reducing the level of CO_2 emissions:

Technology: The continuing reduction in costs and wider availability of renewable energy, substituting for and then replacing fossil fuels; converting surplus renewable energy (when the sun is shining and the wind blowing) into hydrogen or developing new battery technologies for storing surplus electricity until it is needed; LED lights, which use one-seventh of the electricity of incandescent bulbs and last 20 times longer; growing meat in laboratories and factories (this emits no methane and is far more efficient than traditional livestock farming); switching from traditional cars to electric lorries, vans, cars and e-scooters; carbon capture and storage to remove CO_2 emissions from the atmosphere. All these new technologies will significantly help us reduce our emissions while enabling us, on the whole, to maintain our present lifestyle.

Government, which has three roles: firstly, providing incentives and introducing laws, penalties and carbon taxes to facilitate behaviour change by people and by business. Secondly, taking a lead in reducing emissions over the whole of the public sector, for example by requiring zero-emissions schools, hospitals and even armies. And thirdly, by mobilising the huge investment needed for this switch away from a carbon economy.

Behaviour change by all of us – people and business. This is probably the hardest, as we do things the way we do because it is much easier and more convenient. But somehow or other our behaviour and everybody's behaviour all over the world has to change. Continuing as we are and carbon offsetting to reduce our footprint is a diversion as what we are using as an offset would probably have happened anyway!

CO_2 remains in the atmosphere for centuries and we are continuing to add to what's already there. The world needs to limit total CO_2 emissions from today into the foreseeable future to 200 gigatonnes if we are to stand any chance of keeping within 1.5°C of warming. Yet the world's emissions are currently running at around 40 gigatonnes each year.

Switch off for one hour

In 2020, Earth Hour was held on 28 March from 20.30 to 21.30 local time wherever you were in the world. Earth Hour was started by WWF Australia with a demonstration in Sydney, Australia, in 2007, when more than 2.2 million residents and 2,100 local businesses switched off all their lights and all their non-essential electrical appliances for one hour. They did this to highlight the fact that coal-fired electricity is the leading contributor to global warming. What started in one city rapidly turned into a global movement. Today, Earth Hour is celebrated in more than 7,000 cities and towns worldwide.

Are you wondering what you could do when you switch off the lights? Here are some ideas:

↳ Have a dinner by candlelight with your friends (preferably using beeswax candles).

↳ Hold an Earth Hour block party and get to know all your neighbours in your building or on your street.

↳ Go out to a park for a night-time picnic with family or friends.

↳ Go for a romantic moonlit stroll on the beach (if you are by the seaside) or around a lake.

↳ Snuggle up in bed with your partner or just fall asleep (and have sweet dreams).

Earth Hour is to be enjoyed. Do something fun. But while you are enjoying yourself, think about what you can do to reduce your carbon footprint.

DO ALL OF THESE:

1 Calculate your carbon footprint at carbonfootprint.com, then pledge to reduce this immediately by 20 per cent at count-us-in.org.

2 Switch to LED lighting throughout your home.

3 Turn off the lights when you leave a room.

4 Unplug devices when not in use instead of leaving them on standby.

5 Heat or cool only those rooms you use regularly.

6 Turn the heating down 1°C in winter and air conditioning up 1°C in summer.

7 Go meat-free – all the time or just one day a week.

8 Drink tap water, not bottled water.

9 Become an activist. Find an organisation that's right for you – whether it's 350.org, named after 350 parts per million, which is the safe concentration of carbon dioxide in the atmosphere, or Extinction Rebellion.

Or don't do any of these things. Instead, plant a 'Mechanical Tree'. Klaus Lackner, a professor at Arizona State University, has invented a technique for sucking CO_2 from the air using an artificial tree with plastic 'leaves' which have been coated with sodium carbonate and are then rinsed with water to extract the CO_2. This is 1,000 times more efficient than real leaves using photosynthesis. Ten million 'trees' could capture 3.6 billion tonnes of CO_2 a year, which is equivalent to around 10 per cent of annual global emissions.

Mass produced by Carbon Collect, a tree could cost as little as $20,000. The CO_2 could then be sequestered. Or it could become a source of 'green CO_2' for use in food manufacture or putting the fizz into sparkling beverages, replacing industrial CO_2 manufactured by burning fossil fuels; and if the 'tree' is installed locally, this will also eliminate the need for transport and reduce congestion.

Overshooting the Earth's capacity

└→

How we are consuming too much

If everyone in the world lived the lifestyle of
the people in each of the countries below,
then their full, fair ration of available resources
for that year would be used up by the date
shown. Beyond that date, up to 31 December,
they would be living on resources 'borrowed'
from the future.

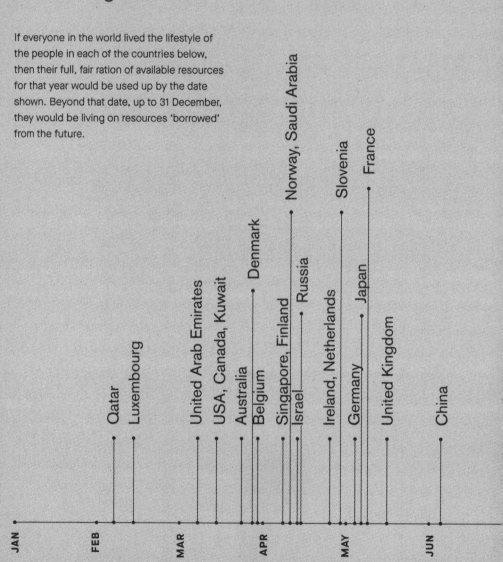

The Earth's resources are finite

For dates before 1 July, citizens of that country consume on average more than twice their sustainable ration. If everybody lived the lifestyle of a US citizen, each year they would be consuming five times this amount. In some countries, such as India and most sub-Saharan African countries, people are consuming less than their share. But averaging across the whole world, each year, we are together consuming 1.7 times the Earth's available resources.

(Figures are for 2021 from Earth Overshoot Day)

The capacity of our planet to provide and to regenerate the resources consumed by the human population and to absorb the waste we create is limited. To live sustainably within our planet's available capacity in the long term, we will need to ration our use of resources.

As a global population, we already use 73 per cent more resources than are available to us each year – to feed us, to fuel us, to build our homes, to clothe us and to satisfy all our consumer demands. Each year, this deficit is increasing, despite the advances of technology which enable us to travel further (due to increased fuel efficiency and now electric cars), grow more (the Green Revolution and now aquaponics, hydroponics and lab-grown protein), manufacture more efficiently (robotics and AI). We have now gone way beyond living within our means.

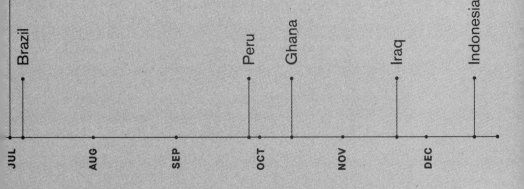

Brazil · JUL
AUG
Peru · SEP
Ghana · OCT
Iraq · NOV
DEC
Indonesia

Our footprint

A 'footprint' is a way of examining the impact that we are having on the planet, either as individuals or as a country or for the whole world. Every individual has their own personal footprint and, as a world, we have a global footprint. There are three footprints which measure the different aspects of sustainable living. These show us the extent of our use of the world's resources and where and how much we might need to reduce our impact and change our way of living. The three footprints are:

Carbon footprint: this measures the amount of CO_2 that we are causing to be emitted directly or that's indirectly embedded in all the things that we purchase. This shows the contribution that we are making towards global warming and the extent that we might need to reduce our emissions if global warming is to be limited to 1.5°C.

Water footprint: this measures the amount of water that we use in our daily lives, including water that is embedded in what we purchase, especially in the food we eat. Agriculture is the largest user of the world's water in a world that is becoming increasingly thirsty.

Ecological footprint: this is a measure of our consumption of the Earth's resources in relation to what our planet can provide us with.

Our ecological footprint is usually measured in global hectares. This is the amount of land required to provide us with the lifestyle we are enjoying. The capacity of the Earth to grow what we need for food, fibres and biofuels, to extract the raw materials we are using in manufacturing and to absorb the waste we are generating is limited. As technologies develop and productivity increases, this capacity will rise. But climate change, reduced fertility, water shortage and desertification are all pulling in the opposite direction – reducing the Earth's capacity to sustain human life. And as the world's population grows – by 2100, it is expected to reach 10.9 billion, 60 per cent more than the present level – this will require an equivalent per capita reduction.

Our personal footprint can be worked out using the Ecological Footprint Calculator: footprintcalculator.org. We can find out about our country footprint using the Ecological Footprint Explorer: data.footprintnetwork.org. Using both these tools we can see whether our personal footprint is above or below the average for our country, and how much higher it is than the average required across the world for 'one planet living'.

The Global Footprint Network calculates that the world's resources available on land and sea for providing for human needs amount to a total of 12.17 billion global hectares (gha). With a world population of 7.88 billion, this gives each person alive a ration of 1.54gha per annum. In the USA, the world's richest country, current consumption per person is 8.6gha, more than five times its fair share. In China, the world's most populous country, it is 3.6gha, more than twice. In Europe, it is around 4.8gha, three times.

For humans to live on the planet sustainably, every person in the rich world will need to find ways of reducing their footprint considerably – which can be done through lifestyle changes and technological advances, both of which will be needed. For most of the poor world, the same will be true but the changes needed will be far less. Some in sub-Saharan Africa will even be able to increase their consumption. For example, in Nigeria, Africa's most populous country, the current footprint is 1.1gha, which means that a fair share will allow a 40 per cent increase in consumption or a 40 per cent increase in population or a combination of both.

The ecological footprint was created in the 1990s by Mathis Wackernagel with William Rees as a PhD thesis at the University of British Columbia, Canada. The Global Footprint Network was set up in 2003, based in the USA, Belgium and Switzerland, to research and provide information on footprints, to develop tools for doing this and to advocate for a more sustainable world.

Earth Overshoot Day

Earth Overshoot Day, which was previously known as Ecological Debt Day, is the date each year on which the human population's consumption of resources for that year exceeds the Earth's capacity to provide these resources. These are the Overshoot Days since 1990:

1990	11 October
1995	5 October
2000	23 September
2005	26 August
2000	8 August
2015	6 August
2021	29 July

As you can see, each year Earth Overshoot Day has been occurring earlier and earlier as we use more of the world's resources faster.

One planet living

'Imagine a world where everyone, everywhere lives happy, healthy lives within the limits of the planet, leaving space for wildlife and wilderness. We call this "One Planet Living", and we believe it's achievable ... But globally we are living as if we have more than one planet. In fact, ecological footprinting shows that if everyone in the world consumed as much as the average person in Western Europe, we'd need three planets to support us.'

This is the manifesto of One Planet Living, an initiative of Bioregional founded by Sue Riddlestone and Pooran Desai in 2003, as a result of their experience in developing the *BedZED* zero-emissions eco-village, a small housing estate in south London. They have developed a framework for thinking about how we can live within the Earth's means and creating plans for increasing sustainability. These are some of the components that need to be considered:

↳ Health and happiness

↳ Equity and local economy

↳ Culture and community

↳ Land and nature

↳ Sustainable water

↳ Local and sustainable food

↳ Travel and transport

↳ Materials and products

↳ Zero waste

↳ Zero-carbon energy

The circular economy

In a 'linear economy', we:

Take raw materials, to …
↳ Make things we want or need …
　↳ Sell these to consumers …
　　↳ Who use them, and then …
　　　↳ Dispose of them when they are no longer wanted or needed …

At which point they end their life, adding to pollution in a landfill or being incinerated.

More people in the world purchasing more goods as their living standards increase multiplies into a huge amount of waste, but, more importantly, a huge burden on the planet to produce all the raw materials involved in making all this stuff. This leads to the idea of a 'circular economy', where at the end of life, the item is reused, recycled, upcycled or used to provide the raw materials for the production of another product. This will become an increasingly important factor in how goods are designed and manufactured. Every time you purchase a car or a refrigerator, discarding your old model (either because you want to update or upgrade to a newer model or because it has broken down), you will be reducing your impact if your old product has been designed to enter a circular economy, where as much of it as possible is repurposed into new products.

The idea of a circular economy emerged in 1976. Also in the 1970s, Walter Stahel, a Swiss architect and co-founder of the Product-Life Institute, coined the phrase 'cradle to cradle' (circular) in contrast with 'cradle to grave' (linear). Today, these ideas have become much more mainstream. In 2018, the Circular Economy Club mapped 3,000 circular economy initiatives in 70 cities in 45 countries.

Bottled water madness

One of the craziest products in modern life is bottled water in countries where tap water is completely safe to drink. This is emblematic of our disregard for the environment. Drinking tap water instead of bottled water avoids the plastic waste of the container and all the energy and pollution created in bringing the product to you. It is far cheaper, costing fractions of fractions of a penny, while some bottled water sells at many times the cost of petrol. Interestingly, in blind taste tests, municipal-supplied water has fared just as well as major bottled water brands. People could not taste any difference. When Coca-Cola launched its Dasani brand in the UK in 2004, the press picked up that it was treated tap water from Sidcup, a suburb of south London, purified by reverse osmosis and remineralised. Health and safety officers found a batch that was contaminated with levels of bromate, which is a suspected carcinogen, in concentrations far above the legal limit. The Dasani launch was a disaster.

People making change

People all over the world are providing advice, ideas and information on how we can live our lives more sustainably. For example, switching from incandescent or halogen lighting to LED lighting will reduce your energy consumption to one-seventh and increase the lifespan of the bulb 20 times. This is a technological solution. But you can also install a dimmer switch, so you can adjust the lighting level to what you need, turn off the lights when you leave the room or have sensors do this for you, and switch to green electricity. You can even install your own solar panel. Each of these actions will reduce your ecological footprint.

Here are three initiatives encouraging more sustainable living in different areas of our day-to-day life.

Green Monday was started by David Yeung and Francis Ngai in Hong Kong to encourage meat-free Mondays in restaurants, meat-eating being a major contributor to global warming. It has now developed a wider agenda 'to construct a global ecosystem of future food that combats climate change, food insecurity, food-related illness, planetary devastation and animal suffering'. Wherever you are, join with David and Francis to have a meat-free Monday every week and then think of ways of reducing your meat and dairy consumption in your daily diet.

The Otesha Project was started by two young Canadians in 2002, Jocelyn Land-Murphy and Jessica Lax, and continued until 2015. They organised cycle tours across Canada visiting schools and community centres where they would perform an interactive play on sustainability issues, raising young people's awareness and asking them to make pledges towards more sustainable lifestyles. Otesha was able to reach out to 150,000 Canadians and train 500 sustainability leaders. 'Otesha' means 'reason to dream' in Swahili. Otesha UK ran from 2008 to 2016.

Both projects produced materials offering simple practical ideas. These concentrated on 'morning choices' – that is, the choices you can make each morning as you get up, get dressed, have breakfast and go off to work or to school. You could choose to contribute to a better world, with the water you use to wash and drink, with the clothing you buy (or don't buy) and wear, with the media you consume, with the tea and coffee you drink, with your breakfast food and with how you make your journey to wherever you are going. With each choice you make, your lifestyle could become that little bit more sustainable. And you can encourage others to do similar things. You can download *From Junk to Funk* and *The Otesha UK Handbook* free from United Diversity Library.

Who Gives a Crap? We can all make a difference through the little things that we do. Take, for example, toilet paper. You can buy a popular brand such as Andrex and be seduced by its advertising, believing that its luxurious softness will give you everlasting pleasure. But what if you were offered an alternative that was 100 per cent recycled, chemical free, with smaller squares and with half its profits donated to global sanitation? This is what Who Gives a Crap? is offering. Or go one better and buy their bamboo premium product. Either way, you will be making a difference.

DO THIS:

Predict the date of Earth Overshoot Day in 2030. Then write a letter to yourself with your prediction (to be delivered to you in 2030) at futureme.org.

DO THIS:

Explore the Earth from space and see how our planet is being affected by human encroachment, climate change and natural phenomena such as earthquakes. Take a look at the images taken by the Landsat satellites at landsat.gsfc.nasa.gov/landsat-galleries.

Eating for the planet

04

The footprint of our food

These figures are total kilos of CO_2 emitted from food consumption per person per year.

The three figures for each country are:

= animals   = plants/veg

and the total for the country.

This table is based on data from the nu3 Food Carbon Footprint Index. It shows the ten countries with the highest and the ten with the lowest food carbon footprint.

Meat is the prime contributor to high emissions. Total emissions for selected other countries: Indonesia 367; China 640; Japan 644; Germany 1,067; UK 1,241; France 1,420.

Large footprints

Argentina
2,141 + 32 = 2,173

Australia
1,896 + 43 = 1,939

Albania
1,734 + 44 = 1,778

New Zealand
1,710 + 44 = 1,754

Iceland
1,706 + .26 = 1,732

Small footprints

Sri Lanka
145 + 15 = 160

Togo
146 + 54 = 200

Ghana
164 + 42 = 206

Malawi
190 + 18 = 208

Mozambique
104 + 104 = 208

Looking to the future

There are three options if we are to going to be able to feed the 10.9 billion humans that are likely to live on this planet by 2100: we can grow more, or we can waste less or we can eat more sustainably, choosing to eat those foods which have a lower impact on the environment. As 30–40 per cent of the world's food is currently being wasted, it obviously makes more sense to waste less rather than putting more energy, effort, water, land, pesticides and fertilisers into growing more. And eating more sustainably is something that we will all have to do if we are to achieve global warming targets – the 2021 National Food Strategy for England proposed a 30 per cent reduction in meat consumption within a decade.

These are some other factors:

↳ A quarter of all carbon emissions arise from growing food. Then there are further emissions from processing it, transporting it along a supply chain starting from the farm and ending in your kitchen, where you cook it. Feeding the world is responsible for around 35 per cent of total greenhouse gas emissions. The more food we grow, the more emissions we create – this is not a good idea when the world is trying to find ways of limiting global warming to 1.5°C.

↳ The same is true for water. Around 80 per cent of fresh water extracted from rivers and aquifers is used for growing food.

Water tables are falling and many areas of the world are becoming water-stressed.

↳ We are eating inefficiently (in environmental terms). Meat is playing an increasingly important part in most people's diets; as people and the world get richer, more meat is being consumed per capita and this means more carbon emissions and more water usage. Meat is a main source of protein and we will need to find alternatives.

↳ We are poisoning the land with effluents from cattle sheds, the run-off from fertilised fields and pesticides (increasingly used with GM foods).

↳ We are losing arable land. According to some estimates, the Earth has lost one-third of its arable land in the past 40 years for a variety of factors, including urbanisation, erosion, drought and desertification, pollution, salination and climate change.

We will need to find ways of growing food more efficiently *AND* we will also need to eat differently. Simply producing more food is not the solution. Felling rainforest to grow soya to feed to cattle to provide us with meat is unsustainable. If we are to meet global warming commitments, if we are to feed the growing population with declining amounts of land and water, things will have to change.

The carbon footprint of food

Worldwide, approximately **13.7 billion metric tons of CO_2** equivalents (CO_2e) are being emitted through the food supply chain per year. The CO_2 equivalent includes the impact of all the other greenhouse gases as well as CO_2. Beef has the biggest impact – methane emission from the animals and land conversion for grazing and production of animal feed being the main contributors. Dairy is high for the same reason. Pork and poultry are much lower. Fruit, vegetables, beans and nuts have the lowest carbon footprints. Transport accounts for around 10 per cent of total food emissions, so moving down from beef to chicken, and chicken to a vegetarian then a vegan diet has a much bigger impact than buying local. The Visual Capitalist website has well-presented data on the carbon footprint of the food supply chain.

These are selected greenhouse gas emissions (including methane) in kilos of CO_2 equivalent per kilo of food consumed (figures from Our World in Data, ourworldindata.org):

Beef	60
Lamb	24
Cheese	21
Chocolate	19
Coffee	17
Pork	7
Chicken	6
Olive oil	6
Farmed fish	5
Eggs	4.5
Rice	4
Caught fish	3
Milk	3
Maize	1
Peas	1
Bananas	0.7
Root vegetables	0.4
Nuts	0.3

Meat also has the biggest **water footprint**, while sea-caught fish obviously has the lowest as no freshwater is needed. The figures are cubic metres of water per kilo of produce (1 cubic metre = 1,000 litres). These are some examples:

Chocolate	20.7
Almonds	19.3
Beef	18.5
Lamb	12.5
Cheese	6.7
Butter	6.7
Chicken	5.2
Tofu	3.4
Strawberries	0.5
Broccoli	0.4

There are lots of tools on the internet for calculating the carbon footprint of food. For example, use the calculator from the Vegan Society, where you assemble all the ingredients to calculate the CO_2 content of the meal you are preparing (which can include meat and dairy as well as vegan ingredients). Calculate the water footprint of your food at waterfootprint.org. And go to the Foodprint website to learn about where your food came from and how it got to you to help you choose products that do less harm.

Too much meat

Meat has been a traditional source of protein, perhaps harking back to our hunter-gatherer beginnings. But farming meat for human consumption is a really inefficient way of providing us with protein compared with eating a vegetarian diet, when vegetable protein is consumed directly instead of being fed to animals and then to us. For example, it takes around 25kg of food to produce 1kg of beef and 4kg of vegetable protein to produce 1kg of beef protein.

Meat consumption has been growing rapidly for two reasons: the world population has been growing, and it has been growing in affluence. There is a direct correlation between wealth and meat-eating all over the world. The richer a population gets, the more meat it eats. The average person in the world today is consuming 43kg of meat per annum, though there are big regional variations: in the USA it is 100kg and in India it is just 5kg. In 2018, more than 72 billion livestock animals were slaughtered for human consumption, of which 68.8 billion were chickens. The total human consumption of animals was 341 million tonnes, five times higher than in 1961. These figures do not include animals raised for dairy produce.

This growth in meat-eating is completely unsustainable. If we as a world are to meet our emissions targets then we will need to eat far less meat and choose different sources of protein. For some, this will be a move towards vegetarianism and veganism. But there are other alternatives for providing people with protein. Will you regret having to eat less meat? Which alternatives do you fancy? Will you be prepared to eat any of these?

Plant-based meat substitutes

One of the first plant-based protein products to be marketed was Quorn, which is produced by fermenting a natural fungus. Today, the race is on to create products that are not only plant-based but look like and taste like, or even better than, their meat equivalents, and which should be ten times cheaper to produce than farm-reared animal protein. Two companies are vying for top spot. Beyond Meat was founded in 2009 and had its initial public offering in 2019, when shares rose by over 800 per cent in the first three months of trading. It is currently valued at $4.76 billion. Impossible Foods was founded in 2011; it is privately owned and was valued at just under $4 billion in 2019.

Both these companies produce and sell a range of products using plant-based 'meat', which they claim tastes as good as or even better than the real thing, which enables people to continue eating meat while addressing four key issues: climate change, depletion of the world's natural resources, animal welfare and human health. Both companies have become part of the global food system, operating on an industrial scale and distributing their products through supermarkets and fast food outlets, where people can enjoy Impossible's Whoppers and Beyond Meat's McPlant burgers.

Eating insects

Insects are a good source of protein; around 2 billion people regularly eat insects as a part of their diet. They are also far more efficient at converting their food into edible protein than traditional farm animals. The most commonly eaten insects are beetles, caterpillars, bees, wasps and ants. When locusts are around, in parts of Africa you see roadside stalls with hurricane lamps to attract the insects, a net to capture them and a vat of hot oil to fry them in. They may be devastating the crops but when caught they become a protein-rich delicacy.

One insect that deserves our attention is the cricket, which is 65 per cent pure protein and rich in iron and vitamin B12. Cricket flour is becoming widely available and with its neutral taste can be used as an additive in cooking.

Eating algae

Algae don't require arable land for cultivation and can be grown anywhere, even indoors. They grow in freshwater and in seawater; they have a high yield and less than half the carbon footprint of rice. Algae could also be a source of food oil; they can produce up to 2,000 gallons of oil per acre, compared with 653 gallons for palm oil.

We already eat algae, including spirulina, chlorella and dunaliella, which are used as food supplements. Algae may have the appearance of green slime but they just might be the superfood of the future, and an ideal source of plant-based protein.

Eating mushrooms

Mushrooms contain protein and fibre. But they are also a source of other nutrients such as B vitamins and selenium, which strengthens the immune system. Different varieties of mushroom have different medicinal properties. White button mushrooms are a good source of vitamin D. Mushrooms can be grown indoors, in unused industrial buildings, garages, basements and sheds. Unlike algae and insects, mushrooms are a food we are used to.

GroCycle has developed a range of online courses to teach people how to grow mushrooms and you can find starter packs on Amazon and eBay.

Innovations in growing food

Food growing is an important part of our economy and innovations are being developed all around the world. These are some initiatives to check up on, and there will be lots of other projects and initiatives to explore.

Katapult is a Norwegian accelerator of start-ups, supporting technological solutions with a focus on health, environment, education and democracy. If you have a great idea, why not contact them? Mission Kitchen does the same for food start-ups in the UK.

EIT Food describes itself as Europe's largest food innovation initiative, building a network of agri-food start-ups, research centres and universities across Europe, working together to create an innovative and entrepreneurial food sector. Check out the innovations they are promoting and what their RisingFoodStars are doing.

The Fish Farm was developed in South Africa by Alan Fleming to create jobs. Each 'farm' is inside a shipping container, which provides a controlled environment as well as security. The main crop is tilapia, which is a vegetarian fish, and the effluent water, rich in nutrients, can be used for vertical vegetable growing. This concept is being developed to provide a business opportunity for urban and township dwellers anywhere.

Freight Farms has developed Greenery S, a vertical hydroponic system housed in a 40ft shipping container capable of growing up to 13,000 plants. They also offer this to schools as an educational package. Other urban farming initiatives include **Jones Food**, **Growing Underground**, **Infinite Acres** and **80 Acres Farms**, all growing salads and microgreens commercially in urban spaces such as empty factories and underground tunnels.

Seed Cooperative, based in the UK, grows, processes and sells organic, open-pollinated seed, and develops new varieties through organic plant breeding to encourage agro-ecological farming. They say: *'Our mission is to sow the seeds of a healthy and resilient organic food system that promotes diversity, democracy and a closer relationship with our food, and those who grow it.'*

Solar Foods, based in Helsinki, makes protein from a primordial soup of bacteria taken from the soil and multiplied in the laboratory, using hydrogen extracted from water as its energy source: 'We've created a revolutionary way to produce a natural protein with just electricity and air. An entirely new kind of food that is natural, can taste like anything and, unlike any other food, is not limited to the availability of land or the use of animals, agriculture and aquaculture. The liberation of protein production is finally possible.'

Because Animals was started by Shannon Falconer and Joshua Errett, who met as volunteers at a Toronto cat rescue centre. They are creating plant-based petfoods but also lab-grown mouse meat (delicious for cool cats!).

Feedback was founded by Tristram Stuart to campaign for food sustainability. Its first event was 'Feeding the 5,000' in London's Trafalgar Square using food which would otherwise have gone to waste. Feedback campaigns for a circular food system, which gobbles up fewer resources to produce the food we need and loses far less food in the form of waste.

DO THIS:

Take a step towards eating differently. Use cricket flour in your cooking as an insect-based protein source. Google it to find a supplier.

DO THIS:

Go vegan for a month. Veganuary, founded by Matthew Glover and Jane Land, asks people to go meat- and dairy-free in January. And if you enjoy it, continue for the rest of the year. In 2021, 582,000 people worldwide signed up to participate in Veganuary.

Trees
of life

Rainforests of the world

The 16 largest rainforests of the world are:

(in thousand sq kms)

1 Amazon rainforest 5,500

2 Congo rainforest 1,780

3 Borneo rainforests 427.5

4 Appalachian temperate rainforest 351.5

5 New Guinea rainforests 288

6 Valdivian temperate rainforest 248.1

7 The South-East Asian rainforests 82

8 Tongass National Forest 68.8

9 Pacific temperate rainforest 60.3

10 Costa Rica rainforests 25.5

11 Sundarbans Reserve Forest 10

12 Sinharaja Forest Reserve 8.8

13 Atsinanana rainforests 4.8

14 Daintree rainforest 2.6

15 Sapo National Park rainforest 1.8

(Source: Wikipedia)

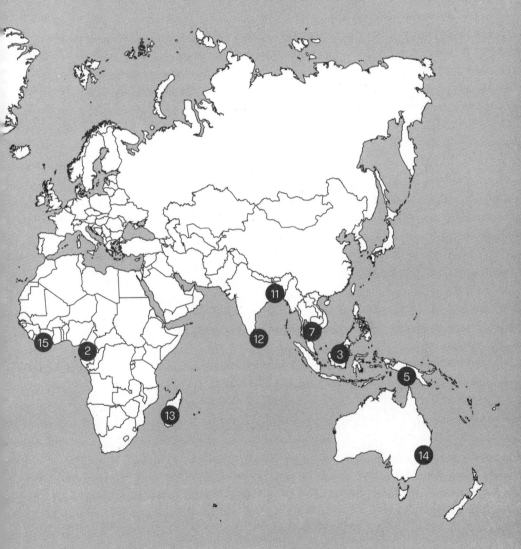

Other forests: The Russian Taiga at 8.15 million sq kms is bigger than the Amazon rainforest.
Other countries in Europe with large forest areas include Sweden, 280,730 sq kms; France,
246,730 sq kms; Finland, 233,320 sq kms; Spain, 184,180 sq kms; Norway, 121,120 sq kms;
Germany, 114,190 sq kms; Italy, 106,736 sq kms; Ukraine, 105,000 sq kms.

The importance of rainforests

A rainforest is defined as an area of usually tall, densely growing broad-leaved evergreen trees that receives high annual rainfall. There are tropical rainforests and temperate rainforests, while forests, mainly found in Europe and Siberia, are slower growing and less biodiverse.

The best-known and largest rainforest (bigger than all the other rainforests combined) is the Amazon. About 60 per cent is in Brazil, with the rest in neighbouring countries. It is critical to the biodiversity of the planet. It covers only 1 per cent of the Earth's surface but is home to 10 per cent of all known wildlife species, with probably many more still to be discovered. There are known to be 16,000 species of trees, 2.5 million of insects, 2,000 of mammals and birds, and 438,000 of plants. It is the world's lung, with its 390 billion trees breathing in CO_2 and emitting oxygen. The trees themselves contain around 140 billion tonnes of carbon. It is also home to around half a million indigenous peoples from hundreds of tribes, many living traditional lives.

The Amazon is under continuing threat as the trees are felled for timber and burned to make way for human settlement and agriculture. About 20 per cent of it has already been lost, and losses continue at around 0.15 per cent per annum. Jair Bolsonaro assumed the presidency of Brazil in 2019 with pledges to roll back protection of the rainforest and to reduce indigenous people's rights and threaten their homes and traditional livelihoods in order to promote economic development.

The Amazon is burning, with fires doubling from 2018 to 2019, partly as a result of a drier climate but also as more land is settled, cleared and prepared for agriculture. How political this is becoming was illustrated by the case of four volunteer firefighters who risked their lives to put out fires in the Alter do Chao region. They were arrested in 2019 and accused of starting the fires deliberately as a device for raising money from a concerned public. This created an uproar, including from Natura, a Brazilian cosmetics company which sources many of its ingredients from the rainforest, which provides a livelihood for indigenous forest dwellers. In the absence of any evidence, a judge ordered the release of the firefighters.

It is not just the Amazon being deforested, it is happening all over the world. According to the UN Food and Agriculture Organization, around 73,000 sq kms of forest are being lost each year. The Arcus Foundation has been tracking forest loss in UNESCO Natural World Heritage sites, with a loss globally of 1.5 per cent of forest in these sites and 2.9 per cent in adjacent buffer zones in the period 2001–2012. Population increase, greed and lawlessness are the main causes.

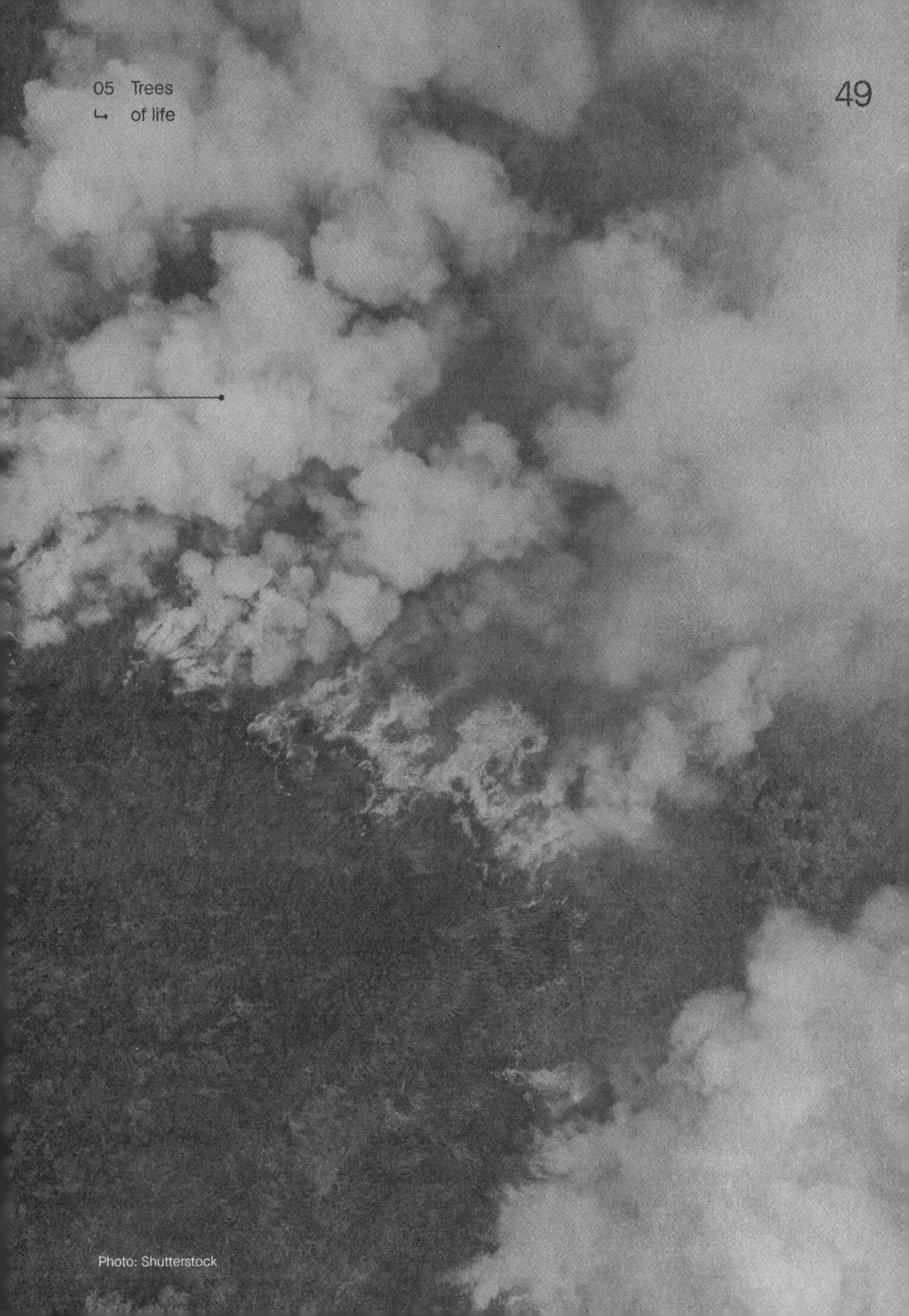

Photo: Shutterstock

Tree and forest facts

Trees enhance the availability of rain, replenish underground water, improve soil fertility, provide clean air, prevent soil erosion and beautify the environment. Here are ten tree facts:

1 A typical tree will produce nearly 118kg of oxygen each year. One hectare of trees removes up to one tonne of carbon dioxide each year. Just two mature trees can provide enough oxygen for a family of four.

2 Forests still cover 30 per cent of the land but deforestation is reducing this.

3 Agriculture is the leading cause of deforestation. Every second, 0.6 hectares of forest is cut down.

4 Forest loss is contributing around 15 per cent of global greenhouse gas emissions, according to the World Resources Institute.

5 At the current rate of deforestation, in less than 100 years the rainforests will be gone.

6 Twenty per cent of the world's oxygen is produced in the Amazon rainforest.

7 Tropical rainforests, which cover 6 per cent of the Earth's surface, contain over 50 per cent of all the plant and animal species in the world. As many as 28,000 species are expected to become extinct by the next quarter of the century due to deforestation.

8 Forest products provide 1.6 billion people with their livelihoods.

9 The rate of consumption of wood for fuel in sub-Saharan African countries is more than three times the annual growth of trees in the region. This is causing deforestation, lack of timber resources and loss of habitat.

10 Tree roots stabilise the soil and prevent erosion. Trees improve water quality by slowing and filtering rainwater, as well as protecting aquifers and watersheds.

If you want to know more about trees, have a look at the Trees Are Good website of the International Society of Arboriculture, treesaregood.org.

Find out about tribes under threat. Survival International is an international NGO fighting for the rights of indigenous peoples: 'We work in partnership with tribes all over the world to amplify their voices and change the world in their favour. We helped the Yanomami people create the largest area of rainforest in the world under indigenous control. We were partners in the "David and Goliath" victory of India's Dongria Kondh tribe against mining giant Vedanta. Alongside the Kalahari Bushmen, we won a landmark case to see them rightfully returned to their ancestral land.' Wikipedia has a list of indigenous rights organisations where you can find one in your own country.

The Trillion Tree Campaign

The United Nations launched the Billion Tree Campaign in 2006. The initial target was to plant one billion trees in 2007 (this was achieved by November 2007). In 2008, the target was raised to 7 billion trees to be planted by the hugely important climate change conference in Copenhagen in December 2009. Three months before the conference, this target had also been achieved.

To build on the Billion Tree Campaign, the idea was extended to a One Trillion Tree campaign at the 2020 World Economic Forum, with a platform for governments, businesses and civil society to participate as part of the UN Decade on Ecosystem Restoration (2020–2030). As of February 2020, more than 13.6 billion trees had been planted.

In 2015, there were about 3 trillion trees in the world. It is estimated that planting 1.2 trillion more trees would counteract 10 years of man-made CO_2 emissions.

By November 2019, 13 years since the Billion Tree Campaign launch, over 13.6 billion trees had been registered as planted in 193 countries. The top 10 countries were:

Ethiopia	4 billion
China	2.8 billion
USA	2.5 billion
India	2.5 billion
Pakistan	1 billion
Mexico	789 million
France	723 million
Turkey	716 million
Peru	646 million
Nigeria	626 million
Kenya	542 million
Egypt	500 million

The men who planted trees

Jean Giono was the only son of a cobbler and a laundress, and an important twentieth-century French writer. His book *The Man Who Planted Trees* is a fable about what one person can do to restore the Earth. The life mission of the hero of the story is planting one hundred acorns each day in a desolate, barren region of Provence, which leads to the total transformation of the landscape – from one devoid of life, with miserable, contentious inhabitants, to one filled with the scent of flowers, the songs of birds, and fresh, flowing water.

Here is a real man who planted trees. Jadev Payeng comes from Assam in north-east India. He wanted to save Majuli island on the Brahmaputra river from disappearing through soil erosion so he started planting trees in 1979. To date, he has single-handedly planted 1,400 acres of forest, an area larger than Central Park in New York City. See his story in the award-winning short film *Forest Man*, available from FilmsForAction.org.

And here is another. Steve Fitch grew up in the Philippines with a love for exploration and nature. Returning to his boyhood home in 1997, he found that the jungles he used to play in had been cut down, the topsoil was eroding into the ocean and the coral reefs he used to explore were being smothered by the soil run-off. He moved to Ethiopia in 1998 and found a similar situation. In 2004, he was asked by President Hailemariam to take over a failed tree nursery and reforestation project. Eden Reforestation Projects was born with the motto 'Plant Trees, Save Lives'. Since then, under Steve's leadership, Eden has planted 700 million trees in 8 countries.

The woman who planted trees

Professor Wangari Maathai won the 2004 Nobel Peace Prize for her efforts in planting trees in Kenya through the Green Belt Movement, which she founded in 1977. She also inspired the Billion (and now Trillion) Trees Campaign. She encouraged local women's groups to create nurseries to raise seedlings, some of which were planted on their farms, but most given away free to neighbouring communities. The women were paid one Kenyan shilling (around two cents) for each exotic tree they distributed and two shillings for each indigenous tree or fruit tree. Through Wangari's initiative, 30 million trees have been planted. She explained her work like this: 'When we plant trees, we plant the seeds of peace and seeds of hope. We also secure the future for our children.'

The boy who planted trees

In 2007, in Germany, nine-year-old Felix Finkbeiner was set an assignment by his teacher to prepare a report about climate change. He found out about Wangari Maathai and what she had done in Kenya. He then shared his idea that the children around the world could together plant 1 million trees across every country on the planet. This was the beginning of the Plant-for-the-Planet campaign. On 28 March that year, the first tree was planted at his school. Students in Bavaria and across Germany got involved and continued to plant trees. After a year, 150,000 trees had been planted. In 2008, Felix was elected to the children's board of the UN Environment Programme, which enabled him to spread his idea more widely.

Plant-for-the-Planet has developed into a worldwide movement. It encourages young people to understand that tree planting is for their future. Each tree planted makes a contribution towards environmental and climate protection. It is also an action for social justice, as those in poorer countries will suffer the most from the effects of climate change. By 2011, Plant-for-the-Planet had achieved its goal of children around the world planting a total of 1 million trees.

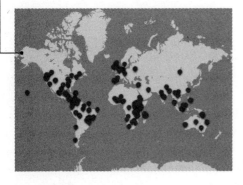

The country that planted trees

Forest cover in Ethiopia fell from 35 per cent of total land area in the early twentieth century to a little above 4 per cent by the 2000s. In 2019, the Ethiopian government launched a £1.1 billion tree-planting project to reverse this deforestation. On 29 July 2019, 23 million people participated in planting 353,633,660 trees. This was a world record.

Become a tree hugger

A 'tree hugger' is somebody who loves trees. People around the world who love trees have done some weird and wonderful things to protect them. Here are two examples.

In Southern California, a giant 400-year-old oak tree known as 'Old Glory' was threatened by the widening of a highway for a new housing development. With the support of other tree-lovers, John Quigley climbed up the beautiful oak and stayed there for over three months until he was removed by police. Nine months later, the tree was moved to a new location.

The Chipko Movement in India became world famous in the 1970s and 1980s. It showed how ordinary people could protect their trees. When a contractor arrived to cut down the trees, local people, including many women, went out and hugged the trees to prevent them being chain-sawed to destruction. This was the birth of the Chipko Movement in a remote village on India's border with the Tibet Autonomous Region.

The movement leader, Chandi Prasad Bhatt, declared their aim: 'Let them know they will not fell a single tree without felling one of us first. When the men raise their axes, we will embrace the trees to protect them.' The loggers withdrew. Over the next few years, many forests were saved by people who had been inspired by the Chipko Movement.

Plant a tree

Trees are good for the environment. Everybody should plant a tree. But what sort of tree should you plant? Each day has a particular tree associated with it. The tree for the day you were born is known as your 'birth tree'.

Your birth tree confers a set of characteristics on you. For example, if you are born on 10 July, your birth tree would be a fir. You might have all the following characteristics:

Don't just plant any tree, plant your birth tree. It could be an apple, ash, beech, birch, cedar, chestnut, cypress, elm, fig, fir, hazelnut, hornbeam, lime, maple, oak, olive, pine, poplar, rowan, walnut or a weeping willow. Find out what yours is and see how well it matches your personality!

↳ good taste

↳ moody

↳ dignity

↳ stubborn

↳ cultivated airs

↳ a tendency to egoism

↳ a love of anything beautiful

↳ caring for those close to you

↳ rather modest, but very ambitious

↳ talented

↳ industrious

↳ uncontented lover, but with many friends, many foes

↳ very reliable.

WATCH THIS:

Green, a film by Patrick Rouxel, tells the story of a sick orangutan in Indonesia, a victim of deforestation for palm oil production, who was evicted from her home and later died. It is a film with no words which tells an important and very moving story. Watch it at: redapes.org/multimedia/films/

DO THIS:

Click to save 7 sq metres of rainforest, with your donation paid for by advertisers at EcologyFund. Do this daily and save 2,500 sq metres in a year, all for free: ecologyfund.com

Where have all the species gone?

06

↳

The world's most trafficked animals

Species under severe threat through trafficking:

1 Pangolin, Malaysia

2 African rhino, Tanzania

3 African elephant, Central Africa

4 Tiger, India

5 Hawksbill turtle, Honduras

6 Orangutan, Indonesia

7 Sumatran serow, Sumatra

8 Helmeted hornbill, Malaysia

9 Gaur, India

10 Snow leopard, eastern Afghanistan

11 Amur leopard, south-east Russia

12 Macaw, Central America

13 Saiga antelope, Kazakhstan

14 Asiatic black bear, northern Pakistan

These are some of the world's most trafficked animals, mainly for meat and medicinal products. Some are severely under threat. Some exist in several regions; they may exist in other locations in addition to that shown here.

A global perspective

There are five main reasons why we are losing species, all caused by humans:

1   Climate change. As the world is warming, we are creating environments where plants and animals may not be able to survive. The bleaching of corals due to ocean warming is threatening a whole marine ecosystem.

2   Habitat loss, as humans clear more and more land for cities and agriculture. The clearance of the Indonesian rainforest to create palm oil plantations is threatening the orangutan.

3   Pollution, which is one possibility given for the decline in the bee population. If we lose our pollinators then our whole food system will come under threat.

4   Hunting, where we are creating extinction through overfishing and killing for food. Whales have been hunted almost to extinction. Atlantic cod were once so abundant that they could virtually be picked up from the sea. Today, they are an endangered species.

5   Trafficking of mostly mammals for food or medicine. Bushmeat is a major protein source for many. Tigers are killed for their teeth and other body parts, rhinos for their horn, elephants for their tusks.

These attributes provided an evolutionary advantage to these animals but are now decimating them through human greed.

There are an estimated 8.7 million species on Earth, with 6.5 million on land and 2.2 million in the ocean. The annual estimated extinction rate is between 0.01 per cent and 0.1 per cent. Most under threat are large mammals. With climate change, the extinction rate is likely to grow rapidly. Each extinction means a loss in biodiversity.

In the last mass extinction 66 million years ago, 75 per cent of species were lost – but the world recovered.

But life on Earth is resilient and will adapt to climate conditions. In the last mass extinction 66 million years ago, 75 per cent of species were lost – but the world recovered. In the 1970s, James Lovelock in his Gaia hypothesis saw our planet as 'a vast self-regulating organism, in the context of which all living things collectively define and maintain the conditions conducive for life on earth'. Read his book *Gaia: A New Look At Life On Earth*.

Life on Earth will continue for billions of years. We humans may be driving ourselves towards extinction but other creatures will rise up and some other species could assume top spot, as we humans did following on from the dinosaurs and all non-avians which went extinct 66 million years ago. But in around 5 billion years, our sun will become a red giant, engulfing Mercury, Venus and probably Earth, and this will mean a complete end to life on our planet.

The Red List

The International Union for Conservation of Nature's Red List of Threatened Species provides the world's most comprehensive information on the extinction risk of animals, fungi and plants.

Currently, there are 142,500 species on the IUCN Red List. Over 40,000 are threatened with extinction, including 41 per cent of amphibians, 37 per cent of sharks and rays, 34 per cent of conifers, 33 per cent of reef building corals, 26 per cent of mammals and 13 per cent of birds. The IUCN aims to turn the Red List into a `Barometer of Life' with assessments of more than 160,000 species. The Red List categorises species as follows:

EW – Extinct in the wild

CR – Critically endangered

EN – Endangered

VU – Vulnerable

NT – Near threatened

DD – Data deficient

LC – Least concern

It is difficult to prove that an animal is extinct. It may not have been seen for a while but it might still be there. But still, each year, species are declared extinct. These were some declarations in 2019:

↳ *Achatinella apexfulva*, a Hawaiian tree snail, with the last known snail, Lonesome George, dying in captivity on New Year's Day.

↳ *Oligosoma infrapunctatum*, Boulenger's speckled skink, a lizard unseen in its native New Zealand for more than 130 years.

↳ *Psephurus gladius*, the Chinese paddlefish, probably died out by 2010 due to overfishing.

↳ *Craugastor anciano*, a frog once common in Honduras, last seen in 1990, probably killed off by habitat loss.

CITES

CITES is the Convention on International Trade in Endangered Species of Wild Fauna and Flora. It is an intergovernmental agreement with the aim of ensuring that international trade in wild animals and plants does not threaten their survival. The illegal wildlife trade is estimated to be worth up to $20 billion annually, including live animals and plants, as well as products derived from them, especially for food, medicine, clothing and decorative items made with leather and wood. Wildlife crime is reckoned to be the fourth most profitable global crime and it has reached crisis point.

↳ Every five minutes a pangolin is poached.

↳ Every 30 minutes an elephant is killed.

↳ Every eight hours a rhino is killed.

↳ There are just 4,000 tigers remaining in the wild, awaiting their turn.

↳ CITES is trying to protect some 37,000 species.

The Wildlife Justice Commission combats wildlife crime: 'Our wildlife is not for sale to the highest bidder. It must be protected from traffickers who turn endangered species into trinkets and jewellery. Our mission is to disrupt and help dismantle the networks that support this destructive industry.'

Jane Goodall: In 1960, aged 26, Jane set out for Tanzania to explore the world of chimpanzees. In the decades that followed, she has demonstrated the urgent need to protect wildlife and has also redefined species conservation to respect the needs of local people and the environment. Now in her late eighties, Jane continues to travel the world, and through the Jane Goodall Institute she urges each of us to take action on behalf of all living things on the planet we share. In 1991, she created Roots and Shoots, with the goal of engaging young people from pre-school to university to work on environmental, conservation and humanitarian issues. Roots and Shoots has local chapters in over 140 countries, with more than 8,000 groups worldwide engaging nearly 150,000 young people. Participants are encouraged to work on problems in their own communities which affect people, animals or the environment.

Science to the rescue

There have been three major scientific advances that have enabled us to better understand biodiversity:

↳ **Evolution:** Charles Darwin published his theory of evolution in his book *On the Origin of Species by Means of Natural Selection, or the Preservation of Favoured Races in the Struggle for Life* in 1859.

↳ **Inheritance:** Gregor Mendel experimented with breeding pea plants and discovered the three principles of inheritance which describe the transmission of genetic traits. He published his findings in 1866 as *Experiments on Plant Hybridization*.

↳ **Molecular biology:** James Watson and Francis Crick discovered the double-helix structure of DNA in 1953, which led to the understanding of how genetic transmission actually works and to the mapping of human and animal genomes.

We now have a range of techniques which could be helpful in conserving endangered species and even in bringing extinct species back to life.

↳ **Cloning:** In 1996, Dolly the Sheep was cloned from one cell taken from the mammary gland of a donor sheep, which proved that a cell taken from a specific part of the body could recreate a whole individual.

↳ **Dicing and splicing DNA:** The Revive & Restore programme aims to enhance biodiversity through the genetic rescue of endangered and extinct species. Its projects include bringing back the passenger pigeon to demonstrate the potential for genomic intervention while helping to restore the ecology of North America's eastern forests.

Revive & Restore's iconic project is the Woolly Mammoth Project. The ultimate goal is to bring back this extinct species to repopulate tundra and boreal forest in Eurasia and North America. The intention is not to make perfect copies of the extinct animal but to adapt Asian elephants to thrive in the cold climate of the Arctic.

According to Revive & Restore, 'A wealth of information exists in the genome of every species. Genomes are an historic record of adaptation to survive billions of years of catastrophes, epidemics and changing conditions. Understanding the information locked in a genome is made possible by observing the living organism's cells, tissues, body, and behaviour. For extinct genomes such organismal interpretation is lost. Reanimation of genes in living cells allows us to discover the function of that prehistoric information in ways that studying genetic code alone can never provide. Mammoth haemoglobin, for example, may reveal information about mammalian blood useful to treating human diseases, and potentially the future of human space exploration (such as surviving cold environments); but the mutations that create mammoth haemoglobin need to be brought back to life for such discoveries to happen.'

↳ **Cryogenics:** James Hiram Bedford, a University of California, Berkeley psychology professor, died of renal cancer in 1967. He was the first human to be cryonically preserved, frozen and stored in the hope that we will be able to create the technology to revive him. This may be fanciful but if this idea can be made to work in the future, then this technique could be used to secure a future for highly endangered species.

↳ **Seed banks:** Seeds are living organisms and through low-temperature storage in dry conditions their life can be extended. Seed banks are being set up in an attempt to preserve biodiversity. Currently, over 6 million specimens are stored in over 1,300 seed banks around the world. The largest are the Millennium Seed Bank, operated by the Wellcome Trust in the UK, and the Svalbard Global Seed Vault, built by the Global Crop Diversity Trust in the permafrost of Spitsbergen, Norway.

Seed banks are being set up in an attempt to preserve biodiversity. Currently, over 6 million specimens are stored in over 1,300 seedbanks around the world.

↳ **Release from captivity:** Some animals are 'extinct in the wild' but specimens are still to be found in zoos, and attempts are made from time to time to release them and re-introduce them into the wild. Watch Mexican grey wolves being released into the wild on YouTube.

Citizen science to the rescue

Citizen science involves volunteers around the world collaborating on a scientific project, and many involve data analysis or wide-ranging research which would otherwise not be possible or practical. Zooniverse is an online platform for accessing these projects. These are some of the wildlife projects that you can engage in along with tens of thousands of volunteers from around the world. It's fun but also a practical thing that people can do to better understand threats to nature and biodiversity:

Chimp&See: The Max Planck Institute for Evolutionary Anthropology in Leipzig, Germany, aims to understand the ecological and evolutionary drivers contributing to behavioural and cultural diversity of chimpanzees. Chimp&See collates systematic ecological, social, demographic and behavioural data from 40 chimpanzee populations.

Skink Spotter NZ: Otago skinks are one of the most endangered lizards in New Zealand. Analysing time-lapse footage will help predict how climate change is affecting their behaviour ... and their chance of survival.

Snapshot Kgalagadi: Classify camera trap images of animals in the 3.8-million-hectare Kgalagadi Transfrontier Park stretching from the Namibian border across South Africa and into

Botswana, famous for its red sand dunes and dry riverbeds. This will help better understand how animals cope with extreme temperatures.

Penguin Watch: Penguins are under threat. Help Oxford University monitor penguin populations in Antarctica and the Southern Ocean to be able to find out why, analysing images from over 100 sites. This is how they invite people to participate: 'The nice thing is that anyone older than about five years old can contribute to penguin conservation. Be warned, it is mildly addictive, but it's for a great cause!'

eMammal: Gather data on animal behaviour for a project managed by the Smithsonian Conservation Biology Institute and the North Carolina Museum of Natural Sciences, validating the identity of animals caught on camera, which will assist in wildlife conservation.

WildCam Gorongosa: Gorongosa National Park in Mozambique was once among the most diverse places on Earth but decades of war decimated its large animal populations. An international conservation effort is restoring the park's wildlife. Help document this.

Mapping Change: Transcribe data from handwritten museum specimen labels to map biodiversity in Midwestern USA, at a meeting place of three terrestrial ecosystems – eastern broadleaf forests, tallgrass prairies and coniferous forests. This will help better understand the impact of climate change.

Endangered languages

It is not just species that are under threat. Languages are too. Diversity of language is important, as a language allows its speakers to express the world as they see it – which differs from community to community. For example, the Inuit are reputed to have 50 words for snow, snow being central to their lives, and their ability to express even small variations may be critical to their survival. The Aboriginal Australians have their own quite different view of time as something that is multidimensional, not linear, which they describe 'as a pond you can swim through – up, down and around', and they need language in order to express this.

Around 6,000–7,000 languages are being spoken in the world today. Half or even possibly as many as 90 per cent are expected to become extinct by 2100. Ainu, spoken on Japan's Hokkaido island, is one of the rarest, with 15 fluent speakers and 300 known users. Imagine there being two speakers and one dies. You are then the last speaker standing, with nobody to speak to! UNESCO has created these categories for endangered languages:

↳ **Vulnerable:** Most children speak the language, possibly restricted to certain domains (such as at home).

↳ **Definitely endangered:** Children are no longer learning the language as their mother tongue.

↳ **Severely endangered:** The language is spoken by grandparents; while the parent generation may understand it, they do not speak it to their children or among themselves.

↳ **Critically endangered:** The youngest speakers are grandparents and older, who speak the language partially and infrequently.

↳ **Extinct:** There are no speakers left.

Attempts are being made to revive languages all around the world. Cornwall is a county in south-west England that had its own language, Cornish. This died out in 1777. Using surviving written documents, descendants of Cornish speakers began to learn their former language and speak it to their children. Road signs have now appeared in Cornish and English, and now there are around 2,000 people who are able to speak Cornish.

Find an endangered language near you and learn to speak it. Here are four resources on endangered languages for you to check out: The Endangered Languages Project; The Foundation for Endangered Languages; Ethnologue, an online resource on lesser-known languages; and the UNESCO Atlas of Endangered Languages.

According to the Bible, the Tower of Babel was built by survivors of the Flood who all spoke a common language. It was a tower reaching up to heaven. God was displeased with this and intervened by giving them a diversity of languages so that they were no longer able to understand one another. Today, English is establishing itself as the 'lingua franca' of the world. There have been several attempts to create a universal language as a way of promoting international understanding. The best known is Esperanto, created by Ludwik Zamenhof in 1873. A much more recent universal language is Emoji, invented by Shigetaka Kurita in 1999, which aimed to be understood by anyone anywhere, and which is said to be the world's fastest growing language. And there is also Klingon for *Star Trek* fans, but fewer than 30 people in the world are able to speak it fluently.

DO THIS:

Become a citizen scientist. Sign up to volunteer with Zooniverse. Go to the projects page and find the one that interests you. Then get stuck in! zooniverse.org

Save
our
soil

The world's biggest deserts:

(in thousand sq kms)

1 Sahara 9,200
(northern Africa)

2 Australian Desert 2,700
(Central Australia)

3 Arabian Desert 2,330
(Saudi Arabia and the Arabian peninsula)

4 Gobi and Taklamakan Deserts 1,632
(China Mongolia)

5 Kalahari Desert 900
(South Africa Botswana Namibia)

6 Patagonian Desert 573
(Argentina Chile)

7 Syrian Desert 520
(Syria Iraq Jordan)

8 Great Basin 492
(south-western USA)

9 Chihuahuan Desert 362
(south-western USA northern Mexico)

10 Karakum Desert 350
(Kazakhstan Uzbekistan Turkmenistan)

11 Sonoran Desert 311
(south-western USA north-western Mexico)

12 Kyzylkum Desert 298
(Kazakhstan Uzbekistan Turkmenistan)

13 Thar Desert 200
(north-western India)

14 Mojave Desert 124
(south-western USA)

15 Atacama Desert 125
(Chile)

16 Great Salt Desert 78
(Iran)

Excluding the Antarctic and Arctic, where the land is largely frozen year round and receives little sunlight.

What is a desert?

The official definition of a desert is a region which receives less than 25cm of rain per year. Using this definition, approximately one-third of our planet's land surface is desert, and deserts are found on all continents. There are four different types of desert based upon climatic conditions: **polar deserts**, which include the whole of Antarctica and the Arctic region extending over Alaska, Canada, Greenland, Iceland, Scandinavia and Russia; **subtropical deserts**, the largest of which is the Sahara; **cold winter deserts**, which are found in China, Mongolia, Central Asia and Patagonia; and **cool coastal deserts**, such as the Atacama in Chile and the Namib in Namibia.

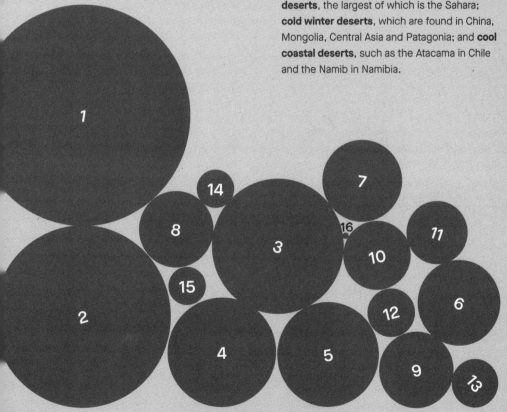

43%
of our planet's *total surface area* is habitable land for living and growing.

The total surface area of land on our planet is about 148 million sq km, 33 per cent of which is desert and 24 per cent mountainous, leaving us with 43 per cent habitable land to use for living and for growing the food we need. This 43 per cent amounts to just under 10 billion hectares or 25 billion acres and is all that we have available to sustain the 7.8 billion people currently living on our planet. But the world population is growing, cities are expanding and the amount of land available for agriculture is reducing, both because of this and due to desertification caused by soil degradation.

collapse of the civilization, and how experience from history might inform and improve agricultural practice in the USA in the wake of the 1930s 'Dust Bowl', caused by drought and inappropriate farming methods. Lowdermilk discovered that soil erosion, deforestation, overgrazing, neglect and conflicts between cultivators and herdsman had helped topple empires and even wiped out entire civilizations. He also learned that careful stewardship of the Earth's resources, through terracing, crop rotation and other soil conservation measures, enabled other societies to flourish over longer periods of time.

The Fertile Crescent in what is now Israel, Lebanon, Syria, south-eastern Turkey and the Tigris and Euphrates valleys in Iraq was the cradle of Western civilisation, where humans developed agriculture and irrigation, created towns and cities, and developed writing and important technologies such as the wheel. Today the Fertile Crescent is largely arid. This is one example from history. The same forces that caused this are currently degrading the land on the fringes of the Sahara and in California's Central Valley, leading to actual or future desertification.

Conquest of the land

Conquest of the Land Through 7,000 Years, Walter Clay Lowdermilk's study made for the US government in 1938–39, explored how agriculture practised by older civilizations might have led to serious soil erosion and then to the

Kiss the Ground

Kiss the Ground by Josh Tickell is a book that explores how current agricultural practice is destroying the environment, degrading the land, poisoning the Earth and

overusing the limited quantities of available water – and how by doing things differently, we might be able to 'reverse climate change, heal our bodies, and ultimately save the world'. His main thesis is that if we do the right things, we will be able to reduce and eventually reverse global warming, save our soils and provide nutritious food for everybody on the planet.

When land is cleared for human habitation or agriculture, the first impact is the disturbance to the local water cycle. When water is channelled, more of it runs off. The second impact is increased heat on the ground and in the air; rather than the sun's rays being used by plants for photosynthesis, they hit the bare ground between crops or the hard surfaces of roads and buildings and this heats the ground. The third impact is topsoil erosion.

Before the advent of agriculture in California, the soil would have held around 100,000 gallons of water per acre. On top of that soil was a mixture of vegetation, all of which drew CO_2 from the atmosphere through photosynthesis, which then ended up in the soil. Microbes used that carbon to build pore spaces which could store the water inside the soil. This was the ecosystem that was removed when the land was cleared for commercial agriculture. California's Central Valley is now 60,000 square miles of mostly flat, open, arid land. Its former ecosystem consisted of mixed oak forest with redwoods in the north and savannah to the south. Today, only a small fraction is covered with vegetation, possibly only as little as 10 per cent. The remainder is

bare, hardened and mostly unplanted, along with reflective urban/suburban surfaces. During the day, this reflects heat into the atmosphere and also absorbs it into the ground. This is turning what was once a vibrant ecosystem into desert.

Watch the award-winning *Kiss the Ground* movie on Netflix, download it for $1 or watch the trailer for free (they aim to reach 100 million people).

The Earth loses roughly 23 billion tons of fertile soil every year. At this rate, all our planet's fertile soil will be lost within 150 years.

No-till agriculture

The Earth loses roughly 23 billion tons of fertile soil every year. At this rate, all our planet's fertile soil will be lost within 150 years, unless we change the way we farm by adopting practices that restore the soil's fertility. One of the biggest contributors to soil degradation is ploughing. Ploughing loosens and removes any plant matter, leaving the soil bare and more likely to be eroded by wind and water. It also displaces or kills off micro-organisms, fungi, bacteria and insects that play an important role in creating a healthy soil. With continual ploughing, what was a healthy growing medium will become lifeless and dependent on chemical inputs for its productivity. Many of these chemical inputs will eventually run off into the water system, then enter into the food we eat or the water we drink.

Increasingly, farmers are beginning to understand the importance of preserving the soil by adopting no-till practices. And manufacturers are designing and selling farm equipment for this purpose. Japanese farmer and philosopher Masanobu Fukuoka was an early advocate of no-till farming. His book *The One-Straw Revolution* advocated no-till, no-herbicide grain cultivation. He claimed that simply by allowing things to grow naturally, the result would be ever-rising yields. And this is what he did and what he found. In his talks, he used to hold up a single straw, which gave the name to his movement. Fukuoka died in 2008.

Regenerative agriculture

Humans can facilitate the process of nature renewing itself and the soil increasing its fertility, rather than using twentieth-century techniques which destroy the soil and degrade the land. The idea of what we now call 'regenerative agriculture' is starting to gain wider acceptance. It combines a number of practices, including:

↪ No-till agriculture, with minimum disturbance to the soil.

↪ Mob grazing, which is short-duration, high-density grazing on each parcel of land with a longer time allowed for grass recovery before being grazed again.

↪ Agro-forestry, including the planting of crop trees and boundary hedges.

↪ Not leaving the soil bare. Planting perennials and cover crops for maximum absorption of sunlight and protection of the soil.

↪ Introducing more intermediate crops, more row intercropping and more grass strips.

↪ No chemical fertilisers, pesticides or herbicides, using biological inputs instead and techniques such as permaculture and biodynamic farming, all working with the land rather than against it.

↳ Improving water management and using organic fertilisers and compost.

↳ Restoring land which is in poor condition and renewing its fertility, especially in the world's arid and semi-arid regions, which are often also suffering population pressure.

Watch *From the Ground Up – Regenerative Agriculture*, a short YouTube video in which three Australian farmers talk about regenerative agriculture and how it has changed their approach to farming. Listen to a series of podcasts hosted by John Kempf, founder of Advancing Eco Agriculture, at regenerativeagriculturepodcast.com.

Solving the climate crisis through regenerative agriculture

Carbon capture, switching to renewable energy and flying less are all ways of reducing CO_2 emissions. A much simpler way is to transform the way we grow our crops and manage our farmland, using natural processes to draw carbon from the atmosphere and inject it into the soil. This is known as 'biosequestration'.

Every year, 30 per cent of our CO_2 emissions is absorbed by plants through photosynthesis. When these plants die and decompose,

A still from the short film *From the Ground Up – Regenerative Agriculture* showing the visual difference between a conventially managed farm (right) and one being managed holistically, with regenerative grazing practices (left).

the living organisms of the soil, such as bacteria, fungi or earthworms, transform the dead plants into organic matter and draw this down from the plants into the soil. This improves the fertility of the soil, helping it to retain water, nitrogen and phosphorus – all essential for healthy growing. The soil in the world contains approximately three times more carbon than is contained in the whole of the Earth's atmosphere. Modern farming techniques interfere with natural processes, through ploughing and crop burning, leading to less organic matter getting into the soil, leaving the fields open to be baked by sunlight, while weedkiller and fungicides kill off the microbes.

If we can change the way we farm, we will be able to increase carbon levels in the soil, drawing down carbon from the atmosphere in the process.

If we can change the way we farm, we will be able to increase carbon levels in the soil, drawing down carbon from the atmosphere in the process. If we are able to increase the capture of carbon into the soil by just 0.4 per cent per annum (which is 4 parts per 1,000 and an achievable target), we will start to stabilise CO_2 levels in the atmosphere. If we do all the other things that we know we need to do to reduce greenhouse gas emissions, then we can begin to reverse climate change. It is not a matter of either/or – we should be doing both. The 4 per 1,000 Initiative (launched in 2015 at the Paris COP21) promotes the idea that we should be looking after our soil for fertility, food security and the climate. Forty-seven states and regions have now signed up to this initiative. Each of them will find their own ways of achieving this goal.

The Carbon Underground was created in 2013 with these two core beliefs:

↳ that there is no solution to climate change that does not include sequestering carbon from the atmosphere and storing this underground;

↳ and that there is no other feasible way to draw adequate amounts of carbon back down to mitigate climate change other than the restoration of soil and shift to regenerative agriculture.

You can access a range of explanatory resources on its website, including videos and podcasts.

The Loess Plateau: 10,000 years of damage repaired in 10 years

The most striking example of how fertility can be brought back to arid land is the transformation of the Loess Plateau in China. Centuries of unsustainable farming had caused massive soil erosion, flooding and crop failure, all of which led to widespread poverty. Today, a large part of the region has been turned into flourishing agricultural land and local farmers are thriving.

In 1995, the Chinese government received $300 million from the World Bank Institute to launch a two-stage recovery process. Transferring state-owned land to the farmers was the first step, giving farmers long-term security and an incentive to manage their land better. This was followed by terracing the fields to reduce soil erosion, increasing vegetation cover and banning free-range grazing and the indiscriminate felling of trees so as to allow natural regeneration to take place. The combination of these regeneration techniques increased productivity and farm incomes, improved crop security and reduced the amount of labour needed to tend the fields – and this in turn enabled the farmers to engage in other income-generating activity.

After only ten years, this approach had lifted an estimated 2.5 million people out of poverty, greened what was once a semi-arid desert and made the Loess Plateau Project one of the biggest success stories for regenerative farming. Watch the video about restoring the Loess Plateau on the World Bank website, worldbank.org/en/news/feature/2007/03/15/restoring-chinas-loess-plateau.

People making change

Circle Carbon, based in Mallorca in the Mediterranean, uses a 1,000-year-old technology called 'TerraPreta', which originated in Brazil's Amazon basin. The main ingredient is biochar, a charcoal made from organic waste residues, tree cuttings and other agricultural waste. The biochar is then mixed with minerals and nutrients and composted to create a nutrient-rich super soil called 'TerraLlum'. This increases both the yield and quality of fruit-bearing trees and vegetables.

The Real Farming Trust is a network of rural and urban growers in the UK who are committed to agro-ecology and regenerative agricultural practices. They organise the annual Oxford Real Farming Conference, which brings together over 1,000 delegates involved in everything from beekeeping to micro-dairies, from organic farms to urban growing. They are helping to create Black Mountains College in Wales to run courses and degree programmes and to demonstrate techniques and share ideas and experiences on regenerative agriculture.

Regeneration International is a global network promoting regenerative farming and land management 'for the purpose of restoring climate stability, ending world hunger and rebuilding deteriorated social, ecological and economic systems'. It runs a programme of online events.

Soil Health Academy runs training programmes in regenerative agriculture to teach farmers and ranchers to learn how to apply soil health-improving principles on their land. They demonstrate 'how to increase profitability, build resiliency into your land, decrease input costs, and improve the nutrient density and marketability of the agricultural products you produce'.

WorldWide Opportunities on Organic Farms (WWOOF, which was originally known as Working Weekends on Organic Farms) is a worldwide movement with branches in over 40 countries which enables people to visit organic farms and gain practical skills in organic farming and gardening.

DO THIS:

Visit kisstheground.com where you are invited to take action under one of these 12 themes (in alphabetical order): activism, business, climate change, composting, fashion, gardening, health and wellness, lifestyle, online courses, regenerative agriculture, soil science, youth education/engagement.

READ THIS:

The Grapes of Wrath by John Steinbeck, a classic American novel dramatising the impact of the Dust Bowl on people's lives in the 1930s.

Our
oceans

Low-lying states

Smaller countries at risk of drowning
due to the rise in sea levels:

These island states have come together as the Alliance of Small Island States (AOSIS) with the main purpose of amplifying the message that these countries are at most risk from climate change, with some even predicted to disappear under rising sea levels and more extreme weather systems.

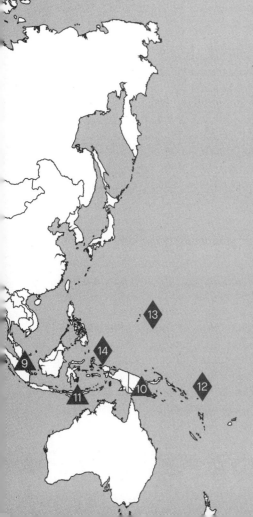

Atlantic ●

1 Cabo Verde

2 Guinea-Bissau

3 São Tomé and Principe

Caribbean ■

4 Antigua and Barbuda, Bahamas, Barbados, Belize, Cuba, Dominica, Dominican Republic, Grenada, Guyana, Haiti, Jamaica, St Kitts and Nevis, St Lucia, St Vincent and the Grenadines, Suriname, Trinidad and Tobago

Indian Ocean/South China Sea ▲

5 Comoros

6 Maldives

7 Mauritius

8 Seychelles

9 Singapore

10 Papua New Guinea

11 Timor-Leste

Pacific ◆

12 Cook Islands, Fiji, Kiribati, Solomon Islands, Tonga, Tuvalu, Vanuatu

13 Marshall Islands, Federated States of Micronesia, Nauru, Niue, Samoa

14 Palau

Rising seas

Sea levels are rising due to global warming.
There are two causes: warmer water is
less dense, so volume expands as the
sea temperature rises; and ice is melting,
particularly in Antarctica and Greenland. If all
the world's ice melted, this would cause the
sea level to rise by 66 metres.

It is estimated that 200 million people in
the world will be living in cities and settlements
that will be below sea level in 2100, with flood
defences needed to keep the sea at bay.
In addition, large numbers of people will be
affected by annual flooding due to rising ocean
levels. It is not just small island states that will
be at risk, but huge centres of population.
The country most at risk is Bangladesh, which
is at the mouth of the Brahmaputra river as it
flows into the Bay of Bengal, which is already
badly affected by flooding and cyclones. It is
estimated that this area will have a population
of 151.4 million by 2100. These are some of
the largest low-lying cities with their estimated
populations in 2100:

Lagos, Nigeria	88.3 million
Mumbai, India	67.2 million
Dhaka, Bangladesh	54.3 million
Shanghai, China	52.4 million
Ho Chi Minh City, Vietnam	15.5 million
Jakarta, Indonesia	18.2 million
Alexandria, Egypt	14.7 million
Bangkok, Thailand	12.14 million
Miami, USA	9.18 million
Houston, USA	7.4 million

Some of these cities may be able to survive
through the building of dykes and levees.
This is what has kept the Netherlands safe.
But Hurricane Katrina destroyed much of New
Orleans in 2005 when the city's flood defences
failed. What is certain is that rising sea levels
will have a devastating impact on the lives of
many hundreds of millions of people and lead
to what is likely to be the biggest migration in
human history.

Warming oceans

The ocean is absorbing most of the excess
heat from greenhouse gas emissions, which
leads to rising temperature of our seas and
oceans. The uppermost part of the ocean,
down to about 75 metres, is warming up
the fastest. The average temperature of the
ocean surface is currently around 17°C but
we are seeing an average temperature rise of
about 0.11°C each decade, and this has been
happening since the 1970s. This warming
is also having a serious impact on marine
ecosystems, especially on coral reefs.

Coral reefs are colonies of polyps held together by calcium carbonate. We think of them as vegetation but in fact they are living animals, secreting calcium carbonate, which acts as an exoskeleton. The vulnerability of corals lies in their symbiotic relationship with microscopic algae embedded in their tissues. These zooxanthellae give the corals the ability to process 90 per cent of their food through photosynthesis, while in return, the corals give the zooxanthellae protection and the carbon dioxide that they require for photosynthesis. This coexistence is fragile; it cannot survive a temperature rise of more than 1–2°C.

Most reefs are found in warm, shallow, clear, sunny waters, where they thrive best. They occupy less than 0.1 per cent of the world's ocean area. Coral reefs are host to one of the most diverse ecosystems on the planet, providing a habitat and shelter for at least 25 per cent of all marine species. They are extremely sensitive to environmental conditions in addition to temperature, especially to acidity (and the sea is becoming more acidic as it absorbs CO_2, as well as becoming warmer). Other threats to corals include blast fishing, cyanide fishing, trawling and the leaching of chemicals into the sea – including fertilisers with excess nutrients and sunscreen from the tourists who are visiting and admiring the reefs. Coral reefs also protect coastlines from the damaging effects of wave action and tropical storms.

The long-term future for corals is precarious. There have been major incidences of coral bleaching in recent years, where the fantastic beauty that tourists come long distances to admire is replaced by dead white exoskeletons – although there can be partial recovery from this. These are some of the most beautiful coral reefs in the world, which you can explore online:

↳ Maldives

↳ Great Barrier Reef, Australia

↳ New Caledonia Barrier Reef

↳ Red Sea Coral Reef, Egypt

↳ Rainbow Reef, Fiji

↳ Tubbataha Reefs National Park, Philippines

↳ Raja Ampat, Indonesia

↳ Palancar Reef, Mexico

↳ Wakatobi Islands, Indonesia

↳ Great Chagos Bank, Indian Ocean

↳ Lord Howe Island, Australia

↳ Belize Barrier Reef

↳ Apo Reef, Philippines

↳ Bonaire Reef, Dutch Caribbean

↳ Grand Central Station and Chimneys, Fiji

World Oceans Day

World Oceans Day is a celebration of the oceans and their importance to the health and wellbeing of the planet. It is held each year on 8 June. These are some ocean facts:

↳ Seas and oceans cover 71 per cent of the planet's surface and hold 96.5 per cent of all its water.

↳ The average depth is 3,790 metres and maximum depth is 10,923 metres (deeper than Mount Everest is high and equivalent to 6.8 miles). Ninety per cent of the ocean has still not been mapped.

↳ Life began in the ocean 3.1 billion to 3.4 billion years ago, and it was only 430 million years ago that animal life migrated from the sea and onto the land. Oceans are now habitat for more than 230,000 known species. Two-thirds of all marine life remains to be identified.

↳ Light is not able to penetrate deeper than 1,000 metres. But creatures have been found living at the bottom of the ocean, deriving energy and nutrients from thermal sources and mineral deposits in temperatures of up to 150°C.

↳ Three times as much rubbish is dumped into the oceans as the weight of all the fish that is caught each year.

Seas and oceans cover 71 per cent of the planet's surface and hold 96.5 per cent of all its water.

To celebrate World Oceans Day, here are some unusual things that you could do:

↳ **Take part in Seasearch**, a project for volunteer scuba divers and snorkellers who want to help protect the marine environment around the coasts of Britain and Ireland by mapping the various types of seabed in the near-shore zone and recording marine life, to see whether it is thriving and to identify any problems.

↳ **Hunt for ghost nets**. Abandoned fishing gear left tangled on rocky reefs or adrift at sea traps fish, dolphins, sharks and other creatures, often leading to their death. The UN estimates that there are roughly 640,000 tonnes of ghost nets in the world's oceans and reefs. A group of divers in Hong Kong led by Harry Chan, now aged nearly 70, have styled themselves as Sea Knights who dive to retrieve and remove ghost nets.

↳ **Buy carpet tiles**. Net-Works takes discarded fishing nets and recycles them into carpet tiles. They work with fishing communities in the Philippines, Cameroon and Indonesia, who are then able to generate an income through this process. So far, they have salvaged enough fishing nets to circle the world six times. They are now creating a supply chain for carrageenan (seaweed extract) in South-East Asia, which will be directly linked to measures for replenishing fish stocks and avert the risk of carrageenan becoming the 'palm oil of the sea'.

↳ **Browse The Ocean Awards**, given annually to honour and celebrate individuals, community groups, organisations and businesses who are creating solutions for the world's oceans. Categories include Local Hero, Science, Innovation, Visionary and Judges Special Awards. In 2021, the Innovation Award went Chris Wilcox for his work on tackling illegal fishing and fishing with explosives using radar, while the Science Award went to Lauren Biermann for using satellite data to find patches of floating plastic litter.

The National Ocean Service in the USA suggests six ways to help the oceans:

↳ Watch for whales: share your sightings so scientists can track trends.

↳ Geocache for a good cause: use GPS to gather information on ocean pollution, including field notes, location data and photos.

↳ Track the tides: record and report to the Environment Agency in the UK or the National Ocean Service in the USA local water levels and flood impacts to enable a better understanding of extreme weather phenomena.

↳ Fight harmful algal blooms: monitor water quality.

↳ Monitor marine debris: record debris on your local beach (and help tidy it up).

↳ Become a sanctuary steward: volunteer at a marine sanctuary or estuary reserve.

A number of citizen science projects are addressing ocean issues, including Seal Watch, Weddell Seal Count, Sea bird watch, Penguin Watch and Floating Forests. Find out about these and how you can participate at zooniverse.org.

Acidification

In one sense, acidification of the ocean is helping us. The ocean is able to dissolve around 30 per cent of the CO_2 being released into the atmosphere. This protects us (a little) from the Greenhouse Effect by reducing CO_2 levels in the atmosphere. But when the CO_2 is absorbed by the sea, it reacts with water to create carbonic acid, which is mildly acidic. The increased CO_2 level in the atmosphere results in more CO_2 being absorbed by the sea, which is becoming more acidic year on year. This gradual acidification will harm marine life which is used to lower acidity levels. The Global Ocean Acidification Observing Network is an international collaboration detecting and better understanding the processes of ocean acidification.

The ocean is able to dissolve around 30 per cent of the CO_2 being released into the atmosphere.

Overfishing

Overfishing is one of the biggest threats to the health of our oceans. Every day, more fish is hauled from the sea that can be naturally replenished.

Enric Sala is *National Geographic* explorer-in-residence. He founded Pristine Seas in 2008 to seek protection for our oceans by creating more Marine Protected Areas, which are 'National Parks of the Sea'. To date, Pristine Seas has created 23 MPAs covering more than 6 million square kilometres. There are different categories of MPA, the most protected being a 'no-take zone', where all fishing and other commercial exploitation is banned. According to Protected Planet, an authoritative source of data on protected areas around the world, currently there are 17,852 MPAs with a total area of 28.6 million square kilometres covering 7.9 per cent of our oceans. The UN target is 10 per cent and scientific consensus is that 30 per cent protection is needed for a sustainable future.

Protection is one way forward. Another is to deal with the issues of how fish are caught and consumed.

↳ We consume 160 million tonnes of seafood each year; just under half is caught and the remainder is farmed. Around 75 per cent of wild fish we eat is caught by commercial fleets, with the remainder caught by small fishing boats and for subsistence.

↳ Each person eats on average 19.2 kg of fish a year, which is around twice as much as 50 years ago.

↳ Twenty-nine per cent of the world's fish stocks are overfished, while 61 per cent are fully fished and 10 per cent underfished. Illegal and unregulated fishing constitutes an estimated 20 per cent of all fishing.

↳ One out of every five fish caught is unmarketable, endangered or too small to land legally. This by-catch amounts to a total of 16 million tonnes of fish being discarded every year.

↳ Over the past 40 years, there has been a decrease recorded in marine species of 39 per cent.

If you eat fish, make sure you eat sensibly. Search the Good Fish Guide website, run by the Marine Stewardship Council, to find out which fish are green rated – from well-managed, sustainable stocks or fish farms – and which are red rated – from unsustainable, overfished, vulnerable or badly managed fisheries, or with high levels of by-catch (fish caught unintentionally alongside the main catch, which are then thrown back dead). Making the right choice does make a difference.

To address the problem of discarded by-catch, Safety Net Technologies has developed a simple system for fishermen to shine lights at the fish they are trying to catch. Some colours will attract the fish that they are looking for while repelling fish they do not want. It claims to be able to reduce by-catch by 90 per cent. It is easy to fit and recharge and is designed specifically for the fishing environment. It retrofits to many types of fishing gear, enabling fishermen to comply with new fishing regulations that reward the use of sustainable gear.

Krill

Krill are small semi-transparent crustacean-like shrimps, about 6cm in length and a gram in weight when fully grown. They float in the water but are not able to swim against the current. Krill are very abundant. Many large animals such as seals, penguins, whales and sea birds feed on krill, which is why the Antarctic is able to support a large animal population.

There have been attempts to catch krill commercially. Large factory ships have been seen in Antarctic waters where they have come to catch and can large quantities of krill. Krill is used mainly in aquaculture and aquarium feeds (as fish food), and also in the pharmaceutical and health foods industry. If ways are developed to feed krill to the human population or as a source of protein for farmed animals, then overfishing krill will become a certainty, threatening the animal populations of the southern oceans.

Books to read

The End of the Line: How Overfishing Is Changing the World and What We Eat by Charles Clover. This describes how modern fishing and overfishing is destroying ocean ecosystems. It examines overfishing in many of the world's critical ocean habitats, such as the New England fishing grounds, West African coastlines, the European North Atlantic fishing grounds and the ocean around Japan. The book was adapted into a successful film in 2009. *The End of the Line* illustrates the disastrous effects of overfishing and shows that farming fish is not a sustainable or healthy alternative.

Bottomfeeder: How to Eat Ethically in a World of Vanishing Seafood by Taras Grescoe. 'Just when opting for omega-3-rich seafood is being recognised as one of the healthiest dietary choices a person can make, the news seems to be full of stories about mercury-laden tuna, shrimp contaminated with antibiotics, and collapsing fish stocks. In a world of endangered cod, pirate-caught Chilean sea bass, and sea-lice-infested salmon, can we really continue to order the catch of the day in good conscience?' Bottomfeeding is all about eating down the oceanic food chain, avoiding the big fish such as tuna, swordfish and salmon, which tend to be full of contaminants, and learning to relish the still-abundant small species that tend to be full of omega-3s and other brain-healthy nutrients.

DO THIS:

Explore how sea level rise and flooding will affect your city (and other cities) at different degrees of global warming: beforetheflood.com/explore/the-crisis/sea-level-rise

READ THIS:

The 2019 Special Report on the Ocean and the Cryosphere in a Changing Climate, published by the International Panel on Climate Change: ipcc.ch/srocc

I want
clean air

The world's most polluted cities

Figures in microns of PM2.5 particulate matter per cubic metre.
Any level of pollution above 55 particulate matter per cubic
metre is deemed unhealthy. Information is taken from IQAir's
2020 World Air Quality Report.

IQAir's 2020 World Air Quality Report found the greatest pollution in Bangladesh, China, India and Pakistan (which together have 49 of the world's 50 most polluted cities). Bosnia and Herzegovina is the most polluted country in Europe, Chile in the Americas: 'Air pollution continues to present one of the world's biggest health hazards to people everywhere, contributing to about 7 million premature deaths annually. 600,000 of these deaths are children. Compounding this staggering health crisis, air pollution is estimated to cost the global economy upwards of $2.9 trillion per year (3.3 per cent of global GDP) due to fossil fuel emissions alone, while also contributing to a range of severe environmental problems.'

Hotan, China 110.2

Ghaziabad, India 108.6

Bulandshahr, India 98.4

Bisrak Jalalpur, India 96.0

Bhiwadi, India 95.5

Noida, India 94.3

Greater Noida, India 89.5

Kanpur, India 89.1

Lucknow, India 86.2

New Delhi, India 84.1

Faridabad, India 83.3

Meerut, India 82.3

Jind, India 81.6

Hisar, India 81.1

Kashgar, China 81.0

Manikganj, Bangladesh 80.2

Agra, India 80.2

Lahore, Pakistan 79.2

Bahawalpur, Pakistan 78.7

Muzaffarnagar, India 78.6

The right to clean air

Clean, breathable air should be the most basic human right. Governments that forget this will lose legitimacy. Yet, according to the World Health Organization:

↳ 91 per cent of the world's population lives in places where the air quality does not meet the recommended safe limits of pollution.

↳ 4.2 million people die each year from outdoor air pollution from a variety of sources, including vehicle emissions, factories and power stations, domestic heating and cooking, cigarette smoking, including passive smoke inhalation, waste incineration, the burning of crop residues after the harvest, and wildfires. This compares with 1.35 million deaths a year from traffic accidents and fewer than 45,000 deaths from terrorism in the peak year of the 2010s.

↳ 3.8 million people die each year from indoor smoke, mainly from burning solid fuel including firewood, crop waste and cow dung in traditional cookstoves and for their heating. This burning, particularly in poor households, leads to respiratory diseases which can result in premature death.

People are not just dying from air pollution; it causes breathing difficulties for the living, too. The Forum of International Respiratory Societies' report 'The Global Impact of Respiratory Disease' says: 'Respiratory diseases are leading causes of death and disability in the world. About 65 million people suffer from chronic obstructive pulmonary disease and 3 million die from this each year, making it the third leading cause of death worldwide. About 334 million people suffer from asthma, the most common chronic disease of childhood affecting 14 per cent of all children globally ... Lung cancer kills 1.6 million people each year and is the most deadly cancer. Globally, 4 million people die prematurely from chronic respiratory disease. At least 2 billion people are exposed to indoor toxic smoke, 1 billion inhale outdoor pollutant air and 1 billion are exposed to tobacco smoke.'

Polluted air is poisoning our lives – 91 per cent of humanity deserves better than this.

Pea-soup green or APEC blue?

Pea soup is a grey-green colour with a gooey consistency. A very thick and often yellowish, greenish or greyish fog caused by air polluted with soot and sulphur dioxide is sometimes known as a 'pea-souper'.

The Great Smog of London covered the city for five days in December 1952. It was caused by a combination of industrial pollution and high-pressure weather. It brought the city nearly to a standstill and resulted in thousands of deaths. This led to the passing of a Clean Air Act in

1956 which meant only smokeless fuels could be burned in certain urban areas.

In November 2014, Beijing hosted the Asia-Pacific Economic Cooperation (APEC) regional economic summit. The Chinese government was determined that Beijing should be smog- and haze-free for the duration of the summit, which was being attended by leading politicians from across the Asia-Pacific region. To achieve this, they put every effort into reducing emissions in the run up to and during the summit. Around 10,000 factories in and surrounding Beijing suspended production; 39,000 factories reduced their hours of working; 60,100 industrial plants and 123,000 other ventures including construction sites and petrol stations were closely inspected; 11.7 million vehicles were kept off the road by introducing a ban on alternate days for cars with even or odd licence numbers; workers in state-owned enterprises, local government offices and educational institutions were told to take six days of mandatory holiday leave.

This achieved the desired result. The sky was blue. 'APEC blue' has come to mean something wonderful but transient. After the summit, the Beijing sky returned to being blue on some days and grey on others. A Beijing resident took a photograph of the view from his apartment window every day for a whole year, laid out the photos to fit on one page and posted this on the internet. This clearly showed the mix of blue days and grey days in Beijing. Although a lot has been done since then to clean up the Beijing air, Beijingers still

wake up wondering whether today will be a blue day or a grey day.

The Covid-19 crisis led to lockdown in many cities across the world. For several months in 2020, there was little traffic on the streets. The *Guardian* reported significant health benefits across Europe: 11,000 fewer deaths from pollution, 1.3 million fewer days off work, 6,000 fewer children developing asthma, 1,900 avoided emergency room visits and 600 fewer pre-term births. A doctor was quoted: 'If air pollution returns to its previous levels my waiting room will once again start filling up with children and adults struggling to breathe.'

What is air pollution?

These are the main constituents of air pollution:

1   **Particulate matter (PM):** Major components include sulphates, nitrates, ammonia, sodium chloride, black carbon, mineral dust and water. It is a mix of solid and liquid particles of organic and inorganic matter suspended in the air. Particles with a diameter of 10 microns or less can penetrate the lungs, though even more damaging are those of 2.5 microns or less, which can enter the blood system. Chronic exposure to particulate matter increases risk of cardiovascular and respiratory diseases.

2   **Ozone:** Increased ozone levels are being created by pollutants such as nitrogen

oxides (NOXs) from vehicles and industry and volatile organic compounds (VOCs) emitted by vehicles, solvents and industry. Ozone pollution is highest during sunny weather and less dangerous during winter or at night. Excessive ozone can cause breathing problems, trigger asthma, reduce lung function and cause lung diseases. Chemically, this is the same ozone as in the ozone layer but it affects all of us in a different way.

3   **Sulphur dioxide:** This mostly comes from burning coal and oil in power plants. It irritates the nose, throat and airways and causes coughing, wheezing and shortness of breath.

Mapping the world's pollution

The United Nations Environment Programme has created a global air quality data platform with IQAir, a Swiss air quality technology company. This was launched in 2020. It brings together real-time air pollution data covering more than 7,000 cities worldwide and reaches over 15 million users. According to Maimunah Mohd Sharif of UN-Habitat, the United Nations programme for human settlements and sustainable urban development: 'Poor air quality is a problem that affects urban populations particularly seriously so the ability to measure and take action to improve the health of those living in our towns and cities

is critical.' Publishing this data should help governments improve air quality and allow citizens to make more informed health choices.

Ma Jun, China's leading environmentalist

Ma Jun has had a significant impact on both water quality and air quality in China, where pollution levels of both water and air had risen to unacceptable levels. He started out in 1993 as a journalist with the *South China Morning Post*. In 1999, he documented and published *China's Water Crisis* and then in 2006 he founded the IPE (Institute for Public and Environmental Affairs) in Beijing and launched the China Water Pollution Map and the China Air Pollution Map the following year, which was the starting point for the World Air Quality Index project.

IPE now provides air quality information for more than 100 countries, using more than 12,000 monitoring stations in 1,000 major cities across the world. In 2017, IPE launched the Blue Map app, which gives citizens information on air quality where they are and lets them know if pollution levels are dangerously high, so they can take any necessary action. On a day when the Air Quality Index pollution level is predicted to be unduly high, the app will tell vulnerable people, such as the elderly, children and those with respiratory or cardiovascular problems, to make sure that they wear a facemask, avoid outdoor exertion or even stay indoors if the pollution level is bad enough. IPE also monitors pollution created by business and makes this data public, through league tables, reports and the app. This shows the businesses which are the worst polluters and creates pressure for them to improve their performance.

IPE invites you to set up your own air quality monitoring station with equipment costing between $100 and $250, depending on specification. This could be an interesting idea for primary and secondary schools. IPE also invites you to contribute your time, energy, expertise and professional skills to this global citizen science project to map, explain and help mitigate air pollution.

Incineration of waste

A lot of rubbish goes to landfill, but as landfill sites fill up municipalities are turning to incinerating waste as a waste-to-energy solution, at least capturing the energy embedded within it. Waste that is to be recycled is, for financial reasons, increasingly being exported to poor countries where, on arrival, it is often dumped and incinerated. So much of what we have carefully sorted for recycling and disposed of in a designated bin is not being recycled at all.

Even with the tallest smokestacks, incinerating waste adds to air pollution and releases toxins into the atmosphere. The Global Anti-Incinerator Alliance (GAIA) promotes action against the incineration of waste and other polluting waste technologies and campaigns for a zero-waste approach, so that there is zero incineration and no trash going to landfill.

In 2017, Burberry incinerated clothing worth over £28 million. This made headlines around the world. In 2018, as a result of public pressure, the company announced that it would discontinue this practice.

The high-end fashion industry has come under fire for incinerating surplus stock. Companies do not want to discount their excess products or donate them to charity shops as they feel that this would impinge on the brand's value. So they incinerate it. In 2017, Burberry incinerated clothing worth over £28 million. This made headlines around the world. In 2018, as a result of public pressure, the company announced that it would discontinue this practice.

For an imaginative use of surplus clothing, check out The Clothing Bank in South Africa, created by two ex-Woolworths executives, Tracey Chambers and Tracey Gilmore. The clothing is upcycled as part of a programme to train women in entrepreneurship. During the training, the women sell the clothes in the townships where they live and use the proceeds to help feed their families as well as to pay for the training. Also take a look at Patagonia's Worn Wear programme, where you can trade in old items of clothing that you no longer need; these are sold second-hand to someone else and in return you receive a credit which you can use to purchase used Patagonia items.

Clean Air Day

There are 'days' for almost every issue or cause spread out through the year. Some are international days, some national days. Clean Air Day is held in the UK in October each year. It brings together communities, businesses, schools and the health sector to raise public awareness of how air pollution is affecting our health. It suggests some simple ideas for reducing exposure and improving health:

↳ Walk and cycle more, especially using the back streets to keep yourself away from polluting traffic. A car driver is exposed to twice as much pollution as a pedestrian and nine times as much as a cyclist travelling the same route at the same time of day.

↳ If you must drive, switch off your engine when stationary; use an electric vehicle if you can; and keep your distance behind the car in front of you when stopped at traffic lights, as the exhaust fumes can get into your car.

↳ Avoid walking along busy roads. Use quieter streets, paths through parks and other green spaces, and pedestrianised areas. Avoid travelling during the rush hour, when the pollution levels are at their highest.

More than 3,700 organisations and hundreds of thousands of individuals participated in Clean Air Day in 2019. The World Health Organization has set targets for reducing air pollution by 2030. Its BreatheLife2030 campaign has four strategies to help achieve this: manage waste, cook and heat cleanly, move mindfully and conserve energy. Greenpeace is actively campaigning for cleaner air, especially reducing emissions from petrol and diesel cars.

Mums for Lungs

Jemima Hartshorn founded Mums for Lungs. She was concerned about the toxic levels of air pollution on London's streets and decided that she wanted to do something about this. Most importantly, she wanted to reduce the levels of pollution that children and babies were being exposed to. She brought together a group of

London parents who were on parental leave and walking the streets with their small babies.

School Streets is their campaign to transform the roads outside schools so that only pedestrians and cyclists can use them at school drop-off and pick-up times. Around 25 per cent of morning rush-hour traffic is parents dropping their children off. Across London, over 800 schools have surrounding air quality above recommended pollution levels, caused mainly by invisible nitrous oxide emissions from diesel vehicles. Young children with their smaller height are especially vulnerable to pollution on busy routes. Closing the roads at set times each day during the school term would help to improve the poor air quality locally and make it safer to walk, cycle and scoot to school, giving the children the opportunity to take exercise. Signs inform drivers of the road closure and barriers or cameras can be used to enforce this. Residents, local businesses and disabled drivers can apply for a permit.

It is not possible for all streets near schools to be closed. It is far easier to do it for schools that are located on quiet side streets than those on busy main roads. Even if it is not possible to close a street, measures can be taken to improve the air quality around a school, such as building a 'green screen' around the perimeter of the school, moving the main entrance to a quieter side street and encouraging parents to switch off their car engines while waiting outside the school gate to pick up their children.

Mums for Lungs is a growing movement that has gained national publicity and branches have been set up in other parts of London.

DO THIS:

Get the latest information on the world's most polluted cities at iqair.com/world-most-polluted-cities. Think about what you would do if you lived in one of these cities.

Become a citizen scientist and start monitoring air pollution in your neighbourhood or around your local primary school. Find out more and order an NO_2 monitoring kit at Mapping for Change: mappingforchange.org.uk.

Clean water, please

10

↳

Access to clean, safe drinking water

Countries rated on a score of 0 (extremely bad for access) to 100 (extremely good for access)

10 best countries for access	10 worst countries for access
1= Canada 100.00	178 Burundi 0.77
1= Finland 100.00	177 Kenya 0.84
1= Greece 100.00	176 Niger 2.68
1= Iceland 100.00	175 Mali 2.71
1= Ireland 100.00	174 Lesotho 3.01
1= Italy 100.00	173 Liberia 4.43
1= Malta 100.00	172 Madagascar 4.47
1= Spain 100.00	171 Benin 6.62
1= UK 100.00	170 Nigeria 6.76
1= USA 100.00	169 Eritrea 7.26

The Environmental Performance Index is published by Yale and Columbia Universities for the World Economic Forum and covers a wide range of environmental issues: agriculture, water, air, climate, fisheries, forest and biodiversity. The table shows the population's access to clean water for the top ten countries (all amongst the richest, with many other rich countries having scores just below 100.00) and for the bottom ten of the 178 countries ranked (some of the very poorest). It clearly illustrates the water divide in today's world.

Water facts

Water is essential to life; without water on our planet we would not be here! When we send spacecraft to other planets, the first thing we look for is water, as we want to know if there was or could have been life on that planet. Here are six water facts:

1   There is a fixed amount of water on Earth – approximately 1.83 billion cubic kilometres. This constantly changes from one form to another – sea water evaporates to form clouds, from which water falls as rain or snow, which forms rivers, which then run into the sea or are absorbed into the earth, to be evaporated once more.

2   Only 2.5 per cent of the Earth's water is fresh water. The remainder is salty, found mainly in the sea but also in salt lakes and salty aquifers.

3   Only 30 per cent of fresh water is available for human use (just 0.75 per cent of all the world's water). The rest is frozen solid.

4   Only a tiny proportion of the world's fresh water is found above ground – just 135,000 cubic kilometres. Seventy times as much fresh water is underground.

5   Water is unevenly distributed throughout the world. In many of the most populous regions of the world, fresh water is in short supply. Around 3 billion people live in areas suffering water stress and 500 million people in areas with chronic water shortage. About 1 billion people only have access to dirty water.

6   Attempts to harvest more of the world's water for human use have often resulted in ecological disaster, such as the drying up of the Aral Sea, reduced flow of major rivers such as the Indus and the Nile as water is extracted for irrigation, and huge migrations of population when big dams are constructed (such as the Three Gorges Dam on the Yangtze river).

How we use water

The average water use in the world is around 1,700 litres per person per day. The total for all of the world's population is 4,000 cubic kilometres per annum. Ten per cent is for domestic use, 20 per cent for industry and 70 per cent for agriculture.

In addition to our daily use of water for things like cooking, washing and drinking, we also indirectly consume water through the goods and services we consume which have used water in their manufacture and to bring them to us. On average, we consume twice as much 'embedded water' as water that we use directly.

An average adult excretes 1.5 litres of urine each day and loses 1 litre of water through breathing, sweating and bowel movements.

The actual amount for an individual depends on size, lifestyle, the amount of exercise, and how hot and humid the climate is. Our food replaces around 0.5 litres of this so we need to drink around 2 litres of fluids each day just to replace the water we lose. Most doctors advise that we drink a little more than this – around 3 litres for men and 2.25 litres for women.

Monitoring water quality

World Water Monitoring Day (on 18 September each year) focuses public awareness on the importance of protecting water resources and engages people in conducting basic monitoring of their local water sources through the EarthEcho Water Challenge. Monitoring can take place any time between 22 March (which is World Water Day) and 31 December. Simple monitoring kits can be purchased by anyone interested in participating. The kit enables everyone, children and adults, to sample local water sources for a set of water quality indicators, including temperature, acidity (pH), clarity (turbidity) and dissolved oxygen.

Public Lab is a US-based citizen science organisation which encourages the public to engage in environmental issues. They have developed a microscope kit, where you can build a microscope by reversing the lens in a webcam (this really works!) and then use this to monitor water samples collected from your tap, puddles in the road, streams and rivers.

Ensuring enough water to meet human needs

These are some ways of doing this:

Reducing demand

Economising on our use of water – for example, by putting a brick in the lavatory cistern so that less is used for each flush, having a shower rather than a bath and limiting the time spent showering.

Recycling the water we use – for example, using the 'grey water' from our bath to water our gardens or installing a WOTA box, which is a home unit for wastewater treatment developed in Japan.

Rationing our access to water through such methods as hosepipe bans, turning off the supply during certain hours of the day or metering with a high price for over-use.

Big ideas for increasing the supply

↳ Pumping water up from underground – but this needs to be done sustainably so that sufficient water remains for future needs.

↳ Diverting rivers to flow to where consumers demand.

↳ Desalination of salt water, which is usually done through a process called reverse osmosis, ideally powered by solar energy.

↳ Transporting water by tanker from water-rich areas to water-poor areas. For example, water is towed out to the Greek islands from the mainland to meet peak summer needs.

↳ Building big dams to hold water falling in the rainy season in reservoirs rather than letting it run into the sea. But this can affect communities downstream and destroy communities where the dam is built.

↳ Towing icebergs from polar regions to water-stressed areas.

Smaller ideas for increasing supply

↳ Rooftop collection of water, stored in water butts or tanks.

↳ Rainwater harvesting by terracing the land and channelling the rainfall into ponds and to replenish aquifers.

More unexpected ideas

↳ Changing our diet so that we eat foods which require less water to grow.

↳ Moving food production to regions where there is sufficient water, rather than growing food in inappropriate areas.

↳ Limiting population growth – more people means more demand for water.

↳ Ending water poverty.

In 2010, the United Nations recognised safe water and sanitation as a basic human right. In 2015, the world community signed up to 17 sustainable development goals, with Goal 6.1 seeking to achieve universal and equitable access to safe and affordable drinking water for all by 2030. End Water Poverty is an international collaboration coordinated by WaterAid in the UK. The WASH Campaign is coordinated by the United Nations to provide water, sanitation and hygiene for all.

Treating wastewater

Effective wastewater management is essential for human health and wellbeing. If we recycle used water for safe reuse, we will not just provide water where it is needed but we will also avoid contaminating our rivers, lakes and oceans.

Currently, approximately 80 per cent of all wastewater produced globally is discharged into the environment untreated. This can be a threat to human life and health. It is not just untreated sewage that is a problem. Agricultural wastewater carries excess nutrients from fertiliser, pesticide residues, and growth hormones and antibiotics used for livestock. Industrial wastewater may include heavy metals and hazardous chemicals.

World Toilet Day

Diseases associated with poor sanitation include cholera, dysentery, typhoid and polio. Around 1.8 billion people in the world today use drinking water contaminated with faecal matter. There are approximately 1.3 million deaths each year from diarrhoeal diseases. Proper sanitation will save lives.

Providing toilets is a gender issue. It will help keep more girls in school. Far too many girls miss out on their education simply because there are no clean and safe toilets. One billion people still practise open urination and defecation (which is harder for girls and women) and many women drink too little in an attempt to delay relieving themselves until after dark, and this can become a major cause of urinary infection.

Singaporean Jack Sim founded the World Toilet Organization on 19 November 2001 to raise awareness of and inspire action to tackle the global sanitation issue, advocating both provision of toilets and adequate wastewater treatment. The initials W-T-O were deliberately the same as those of the World Trade Organization. He held the first World Toilet Summit on the same day and persuaded the United Nations to designate 19 November each year as World Toilet Day. People all over the world celebrate World Toilet Day, campaigning for change and even 'squatting in public' to publicise the issue.

Drinking packaged water

An increasing amount of the water we drink is packaged. In the rich world, bottled water has become a luxury commodity, with water coming from increasingly bizarre sources such as from icebergs (Svalbarði Polar Iceberg Water) and the deep ocean (Kana Deep from Hawaii). Bling H2O brands itself as the world's most expensive bottled water. In the poor world, packaged water is a necessity for some.

Around 1 billion people lack access to safe drinking water; over one-third of these live in sub-Saharan Africa. With growing populations, rapid urbanisation and inadequate investment in urban infrastructure, more and more people need to have an alternative to piped drinking water. One solution common in West Africa and especially in Ghana are water sachets, typically 500ml of filtered and disinfected water sold in heat-sealed polythene bags. These are popular due to their low price, wide availability and a perception that sachet water is purer than tap water (which is not always the case). While meeting people's drinking needs, the sachets generate plastic waste on a large scale, clogging gutters and drains causing flooding in the rainy season, which increases the incidence of water-borne disease.

Following the 2010 Haiti earthquake, a group of New York University students came up with an idea for pedal-powered water purification using reverse osmosis which would provide unpackaged water, and the equipment could double up at night to power a disco. Their idea reached the finals of a social innovation competition, but sadly did not win and never happened.

All around the world people are looking to create affordable ways of providing clean drinking water. Swiss inventor Vestergaard Frandsen created the LifeStraw, a 25cm drinking straw consisting of a 10-inch plastic tube containing seven filters, some mesh, some using chemicals. The drinker simply sucks up water from any source using it as a drinking straw. It costs $3 to make, lasts for a year and provides a person with two litres of water a day.

Michael Pritchard used a similar approach to design his LifeSaver bottle. This filters out particles as small as 15 nanometres, which removes viruses as well as bacteria. It can provide up to 6,000 litres of drinkable water.

At a TED Talk he demonstrated it in front of a live audience – he took river water, pond water containing algae, sewage effluent and rabbit poo, mixed it all up, filtered it and drank it. Tanzanian chemical engineer Askwar Hilonga uses a Nanofilter and sand to filter water, which he markets in East Africa through the company Gongali Model. He wants 'to be a millionaire, not in terms of money, but in terms of impacting millions of lives'.

Doing something

Simon Maddrell and Joshua Mukusya met in Kenya in 1984 on a project to build sand dams and water tanks to improve water access and food production for Joshua's community. Drylands cover 40 per cent of the world's land surface and are home to around 2 billion people. They are characterised by frequent severe droughts. Water scarcity is a daily challenge. When it does rain, water runs off the bone-dry land, taking valuable fertile soil with it. Simon and Joshua designed a solution, building sand dams in dry river beds to trap the rain when it falls. The collected water is used to produce food as well as provide a year-round supply of clean water for people's daily use. In 2002, they founded Excellent Development Kenya, later renamed Otoni Development Organization, which has since built 1,156 sand dams and brought water to over 1 million people in 9 countries. Mukusya sadly died in 2011.

Seth Maxwell was a 19-year-old college student living in Los Angeles. Concerned about the water problem in the world, he asked himself, 'What can one person really do?' He recruited seven college friends, pooled funds and with the $70 he purchased 1,000 bottles of water. They started to give the bottles away free to passers-by, explaining to them that over 1 billion people in the world didn't have access to clean drinking water. They spoke to over 1,000 people on the first day. Almost everybody wanted to give something for the water they took. They turned their $70 into $1,700, which was used to fund the rehabilitation of a well in Eswatini. This was the start of The Thirst Project, which has gone on to raise over $10 million and has funded projects in 13 countries, providing over 400,000 people with clean water.

Autumn Peltier is a First Nations citizen who lives on Lake Huron, one of the world's largest freshwater lakes. At the age of eight, she realised that many of her compatriots in other parts of Canada only had access to contaminated water and she decided she had to do something. She became a 'water protector', fighting for universal clean drinking water for indigenous peoples in Canada and beyond. In a speech to the United Nations, she said, 'Water is the lifeblood of Mother Earth. Our water should not be for sale. We all have a right to this water as we need it.' (You can listen to the speech on YouTube.)

DO THIS:

Learn about solar disinfection (SODIS). This is a simple solution for purifying dirty water and making it fit to drink and is used by people who otherwise have no access to drinkable water. It requires only a PET bottle and sunlight, and can be done by anyone anywhere. Take some dirty water, put it through the SODIS process, and if you are brave enough drink it (at your own risk). Find out more at sodis.ch/methode/index_EN.html.

Nuclear waste and nuclear accidents

11

Nuclear reactors in the world

The number in operation in each country:

1 USA 93

2 France 56

3 China 51

4 Russia 38

5 South Korea 24

6 India 21

7 Canada 19

8 Ukraine 15

9 UK 13

10 Japan 10

There are also nuclear reactors in these
countries: Belgium and Spain, 7 each.
Argentina, Czech Republic, Germany, Pakistan
and Sweden, 6 each. Finland, Hungary,
Slovakia and Switzerland, 4 each. Argentina
and Taiwan, 3 each. Bangladesh, Brazil,
Bulgaria, Mexico, Romania and South Africa,
2 each. Armenia, Belarus, Iran, Netherlands,
Slovenia and United Arab Emirates, 1 each.

According to Wikipedia, in 2020 there were 424 nuclear reactors in the world with a combined generation capacity of 390 gigawatts. In Japan, 17 reactors had suspended operations following the Fukushima disaster, with the possibility of their going live under review. Sixty more reactors were under construction, with 16 of these in China, 11 in Russia and 9 in India. There were 154 more reactors planned and 185 reactors had been shut down or decommissioned or dismantled.

The USA has the most reactors, China has the fastest growing nuclear power sector and France is the biggest per capita.

Nuclear power timeline

1942: The first nuclear chain reaction demonstrated in a Chicago laboratory

1945: The first nuclear weapons test in Nevada; atom bombs are dropped on Hiroshima and Nagasaki to end the Second World War

1949: USSR conducts its first nuclear test

1951: An experimental reactor in Idaho demonstrates that electricity can be generated from nuclear fission

2022: The Zaporizhzhia nuclear reactor in Ukraine, the largest in Europe, comes under attack by Russian artillery

2016: Solar PV becomes competitive with nuclear ($84.7 v $102.8 per megawatt hour)

2011: Onshore wind becomes competitive with nuclear ($96.1 v $114.0 per megawatt hour)

(Figures from US Energy Information Administration)

1952: USA tests its first hydrogen bomb

1953: USSR tests first hydrogen bomb. Fourth months later, President Eisenhower delivers his 'Atoms for Peace' speech at the UN

1954: USSR commissions a 5MW reactor which generates electricity for the grid

1956: UK opens the first commercially viable nuclear power plant at Calder Hall

2011: A third major nuclear accident at Fukushima, Japan, is caused by an earthquake and tsunami. Germany decides to phase out all its nuclear power plants by 2022, with other major nations deciding similarly

1986: A reactor explosion causes the world's worst nuclear accident at Chernobyl, Ukraine

1979: Major nuclear accident at Three Mile Island, Pennsylvania, USA, following a pump malfunction

1958: The Atomium, representing an iron atom, becomes the centrepiece and symbol of the Brussels World Fair

Atoms for peace

'My country wants to be constructive, not destructive. It wants agreement, not wars, among nations. It wants itself to live in freedom, and in the confidence that the people of every other nation enjoy equally the right of choosing their own way of life' – Dwight Eisenhower, US President, speaking at the United Nations in December 1953.

The first nuclear weapons were used by the USA in August 1945 as a way of ending the Second World War. The Potsdam Conference was convened July–August 1945 between the Soviet Union, the USA and the UK to attempt to set an agenda for the post-war world. However, by the following year, Churchill's 'Iron Curtain speech' painted a picture of deep distrust and competition between the two Great Powers and their allies. The blockade of West Berlin from June 1948 to September 1949 and the Korean War, which ran from June 1950 to July 1953, brought the USA and USSR into direct confrontation. The USSR created first a nuclear bomb and then a hydrogen bomb, testing it just 10 months after the USA had tested its first hydrogen bomb, which signalled an increasingly dangerous world with the two nuclear powers racing for supremacy.

But while the world lived in the shadow of the Cold War for much of the second half of the twentieth century, there was another aspect to the nuclear future: the use of nuclear fission (and perhaps, at some stage in the future,

fusion) to generate power. In December 1953, President Eisenhower delivered his 'Atoms for Peace' speech at the United Nations, which became a launchpad for the peaceful use of atomic energy in contrast to the arms race, which led to nuclear stalemate and the concept of 'mutually assured destruction'. Eisenhower advocated a non-proliferation agreement throughout the world and argued for a stop of the spread of military use of nuclear weapons. But alongside this, he wanted to see the peaceful development of nuclear power by all nations, allowing nuclear technology to be used for positive benefit while restricting its military use. An 'Atoms for Peace Award' was launched in 1955 with $1 million from the Ford Motor Company to encourage peaceful uses of nuclear technology. Twenty-three awards were made, the first in 1957 to Niels Bohr and the last in 1969 to Dwight Eisenhower.

We now live in a world where 40 countries either already have or are planning to have nuclear power. The early vision was of abundant non-polluting electricity. But it did not work out quite like this. We have now seen three substantial nuclear accidents and a number of other small incidents, and the problems of decommissioning nuclear plants beyond their use-by dates and disposing safely of nuclear waste remain. And the West remains anxious that 'rogue states' such as Iran and North Korea might use their nuclear reactors to develop nuclear weapons. Meanwhile, in recent years, there has been very rapid improvement in solar and wind technology, such that renewable energy can now outcompete nuclear power with one challenge remaining – that renewable energy supply must be managed to meet demand and not be dependent on the wind blowing or the sun shining.

Atoms for good

Nuclear fission and radiation can also be used for good, to improve people's lives. The World Nuclear University is a network created in 2003 on the fiftieth anniversary of the 'Atoms for Peace' speech that brings together educational and research institutions, academics and professionals who are engaged in peaceful uses of nuclear energy, radio-isotope production and applications of ionizing radiation in medicine and industry. This is not just to promote exchange and collaboration but is an industry initiative for furthering public understanding of peaceful applications of nuclear technologies.

As well as training and leadership programmes, the WNU also organises a Nuclear Olympiad as an international challenge for undergraduates and graduates to showcase their ideas and innovations for nuclear applications and how these could be used to enhance the quality of life. This was first held in 2011 in South Korea as a contest for university students around the world to develop ideas and plans for gaining greater public acceptance of nuclear technology in their own country. Olympiads in 2015, 2016 and 2019 have focused on nuclear applications for global development.

A brief history of nuclear accidents worldwide

The seriousness of a nuclear accident is measured on the International Nuclear and Radiological Event Scale:

↳ **Level 7.** Major accident: Major release of radioactive material, with widespread health and environmental effects, requiring implementation of planned and extended countermeasures.

↳ **Level 6.** Serious accident: Significant release of radioactive material likely to require implementation of planned countermeasures.

↳ **Level 5.** Accident with wider consequences: Limited release of radioactive material likely to require implementation of some planned countermeasures. Several deaths from radiation. Severe damage to reactor core. Release of large quantities of radioactive material within an installation with a high probability of significant public exposure. This could arise from a major accident or fire.

↳ **Level 4.** Accident with local consequences: Minor release of radioactive material unlikely to result in implementation of planned countermeasures other than local food controls. At least one death from radiation. Fuel melt or damage to fuel resulting in more than 0.1 per cent release of core inventory. Release of significant quantities of radioactive material within an installation with a high probability of significant public exposure.

↳ **Level 3:** Serious incident; **Level 2:** Incident; **Level 1:** Anomaly; **Level 0:** Deviation.

To date there have been two level 7 and one level 6 nuclear accidents:

The Kyshtym disaster (level 6) on 29 September 1957 at the Mayak Chemical Combine, USSR, a plutonium processing plant and weapons production facility. The cooling system in a tank containing liquid radioactive waste failed and was not repaired. The temperature rose, evaporating the liquid, and the dried waste exploded with a force of around 70 tonnes of TNT. At least 22 villages were exposed to radiation and around 10,000 people had to be evacuated.

The Chernobyl disaster (level 7) on 26 April 1986 in Ukraine (former USSR). Unsafe conditions during a test procedure resulted in a steam explosion and a fire that released a significant fraction of core material into the environment. This had an eventual death toll of up to 93,000 people. The city of Chernobyl and the nearby larger city of Pripyat were evacuated and then abandoned. A 30-kilometre exclusion zone was established around the reactor.

The Fukushima Daiichi disaster (level 7) on 11 March 2011 in Japan. The starting point was a major earthquake followed by a tsunami. On detecting the earthquake, the active reactors automatically shut down. The electricity supply failed and the emergency diesel generators automatically started. These were powering pumps that circulated coolant to the reactors to remove heat that continued to be produced after the fission had stopped. A 14-metre-high tsunami swept over the plant's seawall and flooded the reactor buildings, filling the basements and knocking out the emergency generators. This resulted in three nuclear meltdowns, three hydrogen explosions and the release of radioactive contamination.

Also of note is the Windscale fire at Sellafield, Cumbria, UK, which occurred on 10 October 1957 when the graphite moderator at a military air-cooled reactor caused the graphite and the metallic uranium fuel to catch fire, releasing radioactive material into the environment. Also the Three Mile Island accident at Middletown, Pennsylvania, USA, which occurred on 28 March 1979, when design and operator errors caused a loss of coolant which led to a partial meltdown. Both of these were classified as level 5 incidents.

Experiencing a nuclear disaster

Here are three ways in which you can learn more about the Chernobyl disaster.

Pay a visit: Visiting places where disaster has occurred is called 'Dark Tourism'. Chernobyl is high up on any list of Dark Tourist destinations.

Both the Chernobyl nuclear site and the nearby town Pripyat have been deemed safe for tourists to visit since 2010. However, you have to be screened before you visit and checked for radioactive particles after you leave. You are also told not to touch objects that have been cordoned off and not to sit down anywhere.

Watch this: *Chernobyl* is a multi-award-winning TV drama mini-series. Created and written by Craig Mazin, the series revolves around the Chernobyl nuclear disaster and the clean-up efforts that followed. While the series was exhaustively researched, some liberties were taken for dramatic purposes but the basic truth shines through.

Read this: *Midnight in Chernobyl: The Untold Story of the World's Greatest Nuclear Disaster* by Adam Higginbotham, which explores life before, during and after what was the world's most serious nuclear accident. It contains images of abandoned homes and playgrounds, the rusting graveyards of contaminated trucks and helicopters too radioactive to be returned to base, the untilled farmland and the ruins of the reactor now enclosed in a concrete dome.

Toxic nuclear waste

Nuclear waste is a radioactive by-product from weapons manufacturing, fuel manufacturing, nuclear power plants and hospital medicine.

Most nuclear waste is created by nuclear power stations. Because it is radioactive, it is harmful to health and needs to be very carefully stored or reprocessed. Some of the radioactive material in nuclear waste has a very long half-life, where it might take as long as 1 million years for the radioactivity to decay to half its present level. If waste is disposed of negligently or criminally, the radioactivity can ruin air and water quality and soil fertility, making it impossible to grow crops safe for human consumption.

There are three categories of nuclear waste: high-level waste, including spent nuclear fuel and waste from reprocessing any spent nuclear fuel; intermediate-level waste; and low-level waste. Only a small percentage is high-level waste but it accounts for 95 per cent of nuclear waste radioactivity.

High-level waste can be vitrified, sealed inside stainless-steel containers and then buried underground in an officially approved site. Low-level waste, often from hospitals or laboratories, can be compacted or incinerated in a container that is subsequently buried in landfill. Intermediate-level waste, including reactor components, chemicals and similar waste which has a higher level of radioactivity, can be encased in concrete or bitumen and then buried deep underground.

Greenpeace estimates that around 250,000 tons of toxic spent fuel in 14 countries are awaiting disposal. France produces more nuclear waste per capita than any other country as over 70 per cent of its electricity comes from nuclear power. This generates

2 kilograms of radioactive waste per person per annum. Only a fraction of this is highly toxic, but after 60 years of nuclear power, there is a lot just sitting there awaiting a decision on how best to dispose of it. France has a plan to bury its high-level waste 500 metres underground in tunnels. A site has been identified in Bure in eastern France. Local residents (not surprisingly) are not happy.

Nuclear fusion: the answer?

Nuclear reactors use a process called nuclear fission to produce energy. A radioactive element such as uranium235 or plutonium239 breaks into smaller atoms which together have a slightly lower mass, with the difference being converted to energy (using Einstein's famous equation $e=mc^2$). Both of these are heavy metals which poison the environment with their toxicity and radioactivity.

But there is another route to nuclear power, nuclear fusion, where atoms combine to produce a bigger atom of slightly lower mass. The basic idea is to take isotopes of hydrogen (deuterium and tritium), heat them to more than 100,000,000°C, at which point a cloud called a plasma will form, then use powerful magnets to fuse the atoms, resulting in a release of energy. This replicates how stars, including our sun,

produce energy. Potentially, this will generate low-carbon power avoiding nuclear waste and without the danger of explosions. The race is on to develop a technology which works. This is hard and it will take time.

The Iter project, involving 35 countries including China, members of the European Union, India, Japan, Korea, Russia and the USA, is constructing a test reactor in southern France. It may take another 30 years until it is operational with power being extracted. There are many other projects around the world seeking to create a solution. The dream is unlimited energy for the whole world.

DO THIS:

Play the game. S.T.A.L.K.E.R.: Shadow of Chernobyl is a video game originally published in 2007. In the game, you assume the identity of 'the Marked One', an amnesiac man trying to find and kill the mysterious Strelok within 'the Zone', a forbidden territory surrounding the Chernobyl nuclear power plant. It is set after a fictitious second Chernobyl disaster, which has further contaminated the surrounding area with radiation and caused strange, other-worldly changes in local fauna and flora, and in the laws of physics.

Death by
chemicals

12

The ten most polluted countries in the world:

Death rate from pollution per 100,000 of the population per annum:

1 **Central African Republic 2,977**

2 **Niger 2,377**

3 **Guinea-Bissau 2,316**

4 **Lesotho 2,252**

5 **Afghanistan 2,083**

6 **Georgia 2,047**

7 **Eritrea 1,976**

8 **India 1,919**

9 **Bulgaria 1,767**

10 **Burundi 1,729**

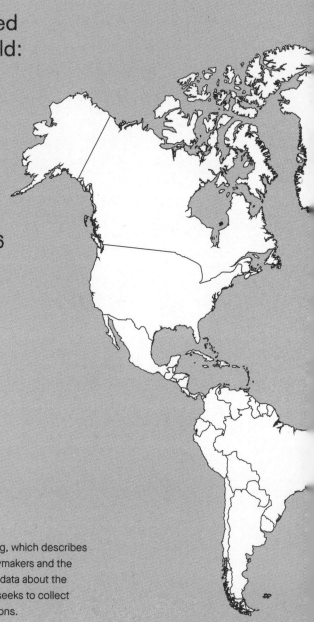

The information comes from Pollution.org, which describes itself as an information source 'for policymakers and the public to find, understand, and interpret data about the pollution crisis affecting us all'. The site seeks to collect data and to exchange ideas about solutions.

People living with pollution

These places are believed to be the eight most polluted sites, posing a real danger to local residents.

1 Houliang village, Shandong, China:
   Dioxin pollution of surface and
   groundwater

2 Chita City, Transbaikalia, Russia:
   Chromium mining

3 Kizel coal basin, Perm, Russia:
   Chromium mining

4 Sirsiya river, Birgunj, Nepal:
   Chromium mining

5 Doyagonj and Ponchoboti, Dhaka,
   Bangladesh:
   Used lead-acid battery recycling

6 Ziguinchor airport, Senegal:
   Chemical storage plant

7 Amman Garh, North-West Frontier
   Province, Pakistan:
   DDT production

8 Paulínia City, São Paulo, Brazil

Chemical plant discharges

Many people live near mines or industrial plants which create huge amounts of pollution, sometimes in countries where plans are approved based on economic benefit only or through bribery and where citizen protest is difficult or impossible. The people living nearby often work for the enterprises that are polluting their lives. Their only options are to live with the pollution or to move (which can be hard or impossible).

Houliang village in Shandong Province, China, is thought to be the most polluted place in the world. Tengzhou Zhenhua is a company that processes waste plastic. The waste plastic is washed and the dirty water is discharged into a pool. Every rainy season, this wastewater spills out and contaminates the surface water and groundwater. Also, the plastic waste is buried in three two-acre pits each about three metres deep and toxins leach out into the groundwater. The plastic is heated to high temperatures, when it emits highly toxic dioxins. Dust in the air contains a variety of pollutants, which, through wind and rain, then pollute the soil and the surface water. Children at the nearby primary school suffer dizziness and vomiting. Dioxins are accumulating in crops and fish, and then enter the human food chain.

Chita is to the east of Lake Baikal in Siberia, Russia, with copper and gold mining causing most of the pollution. A sharp rise in air pollution is observed during the winter, as climatic conditions cause air stagnation with an extraordinarily low rate of dispersion. In spring, the speed of air movement increases but then evaporation from sandy soil creates secondary air pollution. The highest carcinogenic risk is from the oxidation of chromium, which affects both the soil and the drinking water.

Fracking

There are all sorts of industrial processes that are polluting our lives. One is fracking, which promises cheap, clean energy, and which has become a boom industry in the USA.

If we are to avert a climate disaster, we need to reduce our carbon emissions. If we burned all the oil that has so far been discovered, this would create an amount of CO_2 in the atmosphere far greater than the level needed to keep global warming below 1.5°C or even 2.0°C. Yet the oil companies are still exploring for more and more oil and looking for cheaper and cheaper sources. Fracking has transformed the USA from a net importer of energy into a big exporter.

Properly called 'hydraulic fracturing', the process involves drilling down to a deep rock layer (usually more than 1.5 kilometres below the surface) and then drilling horizontally along the rock layer for maybe another 1.5 kilometres. Fluid is then pumped in at extremely high pressure, sufficient to fracture the rock. The fluid contains detergents, salts, acids, alcohols, lubricants and disinfectants at 0.5 per cent to 2 per cent concentration. In addition, sand and ceramic particles are pumped into the well to keep open the fractures, allowing the gas and oil to flow freely out. This is then pumped to the surface along with millions of litres of 'flowback liquid'. This flowback liquid contains contaminants including radioactive material, heavy metals, hydrocarbons and other toxins, all of which has to be safely disposed of – and all too often is not.

Proponents of fracking in the US claim that it is a cheap and safe energy source. They claim that fracking has unlocked massive new supplies of oil and clean-burning natural gas from dense deposits of shale, and that such supplies increase energy security, turning the country from a major importer of fossil fuels to an exporter. But the downside is the risk of contamination. Researchers at Duke University, North Carolina, USA, found that drinking water near fracking wells had levels of methane that 'fell squarely within a range that the US Department of Interior says is dangerous and requires urgent "hazard mitigation" action'. In addition to water quality issues, fracking releases compounds into the air, such as benzene, ethylbenzene, toluene and n-hexane; long-term exposure to these is linked to birth defects, neurological problems, blood disorders and cancer.

Watch the award-winning film *Gasland* on YouTube, which features whistleblowers, congressmen and world-renowned scientists, with some incredibly inspiring and heart-wrenching stories of ordinary Americans fighting for environmental justice against the fossil fuel giants.

Silent Spring

Silent Spring by Rachel Carson was published in 1962. This was a time when there was a widespread belief that science had all the answers to the world's problems. The book documents the problems that were being caused by the widespread and growing use of chemical pesticides on the environment – poisoning people, animals and birds while at the same time helping to feed the growing world population. Carson wrote: 'Over increasingly large areas of the United States, spring now comes unheralded by the return of the birds, and the early mornings are strangely silent where once they were filled with the beauty of bird song.' She saw chemicals as 'the sinister and little-recognised partners of radiation in changing the very nature of the world – the very nature of its life'.

The book was an early warning of the impact of pesticides on the environment and brought environmental concerns to public notice. Its publication led directly to a change in US pesticide policy, including the banning of the use of DDT for agricultural purposes and the establishment of the US Environmental Protection Agency. It was one of the most influential books of the twentieth century and is as relevant today as it was at the time –

although, today, we are poisoning ourselves in many other ways: effluents from chemical factories entering the water supply; mining, extraction and fracking; water run-off from poorly controlled chemical factories and warehouses; industrial activity in built-up areas; aerial spraying and run-off from agriculture; and unsafe disposal in landfill of consumer products, from batteries to computers.

The Environmental Society has a virtual exhibition on its website which shows the impact of Silent Spring in popular culture. Listen to Joni Mitchell's 'Big Yellow Taxi' on YouTube, which exhorts farmers to stop using DDT to save the birds and the bees.

Persistent organic pollutants

Persistent organic pollutants (POPs) include trace metals and organo-metallic compounds. POPs are highly toxic, with serious human, animal and environmental effects. They are resistant to degradation so once they get into the environment they can accumulate in tissues of living organisms and spread through the food chain. They can also travel long distances and reach into remote regions where POPs have never been used.

POPs can cause cancer, allergies, damage to the nervous system and disorders of the immune and reproductive systems. Some POPs also have endocrine-disrupting properties. And they have similar adverse effects on animals.

Many products that we use in our daily lives contain POPs. They are added to improve the product, such as flame retardants or surfactants used to reduce surface tension in detergents and other household products. POPs can be found virtually everywhere in measurable concentrations. We most commonly encounter POPs as organo-chlorine pesticides such as DDT (once used widely to control malaria), industrial chemicals such as PCBs (used as coolants in refrigeration and in carbonless copying paper) and dioxins, which are unintended by-products of many industrial processes.

Pesticides were once thought of as miracles for improving life – increasing crop yields and farm incomes, and eliminating diseases such as malaria. But the hazards to human health from their use are now well recognised. For example:

↳ Organo-phosphates have been linked to higher rates of ADHD in children.

↳ The herbicide atrazine has been linked to birth defects, infertility and cancer.

↳ Women exposed to the pesticide endosulfan during pregnancy are more likely to have autistic children.

↳ Girls exposed to DDT before puberty are five times more likely to develop breast cancer.

↳ The World Health Organization has designated a key ingredient in the widely used herbicide RoundUp a 'probable human carcinogen'.

Now that the dangers of POPs are well known, we need to find ways of reducing their use, and therefore our exposure. The Stockholm Convention on protecting human health and the environment from POPs was agreed in 2004 as an international framework for doing this.

As individuals, we should be trying to find ways of reducing the use of chemicals in our lives. The North-West Center for Alternatives to Pesticides (pesticide.org) and the Pesticide Action Network both offer advice on ways of reducing exposure to pesticides. PAN International coordinates action against pesticides internationally.

Here are five myths which are promoted by agri-business:

↳ Pesticides are necessary to feed the world (they are not).

↳ Pesticides aren't *that* dangerous (they are).

↳ Genetically modified organisms (GMOs) reduce reliance on pesticides (the reverse is true as many are designed to be used with specific herbicides and pesticides).

↳ We are weaning ourselves off pesticides (we aren't; the global pesticide market is estimated at $80 billion and is continuing to grow).

↳ We need DDT to end malaria, combat bedbugs, etc. (we don't; resistance to DDT is growing and other, safer remedies are being found).

Pesticide Action Week takes place at the end of March each year to highlight the problems of pesticides and promote pesticide-free alternatives.

Pesticide-Free Towns Network is a European initiative to minimise the use of pesticides, replacing them with sustainable alternatives so that 'the health of citizens and the environment is safeguarded, and an improved quality of life is achieved'. It is a network of cities and towns which pledge to adopt appropriate policies which:

↳ Ban the use of herbicides and pesticides in public areas under city/town's control.

↳ Extend the ban of pesticides to private areas with public access and agricultural areas next to where citizens live.

↳ Step up greening efforts towards local biodiversity enhancement.

Insignia: One area of worry is the impact of POPs on bee populations, as bees as pollinators are essential to food growing. Insignia is a Europe-wide citizen science project which sees beekeepers collect and monitor pollen samples from honeybee colonies bi-weekly for analysis of pesticide residues and veterinary products.

Volatile organic compounds

VOCs are hydrocarbons that enter the air at ambient temperature. Some are poisonous in themselves; others help create smog by reacting with nitrogen oxides and sunlight. VOCs are produced during fuel combustion (transport powered by fossil fuels is one of the main causes), by burning wood, carbon and natural gas, and through products we use in our daily lives, such as solvents, paints, adhesives, plastic compounds and additives in industrial processes.

Some VOCs have no known effect on human health, others have a high level of toxicity. The toxicity will depend on the particular compound and the period of exposure. Long-term exposure may cause lesions to the liver, kidneys and central nervous system. Short-term exposure may cause eye irritation, nose and throat discomfort, headache, allergic skin reaction, dyspnoea, nausea, vomiting, fatigue and dizziness. Environmental effects include alterations of photosynthetic functions in plants.

Highly toxic VOCs include benzene, styrene oxide and trichloroethylene (which are all carcinogens), and formaldehyde and styrene (which disrupt our bodies' hormone production).

Reducing chemicals in our lives

We know that our immune systems are working less well and that allergies are increasing. One supposition is that this could be a direct result of the chemicals that we have allowed into our lives.

Consumer products companies with their seductive advertising condition us to believe that there is an easy-to-use product which will solve every problem, sometimes even imagined problems, such as body odour and room smells. And we then go out and buy their products, which adds to our chemical overload.

There are lot of steps that we can take to reduce or, better still, eliminate the use of harmful chemicals in our homes and in our everyday lives. We could use natural products and remedies wherever possible. For example, to combat headlice, instead of using anti-lice shampoo, we can comb out the nits. To eliminate houseflies, instead of using toxic insecticides, we can practise careful sanitation and keep door and window screens in good repair. Fly swatters, flypapers and fly traps all help reduce the fly population without using chemicals. To eliminate smells, we can open the window rather than use an air freshener. We can take a brief shower rather than use an anti-perspirant. We can eat organic; this may be more expensive but, if you think about the harmful chemicals that are used to grow non-organic produce, this could be 'the cheap option'.

Here are five simple actions proposed by the Bumblebee Conservation Trust for cutting down on chemicals in your garden and more natural growing:

↳ Plant for pollinators. Grow more nectar-rich flowers, shrubs and trees to provide for pollinators throughout the year.

↳ Let your garden grow wild – wildflowers will grow, making great nesting and feeding sites.

↳ Put away the pesticides – they can harm pollinators and many other beneficial invertebrates. Consider alternatives and only use pesticides as a last resort.

↳ Cut your grass less often and remove the cuttings to let plants flower.

↳ Build a bee hotel (a 'bee and bee'!) and avoid disturbing or destroying nesting or hibernating insects in grass margins, bare soil, hedgerows, trees, dead wood or walls. Friends of the Earth provides instructions on its website.

Photo: Tania Malréchauffé

Microbeads

Microbeads are less than one millimetre in their largest dimension and made mostly of polyethylene, polypropylene and polystyrene. They are used in cosmetics and many personal care products, such as toothpaste. They are not chemically harmful but they often end up being ingested by animals and fish, and are entering our food chain. We are coming to recognise the danger they are causing to wildlife and human health. Microbeads are now being phased out or banned from rinse-off cosmetics and personal care products.

DO THIS:

Beat the Microbead is a campaign, website and app that allows you to explore the microplastic content of consumer products and alternatives that are bead-free: beatthemicrobead.org.

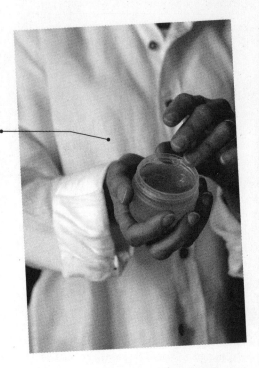

Photo: Nati Melnychuk

The
nitrogen
bomb

13

Nitrogen fertiliser use

Average use in kilograms per hectare of
cropland per annum:

1 Egypt 366.87

2 Netherlands 242.84

3 China 219.74

4 Belgium 198.43

5 Colombia 182.50

6 Armenia 178.39

7 Suriname 174.89

8 UK 168.50

9 Uzbekistan 163.27

10 Costa Rica 159.34

11 Chile 152.24

12 Czech Republic 143.94

13 Trinidad and Tobago 138.30

14 Vietnam 134.37

15 South Korea 133.80

16 Germany 125.02

17 Norway 123.45

18 Switzerland 114.78

19 France 114.77

20 Slovenia 113.78

These figures are from the UN Food and Agriculture Organization for 2017. Selected other
countries: Argentina, 24.27; Brazil, 81.63; India, 100.08; Indonesia, 57.54; USA, 72.61. Marshall
Islands and Nauru recorded no usage of nitrogen fertiliser in 2017 and usage in Guyana, Uganda,
the Congo, Niger, Samoa, Gambia, Central African Republic and Benin was less than 1kg.

Nitrogen is everywhere

Nitrogen is the most abundant of the six chemical elements crucial for life (the others are carbon, hydrogen, oxygen, phosphorus and sulphur). But more than 99 per cent of the Earth's nitrogen occurs as a gas, N_2, which constitutes 78 per cent of the air we breathe (oxygen makes up 21 per cent).

Most living organisms require reactive nitrogen to grow and thrive. The nitrogen in the air is in an inert form which is of no use to life. Reactive nitrogen includes inorganic compounds such as ammonia, nitrous oxide, nitric acid and nitrates, and organic compounds such as urea, amines, proteins and nucleic acids. Before humans emerged, reactive nitrogen was created naturally by lightning and through nitrogen fixation, where some plants use bacteria in their root systems to convert atmospheric nitrogen into reactive nitrogen. As agriculture developed and to feed a growing world population, farmers found that they needed to add nitrogen to the soil to maintain its fertility and crop yields. Progressively, over the past 300 or so years, ways of converting inert nitrogen into reactive nitrogen have been found. There are three main ways of doing this: by increasing the cultivation of legumes, rice and other crops that fix nitrogen; by burning fossil fuels; and by inventing chemical processes that transform nitrogen gas into ammonia and other compounds.

Feeding a hungry world

Feeding the world's population is a priority for the human race. Food security for everybody is an agreed global goal. Whenever and wherever starvation looms, it is seen as an issue which must be addressed. The UN's Sustainable Development Goal 4 is to end hunger and all forms of malnutrition by 2030. Other 2030 targets include doubling agricultural productivity and the incomes of small-scale food producers; ensuring sustainable food production systems and agricultural practices that increase productivity and production; and helping to maintain ecosystems and strengthening resilience to the impact of climate change.

The UN's Sustainable Development Goal 4 is to end hunger and all forms of malnutrition by 2030.

But despite these good intentions, there have been major famines throughout human history and there will continue to be. Some famines are caused by disease, such as the Great Famine in Ireland caused by blight which affected the country's staple food crop, the potato. This famine lasted from 1845 to 1849, causing Ireland's population to decrease by around 25 per cent – with 1 million people dying and another 1 million emigrating (mainly to the UK and USA).

Some famines are caused by drought and other climate effects, the impact of which is often exacerbated by population growth or conflict. The Ethiopian famine of 1983–85, which prompted the Band Aid record and the Live Aid concerts, is a recent example. The United Nations has warned of 20 million people at risk in South Sudan, Somalia, Nigeria and Yemen. The extreme drought in Syria from 2006–2009 was a prime factor in the unrest which led directly to the current conflict in the region.

Some famines are man-made, caused by political suppression or maladministration, such as the Ukraine famine of 1932–33 (3–12 million deaths), a possible cause of which was Stalin's response to an increasingly popular Ukranian independence movement, and the Bengal famine of 1943 (2–3 million deaths), where the government first denied that a famine even existed and then implemented policies which made the situation worse. The largest famine in the twentieth century was in China in 1959–61 (21 million deaths). This was during the Great Leap Forward, caused by officials wildly exaggerating crop forecasts to demonstrate their commitment to the Communist Party, then having to deliver almost all the grain that was actually harvested as the required share of their target to central government, which was used to feed the urban population, leaving the peasants starving.

The growth of the world's population (see chapter 17) has led to an increased need for food. The challenge has been – and continues to be – to find ways of growing more food on what land is available and suitable for agriculture, while at the same time seeking to contain deforestation and sustain biodiversity. At various points in human history, a development in technology has allowed us to significantly increase food production.

Charles Townshend, known as 'Turnip Townshend', was a member of the English aristocracy and leading politician in the early eighteenth century. He devised a crop rotation system which involved growing turnips and clover (as fodder crops for livestock), and barley and wheat (for human consumption). This first 'agricultural revolution' increased land fertility by fixing nitrogen in the soil and enabled agricultural production to rise to meet growing demand.

But much more nitrogen was needed for increasing food production to feed growing populations. Throughout the nineteenth century, nitrate for use as fertiliser was obtained from mining, from guano (bird poo) deposits and from bonemeal from the crushed remains of animals. But towards the end of the century, demand began to outstrip supply. In 1909, Fritz Haber devised a process for converting nitrogen in the atmosphere into ammonia, which could then be used for fertiliser (as well as for explosives). His process was commercialised in 1913 by Carl Bosch, working for the German chemical company BASF, and for the first time artificial fertiliser could be produced economically and on an industrial scale (the Haber-Bosch Process won its inventors a Nobel Prize). This was a second revolution.

Plant science using techniques such as selective breeding and more recently the development of GMOs has created a third food-growing revolution. This has increased production and also enhanced the nutritional value of the food being grown. The Green Revolution in the 1960s created high-yielding varieties of basic crops, which tripled the yield of rice, for example. We have also seen the development of precision agriculture, where water and fertiliser are delivered to precisely where they are needed, which decreases the inputs of water and fertiliser while at the same time increasing productivity.

Food from fertiliser (Source: Our World in Data)

Increasing agricultural productivity has meant that more and more people can be fed from food grown without the use of nitrogen fertiliser. But the number being fed through the use of nitrogen fertiliser has been growing far faster. This is how the use of fertiliser to feed the world's population has grown since the start of the twentieth century:

	Fed with fertiliser	Fed without fertiliser
1900	0	1.65 billion
1910	8.75 million	1.74 billion
1930	103.5 million	1.97 billion
1940	161.0 million	2.14 billion
1950	202.9 million	2.33 billion
1970	888.14 million	2.81 billion
1990	2.13 billion	3.20 billion
2008	3.26 billion	3.53 billion
2015	3.54 billion	3.84 billion

Currently, nearly half the world's population is being fed from food produced with artificially produced fertiliser. The challenge now is to find ways of feeding an extra 2 billion people, the projected growth in the world's population by 2100, while the land available for food growing is depleted through urbanisation and degradation, and at the same time finding ways of mitigating the negative impacts of nitrogen.

Nitrogen poisons our water and contributes to global warming

'Excess reactive nitrogen compounds in the environment are associated with many large-scale environmental concerns, including eutrophication of surface waters, toxic algae blooms, hypoxia, acid rain, nitrogen saturation in forests, and global warming.' – US Environmental Protection Agency 2011 report

Excessive nitrogen and other nutrients in water can lead to:

↪ Algal blooms and eutrophication (where excess nutrients over-stimulate growth in plant life).

↪ Disturbance to ecosystems, with new species becoming dominant in the changed nitrogen-rich environment.

↪ Light limitation, dissolved oxygen reduction and toxin production in aquatic environments, all of which affect plant growth.

↪ Human health effects – for example, from excess nitrates in drinking water.

Alongside this, nitrous oxide (N_2O) is a major contributor to climate change. It is the third most important greenhouse gas, after carbon dioxide (CO_2) and methane (CH_4). N_2O levels in the atmosphere have been rising steadily since the mid-twentieth century. There are three main causes of this: the increased use of nitrogen fertilisers, which stimulates microbes in the soil to convert nitrogen to nitrous oxide at a faster rate than normal; the widespread cultivation of nitrogen-fixing crops (such as clover, soybeans, alfalfa, lupins and peanuts, much of which is used as a protein source for livestock); and the combustion of fossil fuels, but also biofuels, which are categorised as green energy. N_2O is 265 times more effective in trapping heat than CO_2 and remains active in the atmosphere for an estimated 114 years. N_2O is the forgotten greenhouse gas, contributing as much as 6.5 per cent to global warming. Its role in climate change has been on a similar (rising) trajectory to CO_2, according to the Annual Greenhouse Gas Index.

The UN Environment Programme has established the International Nitrogen Management System to explore the consequences of the nitrogen problem and suggest ways of dealing with it. Their conclusion is that we have to halve the amount of nitrogen dumped into the environment by the mid-twenty-first century or our ecosystems will face epidemics of toxic tides, lifeless rivers and dead oceans. To do this will require a doubling of the efficiency of nitrogen use on the world's farms as well as creating ways of recycling as much nitrogen as possible back into food production.

can mitigate the problem but this is an expensive solution. The 1 billion cattle on our planet are also contributing significantly to global warming by belching up to 500 litres of methane gas each day, which is contributing an estimated 2 per cent to global warming. Rainforest is also being cleared for growing soya, which is a major component of cattle feed, and this again contributes to global warming.

Mega-dairies and micro-dairies

Dairies are growing bigger and bigger to take advantage of economies of scale. Mega-dairies may have thousands or even tens of thousands of cows. The Chinese, not a people who have traditionally had milk products in their diet, are building a dairy of 100,000 cows in Mudanjiang City in the north-east to supply the Russian market; this new dairy will be more than double the size of their previous largest dairy.

These huge dairies can create serious environmental problems. The excreta from the cows is often stored in large lagoons which also contain dairy parlour washings, which include chemical disinfectants and other waste. The resulting slurry can become a toxic brew. An open slurry lagoon will give off four main gases: methane, ammonia, carbon dioxide and nitrous oxide. Seepage from the lagoon and run-off from the slurry used to fertilise fields can pollute the water table. Covered lagoons and anaerobic digestion, where bacteria break down organic matter,

Photo: Subtle Cinematics

These huge dairies outcompete and are replacing traditional dairying. People are actively campaigning against mega-dairies, such as the Cows Belong in Fields campaign against the UK's first proposed mega-dairy.

Surprisingly, there is an alternative. Micro-dairies with fewer than 40 cows can produce grass-fed milk for local doorstep delivery, which they can do profitably while at the same time being humane and environmentally sustainable. So the next time you buy milk, you have a choice. See if you can get local milk. This may be a little more expensive but it will taste better and make you feel good. Stroud Micro Dairy in the west of England is one successful example of this.

Growing gliricidia

Gliricidia sepium is a miracle plant, originating from Central America. It improves the soil, with its nitrogen-fixing root nodules pulling nutrients closer to the surface. Its leaves and bark contain fixed nitrogen, which can be used as organic fertiliser and as a pesticide. Farmers no longer need to spend money on agricultural inputs and the water table is not poisoned from chemical run-off. It can be cut or coppiced to produce zero-carbon fuelwood. It can be planted as a shade crop or as a boundary crop, so generating additional income for farmers. The government of Sri Lanka has declared gliricidia its fourth national plantation crop after tea, rubber and coconut.

Lucky Dissanayake was a Sri Lankan publisher and TV producer living in London. She upped sticks and returned to Sri Lanka in 2013 to set up Biomass Ventures to encourage small farmers to grow gliricidia for use in power generation, with the leaves collected as a subsidiary crop to be used as fertiliser. She aimed to use the profits to increase literacy and provide access to IT for rural communities. Sadly, Biomass Ventures went into liquidation in 2021.

Oysters the answer?

Oysters provide habitat for other plants and animals, protect coastlines from heavy wave energy, storm surges and erosion, and are a good source of protein with a high market value. But oyster reefs are under threat due to overharvesting (human greed) and pollution from excess nitrogen, oil, PCBs and heavy metals, as well as through storm surges and hurricanes.

Sea Grant is a national network of 34 university-based programmes which supports coastal and Great Lakes communities in the USA through research and education. Sea Grant suggests that oysters can solve the nitrogen problem through 'bioextraction', using the nitrogen to grow both its shell and its tissues. You could help by eating more sustainably sourced oysters. Enjoy!

DO THIS:

Find out as much as possible about mega-dairies and the campaigns to stop them. Buy organic milk. Or consider switching to vegan alternatives. Oat milk, soy milk, rice milk (in that order) are far better for the environment in terms of CO_2 and N_2O emissions, water use and land use.

Drowning
in plastic

14

↳

Garbage in our oceans

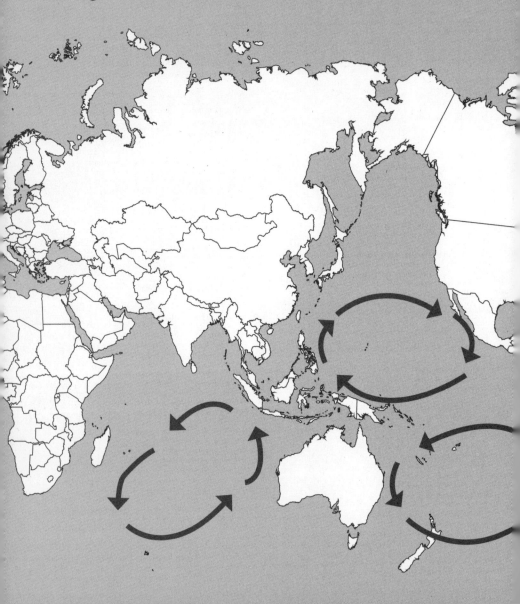

The five gyres

A gyre is a naturally occurring vortex of wind and currents that rotates clockwise in the northern hemisphere and anticlockwise in the southern hemisphere. There are five major gyres in our oceans: the North Atlantic Gyre, the South Atlantic Gyre, the North Pacific Gyre, the South Pacific Gyre and the Indian Ocean Gyre. They have a significant impact on the ocean, driving an oceanic 'conveyor belt' that helps circulate ocean waters. But they also suck the plastic and other detritus floating on the oceans towards their centres, creating garbage patches. With the increasing plastic waste entering our oceans, these patches are growing and growing.

Plastic in our oceans

According to Plastic Oceans International, more than 90 per cent of all plastic is *not* recycled. At least 8 million tonnes is being dumped into the ocean each year – which is equal to a garbage truck every minute. This plastic pollutes the air, the water and the entire food chain, threatening human health, wildlife and the planet.

The North Pacific Gyre has sucked in by far the largest amount of plastic and has come to be known as 'the Great Pacific Garbage Patch'. It covers an area of nearly 1.3 million square kilometres, 1,100 kilometres to the north-east of Hawaii. Today, it is estimated to contain more than 1.8 trillion pieces of floating plastic in the centre of the patch, weighing an estimated 80,000 tonnes, equivalent to 800 jumbo jets, with the amount increasing day by day.

The patch consists mainly of quite small pieces of plastic. Most are invisible to the naked eye and much of it suspended beneath the surface. The vast majority is polyethylene, polypropylene and discarded fishing nets and ropes, ranging in size from tiny (0.05cms) to huge. There is 180 times as much plastic as marine life in the Great Pacific Garbage Patch. Studies have shown that 84 per cent of sea life contains toxic chemicals in excess: sea turtles' diets are composed of up to 74 per cent of plastics and albatross chicks have around 45 per cent of their weight composed of plastics.

Sea turtles' diets are composed of up to 74 per cent of plastics.

This provides a stark reminder of how our throw-away economy is creating products and packaging which may be safe for our own use but failing to consider what happens to all the plastic once it has been used and disposed of. When the plastic also finds its way into the marine food chain, it is killing fish and we are eating the fish that have eaten it.

To understand more about this problem, watch the Ocean Clean Up video at theoceancleanup.com/oceans or perhaps host a community screening of *The Story of Plastic*. There are lots of other films to watch about this and related issues on the Plastic Oceans website – plasticoceans.org/films.

Do something

These are some actions suggested by the Environmental Cleanup Coalition to reduce plastic pollution in our oceans:

↳ Pick up plastic litter whenever you see it.

↳ Use a water filter rather than buying bottled water.

↳ Buy products without unnecessary packaging and buy in bulk wherever possible.

↳ Use reusable shopping bags.

A voyage through the Great Pacific Garbage Patch

'How can we raise awareness of the 73.9 million pounds of plastic floating in our oceans?' This was the question that David Mayer de Rothschild asked himself. He is a British adventurer, ecologist and environmentalist, and the founder of Sculpt the

Future Foundation, which makes small grants to support creative, innovative, sustainable environmental action, and of Adventure Ecology, which uses adventure as a way of inspiring people to live more sustainably and take action on environmental issues. He is a member of the UK Rothschild banking family.

De Rothschild undertakes ecological challenges in order to popularise environmental issues. He has trekked across Antarctica and explored the Greenland ice cap to witness at first hand the consequences of climate change. In 2010, he undertook his most ambitious adventure. He sailed across the Pacific from San Francisco to Sydney on an 18-metre catamaran which he had built from 12,500 two-litre plastic bottles and other recycled PET plastic and waste products. The journey lasted for 129 days and covered 8,300 nautical miles. He wanted to see and report on the evidence of marine pollution, and to drum up global awareness of the reckless damage to the world's oceans being caused by the very same plastic throwaways that his boat was floating on.

He explained, 'You don't have to build a plastic catamaran to make a difference. We're looking for dreamers, curious types, storytellers, rebels and, most important, you! Just let your inner change maker break through, click your mouse, and pledge to better our oceans and planet.'

The trip was broadcast live on the internet and, in order to inspire people to take action, he asked his followers to pledge to do three things:

1   To give up buying items in plastic bottles: 'They're manufactured, packaged, shipped, flown, trucked and then refrigerated for days only to be thrown away ten minutes after they're bought. What a waste!'

2   To give up using plastic bags: 'Can you cross a car park without one? Humans have crossed deserts, oceans and icy landscapes for thousands of years without plastic bags. Give it a try.'

3   To give up anything that is packaged in or made from Styrofoam. 'It's a water resistant, floating, shock absorbing, heat-insulating saboteur of nature: Cups and take-out food containers are the biggest culprits, but there are plenty of alternatives.'

His boat was called *Plastiki*, a reference to the *Kon-Tiki*, on which Thor Heyerdahl sailed the Pacific in 1947 from South America to Polynesia to demonstrate how the inhabitants might have arrived on these mid-Pacific islands.

The circular economy from a circumnavigator

Here is another sailor who is trying to do something to address the problem of ocean plastics. In 2005, Ellen MacArthur broke the world record for the fastest solo circumnavigation of the world. She retired from professional sailing in 2010 and founded the Ellen MacArthur Foundation to accelerate the transition to a circular economy, where we design things from 'cradle to cradle', using and reusing materials from one life to the next. In 2017, the foundation launched a $2 million award fund for innovation in the use of waste plastics, and to help promote the use of these innovations.

The Ellen Macarthur Foundation produced a report for the World Economic Forum called 'The New Plastics Economy: Rethinking the Future of Plastics'. In the twentieth century, plastics were seen as a miracle material for the future. In the twenty-first century they are seen as a curse. The report gives a vision of a global economy in which plastics never become waste and outlines concrete steps that could be taken towards achieving this.

From plastic to diesel

Many plastics are made from oil. It is possible to convert the plastic back to its original form and then into diesel. The first step is to put the plastic waste into a pyrolysis plant. This heats the plastic to a high temperature, which turns the plastic into oil-gas, which then becomes liquid oil when it has been passed through a cooling system. The oil can be used as fuel directly. But it can also be converted into diesel through a distillation process and by adding a bleaching agent. This process can be done in a factory but small-scale converters have been developed, which offers the possibility of community-level collection schemes to produce diesel for local use.

Learn how diesel can be made from plastic waste. Watch *Make Your Own Free Diesel from Waste Plastic!* parts one and two on YouTube to find out how.

What plastic can be recycled?

There is too much plastic in the world. The best approach is to avoid using it wherever and whenever you can. But if you can't, then make sure what you use gets recycled. There are different types of plastic – some are easily recyclable, some less so, some not at all.

The Society of the Plastics Industry created a system in 1988 that enables recyclers to identify what plastic an item is made of, which means it can be recycled more effectively. On most plastic containers, you will find a recycling logo with a number in the middle and sometimes letters underneath stamped into the plastic. These numbers refer to the following plastics:

 Polyethylene terephthalate (PET) is the easiest to recycle. Used for drinks bottles and food packaging.

 High-density polyethylene (HDPE) is also easily recyclable. Used for detergents, bleach, milk, shampoo and motor oil.

Polyvinyl chloride (PVC) is difficult to recycle. Used for pipes, toys, furniture, packaging and much more. Difficult to recycle and a major environmental and health threat.

 Low-density polyethylene (LDPE) can be recycled, usually into the same thing. Used for wrapping and shopping bags.

 Polypropylene (PP) is usually recycled into fibres. Used for clothes, bottles, tubs and ropes.

 Polystyrene (PS) is lightweight, bulky and hard to recycle. Used for packaging and cups.

 Other, may be a mixture of several types of plastic, not recyclable and to be avoided.

If you can't recycle, you can upcycle by turning your trash into something useful. Google 'creative uses of waste plastic' and you will find many ideas for ways to reuse and recycle plastic waste.

Use less plastic

So much of what we eat and what we purchase comes with plastic. It's hard to give it up. Vowing to go plastic-free outright is tempting but it's important to be realistic.

A better strategy for tackling your plastic footprint is to do it in small steps, embedding your new habits in your daily lifestyle bit by bit. Find ways of buying produce which is plastic-free. Take cups and containers with you when buying coffees or food to go. Make a less plastic pledge at lessplastic.org.uk. Join Break Free from Plastic, a global movement for a future free from plastic pollution. Involve your children at kidsagainstplastic.co.uk. They can become next-generation evangelists for a less plastic future.

Send a postcard. Flora Blathwayt is the 'Queen of Condiments'. She founded the social enterprise Rubies in the Rubble to make jams and chutneys from surplus fruit and veg which would otherwise have gone to waste. During the Covid-19 lockdown, she started collecting plastic from the beach and making greetings cards. These are WashedUpCards. Use them to spread the message.

Eat your knife and fork

A lot of plastic is generated by fast food and take-aways. Aditi Deodhar, a postgraduate student in Hong Kong, is developing an ingenious alternative to plastic cutlery. Planeteers is a student-run start-up which aims to address the menace of plastic cutlery waste, mass deforestation due to chopsticks production and health concerns caused by consuming carcinogenic microplastics while eating food with plastic cutlery. They have developed incrEDIBLE!, 100 per cent vegan, natural and edible cutlery for restaurants and take-aways to give to their customers. They would like to 'cultivate sustainable and healthy habits, one set of cutlery at a time!' In a similar way, you can fill an edible Ooho bottle with tap water, drink the water, then eat the bottle. *Bon appetit!*

Just pick it up

In Wales, there is a tradition of referring to people by the job they do. So Alec Jones the milkman would be referred to as 'Jones the Milk'. This is the story of Robin Kevan, a retired social worker, who became known as 'Rob the Rubbish'.

What concerned Rob was litter on the streets of his town. Some people would do nothing. Others might ring up the council and ask them to clean it up. Not Rob. He decided to do something himself. So every day, Rob went out in the morning in the tiny Welsh town of Llanwrtyd Wells (which happens to be the smallest town in Britain) to pick up litter, using the simplest of equipment – gloves, a pick-up stick, yellow jacket and black bin bags.

Then he decided to clean up the countryside. After breakfast, he drove to the surrounding mountains to pick up the litter that the visitors and ramblers had left. His litter-picking activity began to attract publicity. Word spread. He started to receive invitations to clean up other mountains – Snowdon, Wales's highest; Ben Nevis, Scotland's highest; and then Everest

base camp – which must count as 'the peak' of his mission to make the world a cleaner place.

Take it back

In 2006 in the UK, the Women's Institute decided to take action against excessive packaging. The WI, as it is known, is the largest women's organisation in the UK, with over 200,000 members. Monthly meetings give members the chance to meet up in person, try new activities, listen to speakers and campaign on issues that matter to them.

The WI is normally quite conservative and known for its baking and jam making. In 2006, members decided that supermarket packaging was excessive, so they organised a 'Take Back' campaign, asking members to take back all the packaging to the store where they had purchased the item and to tell the store manager that they should be responsible for disposing of this packaging (on the basis that the polluter should pay). Some even wrapped themselves in clingfilm, stood outside the store and handed out leaflets.

The WI chair said: 'WI members want supermarkets to reduce unnecessary packaging and put the environment first. I urge the public to join our campaign and return unnecessary and excessive packaging to supermarkets. Climate change is one of the biggest threats facing our world today. Supermarkets must take action now to reduce the packaging which, as landfill waste, releases greenhouse gases.'

Next time you're headed out to the beach ... take along a plastic bin bag and pick up all the litter that you find.

Clean up the beach

The ocean's wildlife is now choking on the plastic that we have polluted the sea with. International Coastal Cleanup started in 1986 when Linda Maraniss met Kathy O'Hara when they were both working for Ocean Conservancy. The first Cleanup had 2,800 volunteers. Since then, it has grown into an international event taking place each September with more than 500,000 volunteers in more than 100 countries who collect over 5 million kilos of trash – everything from cigarette butts to junked kitchen appliances.

Next Cleanup day, go down to the beach or the lakeside with your friends and clear up as much rubbish as you can. But remember that beaches need cleaning more than just once a year. So next time you're headed out to the beach, or to a lake, the riverbank, a canalside or a park, take along a plastic bin bag and pick up all the litter that you find.

Photo: OCG Saving The Ocean

The top 10 items by quantity picked up by Coastal Cleanup in 2019

4,771,602
food wrappers

4,211,962
cigarette butts

1,885,833
plastic drinks bottles

1,500,523
plastic bottle caps

942,992
straws and stirrers

754,969
plastic cups and plates

740,290
plastic grocery bags

678,312
plastic take-away containers

611,100
other plastic bags

605,778
plastic lids

DO THIS:

Join the Litter Movement. Make a commitment to pick up one piece of litter every day and invite one other person to do the same: roskapaivassa.net/littermovement.htm.

Zero
waste

↳

23 Zero-waste cities

Pioneering cities and regions pledging to
reduce waste:

Toronto

Montreal

Vancouver

Portland, Oregon

San Francisco

San Jose, California

Santa Monica, California

Newburyport, Massachusetts

New York City

Philadelphia

Washington DC

These cities and regions each made this pledge at the 2018 Global Climate
Action Summit: 'We pledge to advance towards zero-waste cities by: (a)
reducing the municipal solid waste generation per capita by at least 15 per
cent by 2030 compared to 2015; and (b) reducing the amount of municipal
solid waste disposed to landfill and incineration by at least 50 per cent by
2030 compared to 2015, with less than 30 per cent going to landfill and
incineration by 2030.' Zero-waste cities are pledging to waste less, moving
towards zero-waste rather than actually getting there.

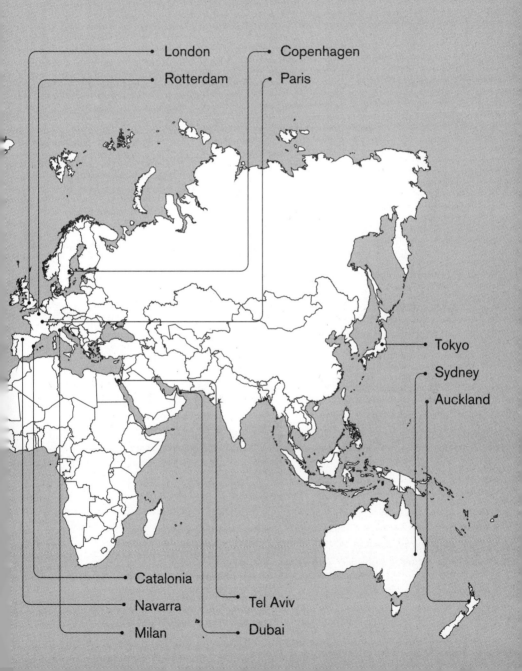

London
Copenhagen
Rotterdam
Paris
Tokyo
Sydney
Auckland
Catalonia
Navarra
Milan
Tel Aviv
Dubai

Cities committing to waste reduction

There is a widespread recognition that we waste too much. More and more individuals, communities, businesses, institutions and governments are declaring zero-waste commitments, implementing policies to foster waste reduction and to ensure that as much waste as possible is diverted away from landfill and incineration. In the case of waste, less is more – a more healthy and sustainable environment for people and planet.

C40 Cities is a network of 96 cities across the world which have committed to taking action to reduce waste and address climate change. Their pledge includes these statements:

'Global waste generation is increasing faster than any other environmental pollutant. Therefore, action in this sector can have a much greater impact on reducing greenhouse gas emissions (GHG) than the current emission inventories suggest. The International Solid Waste Association estimates that when all waste management actions, including disposal, recycling, composting and treatment, are considered, the waste sector could cut 10 to 15 per cent of GHG emissions globally. When actions to reduce waste generation are also taken into account, the sector could reduce up to 20 per cent of the global emissions.'

'Cities are also embracing the concept of the

circular economy, by not just reducing the amount of waste disposed of in landfills and incinerators but also working to decouple economic activity from the consumption of finite resources. These cities are taking action to keep resources in the economic system for as long as possible and phase waste out of the system. Circular economy initiatives can protect natural resources, clean the air that citizens breathe and the water they drink, while also making cities more efficient, prosperous and competitive.'

The waste problem

Waste is both a physical problem (how and where do we dispose of the huge amounts of waste that we create?) but also an environmental problem (we know it's contributing to climate change). Waste is mostly created in the richer countries and in cities. High-income countries generate about 34 per cent of the world's municipal solid waste – the everyday trash or garbage thrown away by people. According to the European Union, Europe generated over 905 million tonnes in 2016 (excluding mineral waste from mining and quarrying operations). This works out at around 5,750 kilos per person per year – with the average weight of a person at just 62 kilos. We are generating over 90 times our body mass in waste each year.

The World Bank estimates global municipal waste at 2.01 billion tonnes annually and expects this to increase by 70 per cent by 2050. The fastest growth will be in sub-Saharan Africa, South Asia, the Middle East and North Africa, where waste is expected to at least double.

Globally, some 37 per cent of waste is disposed of in some form of a landfill, only 8 per cent of which is disposed of safely, with the methane and CO_2 being emitted through the decomposition of organic matter being collected. Nineteen per cent of waste is recovered through recycling and composting and 11 per cent is incinerated. At least a third of municipal waste is not being managed in an environmentally safe manner. Open dumping accounts for about 31 per cent of all waste generated. Around 5 per cent of waste generated in Europe is exported, mostly to poorer countries where it is often illegally dumped or incinerated. And there has been a growing resistance to the export of waste from the rich world to the poor world.

The proper disposal of waste is not just a matter of health and safety. It has important environmental benefits. An estimated 1.6 billion tonnes of CO_2 equivalent greenhouse gas emissions are generated annually from solid waste treatment and disposal, which represents 5 per cent of global emissions. This primarily comes from disposing of waste in open dumps and landfills without gas collection. The incineration of waste is also an environmental hazard. Check out the Global Alliance for Incinerator Alternatives.

It is obvious that something needs to be done! The Zero-Waste Movement encourages cities to reduce waste generation and find ways of diverting more waste to recycling, while also encouraging people to live less wasteful lives. You will find zero-waste groups in many of the world's large cities.

These are some categories of waste that can be reduced:

↳ Packaging waste. Much of this is plastic waste from consumer products, and cardboard waste has increased significantly with the growth of online retail.

↳ Food waste, which can be reduced by behaviour change or composted.

↳ Office and factory waste, where businesses can put in place plans for waste reduction.

↳ Electronic waste, which can be reduced by manufacturers giving their products a longer life, and also through end-of-life recycling.

Landfills into landscapes

We have been sending garbage to landfills for many years now, and those landfills are often close to cities so as to minimise transport costs. But what happens when a landfill becomes full up and is unable to take any more garbage? Can it be repurposed for public benefit? Here are two examples of turning an eyesore into must-go-to attractions.

Take the free Staten Island ferry from Manhattan, with a wonderful view of the Statue of Liberty on the way. When you arrive on Staten Island, there is a surprise waiting for you. It was once the site of world's largest landfill, which operated from 1948 up to its closure in 2001. From the 1990s, it was the city's only landfill and 20 barges a day brought trash to there to be dumped. It is now the 2,200-acre Freshkills Park 'built on top of 53 years of New York City's garbage'.

Travelling into Jerusalem on the highway from Ben Gurion Airport, you used to see a mountain of garbage with a stench so great that you'd have to hold your nose, with gases rising into the blue sky and vultures circling above. This was not the sort of image to impress visitors to Israel's main city. It too has now been converted; the Ariel Sharon Park has been built on top of 25 million tons of garbage.

People helping people reduce their waste

These are some social innovators who are creating less wasteful ways of making, selling, using, disposing of, repairing, reusing and recycling the products we consume in our daily lives.

Let's repair it: In 2003, Kyle Wiens was unable to find an Apple iBook G3 repair manual. So he decided to create his own repair guide. This led to him setting up iFixit, which sells parts and publishes free Wiki-like online repair guides for consumer electronics and gadgets on its web site. Kyle explains: 'We're working on right to repair laws. Let's take back our right to use, modify, and repair however we want. Defend your right to fix. Products that can be repaired, should be repaired. Refurbished cell phones can be sold to someone new. Repairing creates jobs for the future: for every 1,000 tons of electronics, landfill creates 1 job, recycling 15 jobs, repairing 200 jobs. Repair jobs are local. They won't ever be shipped overseas. Repaired computers bridge the digital divide.'

Let's find it: Dian Hisham is a graphic designer from Singapore who lives in London. She runs a Facebook page called ZeroWasteNearMe to help people find local outlets which sell unpackaged produce. The Zero Waste Network has also created a directory of zero-waste suppliers. Check these out. If you live somewhere outside the UK, find or create similar online resource.

Let's do it: Alexander Furey founded Zero Waste Mindset to spread the idea of reducing waste, especially to business. With Delia Gadea he co-founded Zero Waste London, which facilitates, hosts and promotes zero-waste-related events and activities, including socials, talks, panel discussions, tours, film and documentary screenings and workshops using MeetUp as a platform for doing this. Zero Waste London also supports and promotes a variety of zero-waste and sustainability events organised by others and acts as a platform for everything related to zero waste in London and further afield. It has become the largest zero-waste community in the UK, with over 2,000 members.

And even in poor countries: Sensible solid waste management can also be organised in villages in poorer countries. The RoundGlass Foundation was set up by Sunny Singh, a Punjabi-origin health-tech entrepreneur working in Seattle. His foundation aims to improve lives and livelihoods in some 360 villages in the Punjab. Most household waste is food waste with a very limited quantity of packaging waste. The foundation runs a daily collection service in villages. It composts the food waste and recycles the paper and plastics. Households pay 40 rupees per month for this service, which covers costs, and the sale of the compost to farmers generates a small profit for the village. The next challenge is to treat the sewage which currently ends up in village ponds. The foundation plans to replicate this in all 360 villages.

Three zero-waste people

Most of us don't even think about the waste that we create. We eat a take-away lunch and then toss everything into the trash, some perhaps for recycling, but a lot not. The uneaten food, the plastic containers, the paper plates and napkins, the wooden chopsticks. Making all of this consumes resources. Far better in today's world to waste less and, by doing this, to begin to understand the issue of waste a little bit better.

Bea Johnson: In her book *Zero Waste Home: The Ultimate Guide to Simplifying your Life by Reducing your Waste*, Bea suggests five Rs: refuse, reduce, reuse, recycle, rot (compost it). She has used this to reduce her family's annual trash so that it fits into a pint jar.

Lauren Singer: Laura, who styles herself as the 'Zero Waste Woman', has been trying to live a lifestyle without waste in order to show that this is possible and to spread the message through the publicity that she has been able to get. Read Lauren's blog and take her advice on how you can start to reduce the amount of waste that you create.

Kathryn Kellogg: When Kathryn moved to California, she says, she was shocked to see all of the litter and plastic lining the streets, so close to the ocean. This was Kathryn's starting point for creating her Going Zero Waste blog, which has lots of tips, including '10 things I don't buy anymore' and '17 zero-waste make-up brands'.

Many others have followed their lead and have created their own blogs on zero-waste living in other countries. Could you become a zero-waste person? Perhaps. Would you want to? Maybe. Would you like it? Not a lot. But will you do it? Why not give it a try? You will be making a difference and you will also inspire others.

The Story of Stuff

The Story of Stuff project started with an animated film by Annie Leonard about our consumption-crazed culture, the ways in which we are drowning in stuff and what we can do about it. Annie and her team have now made eight other films with more than 50 million online views around the world, which have encouraged viewers to support hundreds of environmental projects and campaigns with their time, energy and money. Watch *The Story of Stuff* and other short films suggesting ways towards a more sustainable future. Annie says, 'We have a problem with Stuff: we have too much of it, too much of it is toxic, and we don't share it very well. But that's not the way things have to be.'

Waste less

To step away from a 'convenience lifestyle', where you do what is easiest and most enjoyable, will always require determination. Giving up throwaways and making sure that you recycle or upcycle what you no longer need or want requires effort, and it is probably much more fun to go shopping for new things than continuing to use what you have.

The challenge is not to become a zero-waste person but to waste less, a lot less, by doing some simple things:

1   Take your own cup to Starbucks or Costa and your own reusable containers to your favourite take-away shops. Refuse to take their plates, cups, knives and forks, napkins and bags. Tell them why you are doing this.

2   Take shopping bags with you when you go shopping and give preference to buying goods which use less packaging. There are more and more zero-packaging shops where you fill your own containers with dry goods rather than buying everything pre-weighed and neatly packaged.

3   Buy only as much as you need. Don't be tempted to buy more by 'special offers'.

4   When you think about buying a new piece of clothing, think whether you really need it. If you don't, then don't buy it. But if you really do, then you can donate your used item to somebody who needs it. There are schemes like Dress for Success where you can donate clothes you no longer need to people looking for a job, so that they will be better dressed for their interview and stand a better chance of getting employment. There are swishing parties, where you exchange what you don't want for what somebody else doesn't want.

5   Join the sharing economy, whether it is fashion, books, tools, travel or holidays.

DO THIS:

Search zero-waste ideas on Pinterest to find a wide range of practical advice. Have fun exploring a wide range of ideas.

The food
we don't eat

16

↳

Per capita food waste per annum

Figures are kilograms of food waste per person per annum:

	Worst in the world		Best in the world
1	USA 95.1	67	Rwanda 1.0
2	Belgium 87.1	66	Mozambique 1.2
3	Canada 78.2	63=	Ethiopia 1.4
4	Australia 76.3	63=	Zambia 1.4
5	Austria 73.6	63=	Ghana 1.4
6	Denmark 71.6	61=	Kenya 1.5
7	Finland 69.5	61=	Nigeria 1.5
8	Lithuania 68.5	59=	Sierra Leone 1.6
9	France 67.2	59=	Zimbabwe 1.6
10	Italy 65.1	58	Cote d'Ivoire 1.7
11	Ireland 63.6	57	Senegal 1.9

These figures for end-user waste are taken from the 2018 Food Sustainability Index commissioned annually by the Barilla Center for Food and Nutrition Foundation and the Economist Intelligence Unit (Barilla is a food company specialising in pasta and sauces). Fifty-seven countries were surveyed. These are the figures for selected other countries: China, 33.7; India, 4.8.

The index also ranks countries on food sustainability using metrics that measure sustainability across three categories: food loss and waste, sustainable agriculture (water use, land use, air quality and greenhouse gas emissions) and nutritional challenges (life quality, health, life expectancy, dietary habits). The best countries for waste (not just end-user waste) are France, Argentina and Luxembourg; the best for sustainable agriculture are Austria, Denmark and Israel; and the best for nutrition are Japan, South Korea and Denmark. France achieved the best overall score.

Waste and hunger

How can we get food to everybody who needs it? And if we need more to feed a growing population, should we be growing more? Or wasting less?

An estimated 30–40 per cent of all the food grown in the world is currently wasted, with waste occurring along the whole of the food chain from farm to shop to home and into the waste bin. When prices fall so low that it is not worthwhile to harvest the crop or there is nobody available to do the picking it may simply be left in the field; harvesting may be done inefficiently such that not everything is collected; produce can rot at all points along the supply chain due to inadequate storage facilities; produce is unnecessarily trimmed to fit supermarket packs; stock in warehouses and supermarkets can pass its sell-by date; consumers may be buying more than they need, possibly encouraged by special promotions; restaurants and take-aways give oversize portions; we may be peeling our vegetables too zealously; our cooking might be a disaster; food from the fridge and leftovers on our plates are being binned.

While enough food is being grown in the world to feed its population, people are still going hungry. The UN Food and Agriculture Organization estimates that more than 820 million people in the world (over 11 per cent of total population) suffer from lack of sufficient food, and not just in poorer countries. At the same time, 1.3 billion tonnes of potential nourishment doesn't get consumed each year, including the equivalent of 1 billion sacks of potatoes, 3.7 trillion apples, 574 billion eggs and much else. See how many tonnes of food have been wasted so far this year at TheWorldCounts.com.

Huge amounts of energy and water are embedded in the production of all this wasted food.

What can shops, restaurants, cafeterias, schools, hospitals, other institutions with dining facilities and households do to reduce food waste? And if food is unsold or unused, can anything be done with it?

Here are some surprising facts:

1   The annual value of food wasted globally is $1 trillion and it weighs 1.3 billion tonnes.

2   The world's nearly 1 billion hungry people could be fed on less than a quarter of the food that is being wasted in the USA and Europe.

3   An area larger than China is used to grow food that is never eaten.

4   25 per cent of the world's fresh water supply is used to grow food that is never eaten.

5   If food waste were a country it would be the third largest emitter of greenhouse gases after China and the USA.

6   One tonne of food waste prevented would save 4.2 tonnes of emissions.

7   2.3 billion people will be joining the planet by 2100, which will require a 60–70 per cent increase in global food production.

Different solutions to this problem will be needed in different parts of the world. In developing countries, the food waste tends to occur early on in the process so improving farming techniques, storage and supply chains is a priority. In higher-income nations, food waste will be occurring later in the supply chain, so it is retailer practices and consumer behaviour that will need to change.

What if there's a global catastrophe?

What if food production is severely affected by abrupt climate change, a superbug or an erupting super-volcano? Allfed, the Alliance to Feed the World in Disasters, explores many scenarios where we move from surplus to insufficient food. Food waste is not then the issue – human survival is. Founders David Denkenberger and Joshua Pearce offer a range of solutions in their book *Feeding Everyone No Matter What*.

People making change

Here are a few people who are doing really creative things with surplus food:

Ronni Kahn is a South African who emigrated to Australia. In 2004, she founded OzHarvest to rescue food which would otherwise go to waste. Starting with one van, she delivered 4,000 meals in the first month. Today, OzHarvest rescues over 180 tonnes of food each week from over 3,500 food donors including supermarkets, hotels, airports, wholesalers, farmers, corporate events, catering companies, shopping centres, delis, cafes, restaurants, film and TV shoots and boardrooms. OzHarvest has grown into Australia's leading food rescue organisation, delivering surplus food to more than 1,300 charities. It operates a rescued food supermarket (the OzHarvest

Market in Sydney) on a 'take what you need, give if you can' principle, selling produce that has either been donated or would otherwise go to waste. It has set up parallel operations in New Zealand, South Africa and the UK.

Joseph Gitler was an immigrant to Israel from the USA. In 2003, he started rescuing meals from catering halls and corporate cafeterias, storing the food in refrigerators lining his driveway. He then delivered to local non-profits to feed the needy. An old chicken coop became Leket's first warehouse, housing five domestic refrigerators. This was the starting point for what has become possibly the best food rescue organisation in the world. Leket now harvests surplus agricultural produce from farms through its Agricultural Gleaning Project, grows food through its Self-Growing Farm Project and collects surplus cooked meals from restaurants and canteens through its Meal Rescue Project. Its Nutrition and Food Safety Department ensures that everything complies with food safety regulations and that its donated food is nutritious. The food is delivered to partnering non-profits, which then distribute it to people in need. In 2020, Leket rescued 19,916 tonnes of food, providing 2,360,000 hot meals to 330 non-profits feeding 246,000 needy people each week.

Tessa Clarke (UK-based) and **Saasha Celestial-One** (USA-based) started OLIO as an app to connect neighbours with each other and with local businesses so surplus food could be shared and eaten, not thrown away. This included food from local stores nearing its sell-by date, spare home-grown vegetables, bread you baked or from the local baker or the produce in your fridge when it is too much or when you go away. The app can also be used for non-food household items. To advertise an available item, you simply open the app, add a photo and a description, and say when and where the item can be picked up. To get an item, you browse the items listed near you, request whatever takes your fancy and arrange to pick it up.

Lotti Henley was in her mid-eighties when she co-founded Plan Zheroes with Maria Ana Neves and Chris Wilkie. Plan Zheroes is a food donation platform to help food businesses easily and safely donate their surplus food to nearby charities and community groups who can use it. Any business that wants to donate creates an account and posts its donation. The platform informs all nearby charities that food is available. The first organisation that claims it then collects it. It was Lotti's experience of hunger as a refugee during the Second World War that led her to want to see a world where 'one day no good food will go to waste and no one will have to live in food poverty'.

Robert Egger wanted to use recycled food from Washington DC to train unemployed adults and homeless people to develop work skills which would lead to employment. His DC Central Kitchen, set up in 1989, has inspired people in other cities to open similar kitchens. Then, in 1999, two Wake Forest University students, Jessica Shortall and Karen Borchert, started a small student-run organisation on their campus called

Homerun to engage students in cooking and delivering dinners in the local community. After graduation, Karen got a job at DC Central Kitchen and what she had started at Wake Forest developed into the Campus Kitchen Project, where students use donated kitchen space plus surplus food from the campus kitchen plus their own donated time to prepare and deliver meals to homeless shelters, food banks, soup kitchens and individuals or families in need. The Campus Kitchen Project is now part of the Food Recovery Network.

Kelvin Cheung. In 2006, Jessica Shortall gave a talk at a supper club in London, telling the story of the Campus Kitchen Project. A group of London-based social entrepreneurs who were concerned about food waste and liked the idea of a 'triple donation' – volunteer time, surplus food and kitchen space – decided to create something similar for the UK. They invited Kelvin, a sustainability enthusiast who was just completing his master's degree, to create FoodCycle. Local groups are asked to find the food, find kitchen space for preparing it and find hungry people to feed it to. The first FoodCycle group was started in 2008 by LSE students using the Fleet River Café to cook meals on Monday evenings which were served the next day to an opera project for homeless people. Groups sprang up around the UK. In 2020, there were 43 FoodCycle groups which served 775,664 meals and salvaged 359 tonnes of surplus food.

Nat Jenkins was a FoodCycle volunteer interested in exploring more ways of using surplus food. What if a restaurant agreed to serve one meal a fortnight cooked from at least 75 per cent surplus ingredients which he would help source for them? This would find a use for perfectly good produce as well as adding to the restaurant's 'green credentials'. This is how Zero Restaurants was born in 2021. Customers pay what they want and any surplus income after running costs is donated to an environmental cause. Nat hopes that this will become standard practice for any 'sustainable restaurant'.

Emilie Vanpoperinghe and **Deepak Ravindran** were in a Portuguese market admiring the fresh, beautiful, but sometimes (to them) funny-looking fruit and vegetables on display. It struck them that they only ever saw identical, perfectly formed produce in UK supermarkets. Why was this? One reason is that the supermarkets do not sell produce that is too small, too big, or not perfectly formed. Another problem is that too much food has been grown and the growers have a surplus which they cannot sell. Emilie and Deepak decided to do something. They created a box scheme to supply odd-shaped and surplus produce which is nonetheless fresh and tasty. Customers can sign up for an Oddbox delivery of fruit or vegetables or a mix of both in one of three sizes which is delivered once a week or once a fortnight.

Larry Green founded Bokashi Cycle, a composting system which uses a sealed bin to ferment food waste, including meat and dairy, using inoculated bran, turning it into a nutrient-rich liquid fertiliser and compost which, when added to the soil, is slowly taken up by microbes, fungi and plants. It is simple, fast and cheap. It produces no heat or gases so avoids nuisances such as odours and vermin and can be done in any kitchen.

Sell-by dates

A fruit cake was found in Antarctica's oldest building which is believed to have been from Robert Falcon Scott's 1910–13 Terra Nova Expedition. The tin was rusted and falling apart, but the cake inside looked and smelt edible (according to the Antarctic Heritage Trust, which owned the building). The cake was an ideal high-energy food for Antarctic conditions – and fruit cake remains a favourite item on modern trips to the Antarctic. The cake was seen as a valuable and fascinating artefact, and was taken with its tin to the Canterbury Museum in New Zealand where it was restored and is now on display. But is this cake too old to be eaten? Could it theoretically be eaten safely? Today, health and safety issues dominate our thinking, so almost nobody would be prepared to eat it. Our 'use-by' and 'best before' dates may be well-intentioned, but they are causing food wastage on a huge scale as consumers throw away food which may not be fresh but which is perfectly safe to eat.

In October 2016, Scott Nash, founder of MOM's Organic Market grocery stores, wanted to make a smoothie. He was staying at his holiday cabin in Virginia. The only yogurt to hand was a pot that he had left behind six months earlier. He opened the pot. He could discern no mould or smell. So he put the yogurt in the blender, made a smoothie and drank it. It tasted good. Nothing happened. He wasn't food poisoned.

This incident triggered Scott's interest in out-of-date food. He started using it in his cooking, documenting his experiences and posting what he was doing on his blog. Smoked trout 24 days past its 'sell by' date, chicken broth three months beyond its 'best before' date, year-old tortillas. All looked perfectly safe. He ate them. Nothing happened.

There are two big issues. The confusion between 'use by', which advises not to use the product after that date, and 'best before', which indicates that it will be less good after. Most people do not notice the difference and throw out any product after its marked date. Scott had shown that food safety experts are being over-cautious and that food is safe to eat well beyond its 'use-by' date. And a survey has shown that 30 per cent of food being binned was past its 'best before' date. Date labelling leads to a huge amount of food waste.

Buy one, give one free

There are all sorts of offers in stores and supermarkets to encourage you to buy, and buy more. One is 'buy one, get one free' (often referred to as BOGOF). For every item you purchase at full price, they will give you a second item completely free of charge. In effect, you are paying half price but you have to buy two when you may only need one. This is a highly effective form of sales promotion because people feel they are getting something for free. But it encourages people to buy more than they need, which leads to wastage.

DO THIS:

Next time you see a buy one, get one free special offer, instead of taking both items for yourself, why not donate your free item to someone who needs it but who can't afford it? Turn 'buy one, get one free' into 'buy one, give one free'.

Too many people in the world?

17

↳

Annual population growth

Percentage annual population increase in different countries:

⬆ Highest growth rates

1. Niger +3.84
2. Bahrain +3.68
3. Equatorial Guinea +3.47
4. Uganda +3.32
5. Angola +3.27
6. DR Congo +3.19
7. Burundi +3.12
8. Mali +3.02
9. Chad +3.00
10. Tanzania +2.98

⬇ Highest negative growth rates

1. Puerto Rico -2.47
2. Lithuania -1.35
3. Latvia -1.08
4. Bulgaria -0.74
5. Romania -0.66
6. Croatia -0.61
7. Bosnia and Herzegovina -0.61
8. Ukraine -0.59
9. Greece -0.48
10. Lebanon -0.44

These are the countries with the highest annual population growth rates and rates of decline calculated by fusing data provided by the UN in 2021. The population figures include inward migration (adding to the population) and outward migration (reducing the population). The largest increases are seen across sub-Saharan Africa, despite significant levels of outward migration. There is negative growth in countries that are in crisis (Lebanon, Ukraine) and countries exporting labour (Eastern Europe mainly, but also Puerto Rico). Japan is the forerunner in negative growth of its indigenous population and is having to create ways of adapting to an ageing population. You can watch the world's population grow at wordometers.info.

How many people are there?

The world population at time of writing is 7.88 billion and is growing at 1.05 per cent per annum. The annual growth rate peaked at 2.1 per cent in 1969. At present, an additional 81 million people are being added to our already crowded planet each year.

World population in history

This is how the world population has grown since homo sapiens first appeared:

90,000 BC	The first humans evolve
10,000 BC	**4 million**
Year 0	**190 million**
1700 AD	**600 million**
1804 AD	**1 billion** it has taken all human history to reach one billion
1930 AD	**2 billion** 126 years to reach second billion
1960 AD	**3 billion** 30 years to reach third billion
1974 AD	**4 billion** 14 years to reach fourth billion
1987 AD	**5 billion** 13 years to reach fifth billion
1999 AD	**6 billion** 12 years to reach sixth billion
2011 AD	**7 billion** 12 years to reach seventh billion
2023 AD	**8 billion** an estimated 12 years to reach eighth billion
2037 AD	**9 billion** an estimated 14 years to reach ninth billion
2057 AD	**10 billion** an estimated 20 years to reach tenth billion
2100 AD	**10.9 billion** The UN estimate of the world's peak population

Around 106 billion people have been born since the emergence of homo sapiens. The world's current population is estimated at 7 per cent of all humans who have ever lived. Around half the world's population lives in just six countries: China (1.44 billion people, growing at 0.39 per cent per annum); India (1.38 billion people, growing at 0.99 per cent); USA (331 million people, growing at 0.59 per cent); Indonesia (274 million people, growing at 1.07 per cent); Pakistan (221 million people, growing at 2.00 per cent); and Brazil (213 million people, growing at 0.72 per cent). Nigeria is Africa's most populous country (206 million people, growing at 2.58 per cent).

During the twentieth century, the world's population grew to nearly four times the 1.65 billion population at the start of the century. It has doubled since 1970. What looked like exponential growth up until 1969 when the population growth rate peaked is now slowing right down. In many countries, populations are diminishing.

In Genesis 1.28, on the Sixth Day of Creation, God said to man (male and female): 'Be fruitful, and multiply, and replenish the earth, and subdue it: and have dominion over the fish of the sea, and over the fowl of the air, and over every living thing that moveth upon the earth.' Multiplication means exponential growth, which is broadly what has happened. But over the long term, exponential growth is not sustainable. Multiply this by exponential growth in living standards as countries seek to increase their gross national income year on year, and this becomes even less sustainable.

Would the world have been any different if God had simply said, 'Be fruitful and add'?

Many reasons are suggested for the slowdown in population growth, including:

↳ Women's education and empowerment, with confidence in making their own choices.

↳ Better health provision, leading to lower infant mortality and more children surviving into adulthood. And as more children survive, more people have smaller families.

↳ Changing cultural norms. For example, in India, large families traditionally helped provide security in old age; today, instead of having lots of children, middle-class families focus their energy and resources on making their one child succeed in the world. But there are also unchanging norms. In Africa, large families are still seen as a blessing. Certain sects in many religions encourage large families.

↳ An affluent and educated society, where 'me' and spending on 'what I want' have become important to some people. You are materially richer single or as a childless couple than as a family. Italy is a good example of this, with a low birth rate despite being a Catholic country.

↳ Better and more available contraception and sexual health education, which has been provided in part through efforts to address the spread of AIDS.

↳ Lower sperm counts in men, possibly caused by chemicals in our lives or oestrogen (from contraceptive pills) in our water supply.

↳ High land and property prices in densely populated cities, where young people cannot afford their own accommodation, and may therefore not be able to contemplate having a family.

Populations in most sub-Saharan African countries and many Muslim-majority countries are still expanding – a 3 per cent annual increase means a doubling of a country's population every 24 years. At present, 31 per cent of the world's population are Christian, 23 per cent are Muslim, 16 per cent no religious affiliation, 15 per cent Hindu, 7 per cent Buddhist, 6 per cent indigenous religions and 2 per cent other religions, including Sikhism, Shintoism, Daoism, Judaism. Differential growth rates mean that the balance of the world's population and religions will shift considerably over the coming years.

Missing girls

The gender ratio at birth is normally around 105 male children being born for every 100 female children. But this gender ratio is skewed in some countries because of a preference for boy children, often for cultural or religious reasons. Sex determination early on in pregnancy followed by abortion or even foeticide at birth are the causes. Then there is the issue of excess girl mortality in the first years of life, as the wellbeing of sons and preferential medical care and feeding given to them will affect the survival of daughters. The biggest differences in the normal gender ratio of children are in the world's two most populous countries:

China	115 boys per 100 girls at birth; 117 at age 5
India	111 boys per 100 girls at birth; 111 at age 5

With 14.6 million live births per annum in China and 28.0 million in India, this means that there are more than 1.5 million 'missing girls' each year just in these two countries.

Is there an optimum population?

Would our planet be a happier, healthier place if there were fewer humans on it? This is more about envisioning a future world than any systematic planning or policies for how to get from where we are (on course to 10.9 billion on the planet) to a less densely populated world.

Thomas Malthus was an English economist. In his seminal 1798 book *An Essay on the Principle of Population*, he observed that an increase in a nation's food production improved the wellbeing of the populace, but the improvement was temporary because it led to population growth, which in turn restored the original per capita production level. This became known as the 'Malthusian Trap': 'The power of population is indefinitely greater than the power in the earth to produce subsistence for man.'

Paul Ehrlich wrote and campaigned against continuing population growth in a world of limited resources. His books *The Population Bomb* (1968) and *The Population Explosion* (1990) tried to alert the world to a looming population crisis. In 1994, he proposed that a world population of between 1.5 and 2 billion could provide decent wealth and resources with basic human rights to everybody, while preserving biodiversity and culture and allowing for intellectual and artistic creativity and technological progress.

In 1991, the Optimum Population Trust was founded by David Willey 'to collect, analyse and disseminate information about the sizes of global and national populations and to link this to a study of carrying capacities and inhabitants' quality of life in order to support policy decisions'. The trust suggested an optimum world population of around 2.5 billion. Today, the organisation concentrates on sustainability and maintaining biodiversity rather than proposing any optimum figure, and has been renamed Population Matters.

The United Nations Population Fund (UNFPA) is concerned with reproductive health and rights with a mission to deliver a world where every pregnancy is wanted, every childbirth is safe and every young person's potential is fulfilled.

Limiting the world's population

Here are two approaches to limiting population in the world's two most populous countries.

China: The One-Child Policy was introduced in 1979 when the population of China was 969 million. Today it is 1,440 million, an increase of nearly 50 per cent, but the policy is estimated to have prevented up to 400 million births. Its goal was to ensure that population growth did not outpace food and natural resource availability. Abortion was available for those that needed it or who did not want to fall foul of official policy. The One-Child Policy was targeted at the Han majority population. There have been two consequences: an ageing population with 30 per cent now aged over 50, and many married couples being responsible for the wellbeing of their four parents and eight grandparents in old age. Although the One-Child Policy has now been relaxed, many couples are still choosing to have only a single child.

India: The government created the world's first forced sterilisation programme, which began in the early 1970s with support from the UN and international development agencies. The programme really took off in 1976 when Sanjay Gandhi, the younger and favourite son of the then prime minster, Indira Gandhi, herself the daughter of India's founding prime minister, Jawaharlal Nehru, was given responsibility for its implementation, a task which he fulfilled with zeal. This led to 8.3 million mostly forced sterilisations during a single year, 1976–77. This took place during 'The Emergency', when civil rights had been suspended, and it created widespread hostility. Despite this and continuing efforts to slow population rise and a widespread network of women's health services in villages across the country, India's population has risen by 118 per cent from 636 million in 1976 to an estimated 1,387 million in 2020.

Here are two organisations campaigning with an attempted sense of humour to limit the world's population. Do not take them too seriously:

↳ **The Church of Euthanasia.** Their First Commandment is to 'Vow never to procreate'. They have four pillars to help people fulfil this promise: Suicide, Abortion, Cannibalism and Sodomy. They could also add Abstinence and Contraception.

↳ **The Voluntary Human Extinction Movement** seeks to phase out the human race by voluntarily ceasing to breed, and this will allow Earth's biosphere to return to good health as crowded conditions and resource shortages reduce as the world's population progressively becomes less dense. Their motto is 'Save the planet, kill yourself'.

Marie Stopes

Marie Stopes was an accomplished scientist and campaigner for women's rights who founded the first birth control clinic in Britain. She published a sex manual, *Married Love*, in 1918 and brought the idea of birth control into the public domain. Publicly she opposed abortion, preferring the idea of prevention of conception. She was also a supporter of eugenics, which was a fashionable viewpoint in certain circles at the time, wanting to explore ways of improving the genetic quality of the human population. And another issue that she felt strongly about was the differential birth rate between the rich and the poor.

Marie opened her first clinic in Holloway, north London, in 1921. It was run by midwives with visiting doctors. It offered mothers free birth control advice, taught birth control methods and dispensed cervical caps. It was open to all married women wanting guidance and help. She built up a network of birth control clinics. This work continued after her death in 1958.

In 1975, the Marie Stopes clinics went into liquidation, which led to the founding in 1976 of Marie Stopes International (MSI), a charity which (along with PSI, see below) is one of the two leading family planning organisations in the world. MSI's overseas work began with the Dublin Well Woman Centre in 1978, followed by a Marie Stopes Centre in New Delhi. MSI currently operates in 37 countries.

Population Services International

PSI was founded in 1970 to improve reproductive health, initially working mostly in family planning. In 1985, PSI started promoting oral rehydration therapy. In 1988, PSI started its first HIV prevention project, which promoted abstinence, fidelity and condoms. PSI added malaria and safe water to its work in the 1990s and tuberculosis in 2004.

'With offices in over 50 countries, we work to make it easier for people in the developing world to lead healthier lives and plan the families they desire by marketing affordable products and services. Think mosquito nets, condoms, HIV testing and more. There are over 8,000 "PSI-ers" around the world with an unusually wide range of backgrounds – from the medical industry to the music business – all with unique skills we bring to the job.'

DKT International

DKT's condom brand Prudence is the bestselling condom in Brazil, and comes in a variety of flavours and textures, including a Caipirinha condom launched to coincide with the 2014 World Cup football tournament. Prudence was designed and produced by DKT Brazil, and caipirinha is Brazil's favourite cocktail. DKT is unusual in several respects. It was created in 1989 by senior leaders

at Population Services International and Marie Stopes International as a not-for-profit enterprise providing a range of family planning and AIDS/HIV prevention products, services and information. It has become a major condom manufacturer, using social marketing to communicate with its customers and making its products fun and aspirational rather than telling people to be sensible. Its flavoured condoms are illustrative of this. It generates 70 per cent of its revenue from sales and has offices in 24 countries.

The business is named DKT is in honour of DK Tyagi, who was Assistant Commissioner of Family Planning for the government of India. He designed an extensive communication and behaviour change programme, introducing modern family planning methods into rural areas where modern contraception methods were virtually unknown.

DO THIS:

Hans Rosling was a Swedish professor of international health famed for his ability to analyse and present data. He set up the Gapminder Foundation to create a more 'factful world'. Take the Gapminder Test, which will expose your misconceptions: upgrader.gapminder.org.

LISTEN TO THIS:

Hans Rosling's TED Talks, especially his talk on global population growth: ted.com/playlists/474.

Where will we all be living?

18

The world's megacities

Today's largest cities and urban areas:

City	Population
Tokyo-Yokohama, Japan	39.1 million
Jakarta, Indonesia	35.4 million
Delhi, India	31.9 million
Manila, Philippines	24.0 million
Sao Paolo, Brazil	22.5 million
Seoul-Incheon, South Korea	22.4 million
Mumbai, India	22.2 million
Shanghai, China	22.1 million
Mexico City, Mexico	21.5 million
Guangzhou-Foshan, China	21.5 million
New York, USA	20.9 million
Cairo, Egypt	19.8 million
Beijing, China	19.4 million
Kolkata, India	18.7 million
Moscow, Russia	17.7 million
Bangkok, Thailand	17.6 million
Dhaka, Bangladesh	16.8 million
Buenos Aires, Argentina	16.2 million
Osaka-Kobe-Kyoto, Japan	15.5 million
Lagos, Nigeria	15.5 million
Los Angeles, USA	15.5 million
Istanbul, Turkey	15.3 million
Karachi, Pakistan	15.3 million
Kinshasa, DR Congo	15.1 million

These cities and urban areas all have a population of over 15 million. There are 12 more cities with populations over 10 million: Shenzhen, China (14.7 million); Johannesburg, South Africa (14.2 million); Bangalore, India (14.0 million); Ho Chi Minh City, Vietnam (14.0 million); Tehran, Iran (13.8 million); Rio de Janeiro, Brazil (12.5 million); Chengdu, China (11.9 million); Chennai, India (11.6 million); Lahore, Pakistan (11.1 million); London, UK (11.1 million); Paris, France (11.0 million); Tianjin, China (10.9 million). The world's human population is now more than half urban, with 51 per cent living in towns and cities in 2021. There are 90 cities in the world with populations of over 5 million. China has 16 urban centres of this size, the USA has 11 and India 7.

(Data from the Demographia World Urban Atlas, June 2021)

From settlement to megacity

Humans started out as hunter-gatherers. With the development of agriculture, the first human settlements appeared. And as societies evolved, people accumulated in villages, then in towns, then in cities and today in megacities. These are some of the largest cities in history (note how the centres of global economic success change over time):

2100 BC	Ur, Mesopotamia, 100,000
1300 BC	Yinxu, China, 120,000
700 BC	Babylon, Iraq, 100,000
300 BC	Carthage, Tunisia, 500,000
200 AD	Rome, Italy, 1,200,000
600	Constantinople, Turkey, 600,000
900	Baghdad, Iraq, 900,000
1500	Beijing, China, 1,000,000
1825	London, UK, 1,335,000
1925	New York, USA, 7,774,000
2021	Tokyo-Yokohama, Japan, 39,105,000

Today, 2.27 billion people are living in cities with over 500,000 inhabitants, amounting to just under 40 per cent of the world's total population. These cities are spread across the globe as follows:

	No. of cities	Total population
Africa	118	277 million
Asia	519	1,285 million
Europe	142	215 million
North America	131	295 million
South America	68	181 million
Oceania	7	17 million
World	**985**	**2,270 million**

The Global Cities Institute has projected the growth of cities into the future. These are their top eight megacities in year 2100, all with unbelievably huge populations with people needing to be housed, serviced, fed and kept healthy. How will we manage cities with up to 90 million people? What will life be like for the people living there?

Lagos, Nigeria,	88.3 million
Kinshasa, DR Congo	83.5 million
Dar Es Salaam, Tanzania	73.7 million
Mumbai, India	67.2 million
Delhi, India	57.3 million
Khartoum, Sudan	56.6 million
Niamey, Niger	56.1 million
Dhaka, Bangladesh	54.3 million

Overcrowding

There is a huge variation in population density of big cities around the world. The two most crowded megacities are Dhaka, Bangladesh, with 36,941 people per square kilometre, and Kinshasa, DR Congo, with 32,295. Compare this with the luxury of living in these more affluent big cities (all top 50 cities): Chicago, 1,286; New York, 1,728; San Francisco, 2,100; Los Angeles, 2,437; and Nagoya, Japan, 1,286.

Not all of a city's population lives in the urban core. Many live in suburbs of much lower density outside the centre. There may be townships – areas distant from the centre as reserved accommodation for poorer people. There may also be urban slums – informal settlements that have sprung up on vacant land (whether around an airport, under a freeway, next to a railway, abutting middle-class gated communities or just on pavements) where those without housing have created their own accommodation.

Over the years, and as cities have grown, there have been efforts to move people out from cities:

The Garden City movement: This was started by Ebenezer Howard in the UK, who created settlements in the countryside around London. The first in 1905 was Letchworth Garden City. Basildon New Town was created in 1949, emerging from informal settlements established by soldiers returning from the First World War in Pitsea and Laindon, and was featured by planner and anarchist writer Colin Ward in his published paper 'The Do-It-Yourself New Town'. Milton Keynes, between London and Birmingham, was the most ambitious new town and has a current population of 250,000. Its name was based on an original village name in the area, and chosen partly because it combines the name of the famous poet John Milton and the economist John Maynard Keynes.

New capital cities: A newly built seat of government can act as a magnet for attracting population away from big cities. Canberra was established in Australia in 1913, Chandigarh as capital of both Punjab and Haryana states in India in 1952 and Brasilia in Brazil in 1960, with both Chandigarh and Brasilia designed by world-famous architects (Le Corbusier and Oscar Niemeyer).

Settlements: One of the abuses of the South African apartheid government was to create settlements for non-whites on land outside the city. The most famous is Soweto (south-west-township) in Johannesburg, which currently has a population of 1.27 million. The most infamous instance is the clearance of District 6 in Cape Town, where over 60,000 people from the city centre were forcibly removed to the Cape Flats, many kilometres from the city centre and its employment opportunities. The townships that sprang up here include Khayelitsha and Philippi.

More ambitiously, the Chinese government created Shenzhen from a fishing village as a 'special economic zone'. Today, it is one of China's top five cities, with a population more than double that of neighbouring Hong Kong. China is now planning a new city near to Beijing as a way of stopping the capital's inexorable growth. Xiongan, along with Tianjin and Beijing, will become a three-city capital area for China.

Township tourism

There are two sides to most cities: the city for the rich and the city for the poor. These are some attempts to show the rich how the other half lives:

Reality Tours in Mumbai organises tours to Dharavi, Asia's second biggest slum, housing 1 million people. The streets are so narrow that sometimes there is insufficient room for two people to pass. But it is a hive of activity, and especially recycling and upcycling. If you can't get to Mumbai, read *Maximum City* by Suketu Mehta and watch the film *Slumdog Millionaire*; both provide a portrait of the real Mumbai.

Kibera Tours: Kibera is Nairobi's largest slum. Guides show you daily life in their 'City of Hope', visiting a bead factory, a typical house, an orphanage, a women's centre, a biogas plant and a market.

Unseen Tours: London has around 170,000 homeless people, most living in hostels and temporary accommodation. But around 2,000 sleep rough on the streets every night. Unseen Tours are led by a homeless person who shows you their London, and not the London of fancy shops, coffee bars and night clubs.

Take part in the UK's annual Big Sleep Out to help raise money and awareness about homelessness and experience for yourself what it feels like to sleep on the streets for a night. 'On the 7th of December 2019, in backyards, hometowns and iconic locations across the globe, thousands of people slept out in unison to create the world's largest display of solidarity with and support of those experiencing homelessness and displacement.' This is how the Big Sleep Out reported its 2019 global event, which raised $10 million for homeless charities.

SDI is Slum/Shack Dwellers International, a network of community-based organisations of the urban poor in 32 countries and hundreds of cities and towns across Africa, Asia and Latin America. In each country where SDI has a presence, affiliate organisations come together at the community, city and national level to form federations of the urban poor. Know Your City is a global campaign that SDI runs in partnership with United Cities and Local Governments of Africa (UCLG-A) and the Cities Alliance. Around the world, slum dwellers collect city-wide data and information on informal settlements. This provides information and a voice for the urban poor about their city and how it might be managed better. The campaign has profiled 7,712 slums in 224 cities.

What makes a city sustainable?

The international standard ISO 37120 provides a set of indicators for city services and quality of life. These include:

The economy, including the unemployment rate and the percentage living in poverty.

Education, including the percentage of students completing primary and secondary education, and student-teacher ratio.

Energy, including residential energy use per capita and percentage from renewable sources.

Environment, including greenhouse gas emissions per capita and air quality.

Finances, measured by the debt servicing costs as a percentage of municipal revenue.

Governance, measured by voter participation and percentage of women elected at city level.

Health, measured by average life expectancy, physicians and hospital beds per capita, under-five mortality and suicide rates.

Recreation and planning, measured by public outdoor and indoor recreation space and green space per capita.

Safety, measured by number of police officers, and the number of homicides and violent crime rate per capita.

Shelter, measured by the percentage of city population living in slums and the percentage of homeless people.

Solid waste, measured by percentage of population with access to regular waste collection, the total municipal waste collected and its safe disposal.

Communications, measured by internet connections and landline phones per capita.

Transport, measured by kilometres of public transport and percentage of commuters not using a personal vehicle.

Water and sanitation, measured by the percentage of the population with wastewater collection and treatment, with clean drinking water and with access to proper sanitation.

Smarter cities

As cities grow, far too many people want to access the city's limited services all at the same time. Roads and public transport at peak hours come under strain. From Beijing to Lagos, congestion and pollution make life harder for everybody. The idea is emerging to use technology to manage a city's limited resources more efficiently.

The term 'smart city' is now in common use. The idea is to use information technology, 5G networks, the internet of things (IoT), big data and machine learning to make more efficient use of the physical infrastructure, and also to obtain and use feedback from citizens and consumers for the benefit of everyone. For example, a mobile app with immediate access to real-time data can help motorists avoid traffic jams and congestion blackspots, and ensure that traffic lights and traffic lanes are managed better. A smart city is as much about the smartness of its residents and solutions that they come up with alongside the infrastructure and technologies provided for them.

Amsterdam: The Amsterdam Smart City initiative began in 2009. It now includes over 170 projects which have been developed collaboratively by local residents, government and business, with the aim of managing traffic, saving energy and improving public safety. To capture ideas from local residents, the city runs a Smart City Challenge each year, seeking proposals for ideas and developments that will improve the city's smartness. One outcome has been Mobypark, enabling owners of parking spaces to rent them out to people for a fee. The data generated helps determine parking demand and predict traffic flows. Another initiative allows municipalities to control the brightness of street lights.

Tallinn, the capital city of Estonia, is an e-city. It has embraced the internet as the key to its future, offering free Wi-Fi to everybody and encouraging e-literacy. Much of the business of government is done using digital solutions. X-road, e-Land Registry and Population Register combine information on public services, land and population; identity and residence cards are all digital; blockchain technology is used to ensure security and provide services across the health and justice sectors; e-governance allows citizens to express their views and participate in decision making; there is e-banking and e-finance; in education, e-Kool and Studium improve pupil outcomes, and the number of students pursuing IT careers is double the average.

Resilient Cities are cities future-proofed for environmental sustainability, adaptation to climate change, disaster preparedness and economic viability. Ninety-six cities have joined the Resilient Cities Network from Accra in Ghana to Wellington in New Zealand.

Slow Cities present a completely different idea for how cities should be run. The idea stemmed from the Slow Food movement. The CittaSlow Manifesto describes these as 'towns animated by people "curious about time reclaimed", rich in squares, theatres, workshops, cafes, restaurants, spiritual places, unspoilt landscapes and fascinating craftsmen, where we still appreciate the slow, benevolent succession of the seasons, with their rhythm of authentic products, respecting fine flavours and health, the spontaneity of their rituals, the fascination of living traditions.' There are now 278 slow cities around the world committed to creating a slower, more relaxed, more enjoyable environment for people.

Affordable accommodation

One of the biggest future challenges for cities is not the delivery of efficient services but the ability to provide affordable housing. Migration into cities puts continuing pressure on the availability and cost of housing. In many big cities, young people are being priced out of the market. The well-off can ensure that their children find housing. For the less-well-off, prices are far too high for both renting and taking a first step on the housing ladder. For incomers with no money, finding affordable accommodation can be just a dream. And without access to housing, young people find themselves unable to leave home or start a family.

A possible solution is to provide 'capsule housing', a tiny space for sleeping and personal activity, with shared facilities for cooking and relaxing. This is an option seriously being considered by municipalities such as Hong Kong. It is also something that entrepreneurs are looking at. PodShare is a start-up providing customers with a single bed, private storage space and access to shared facilities including kitchen, bathrooms, living rooms and an outside yard for around $50 per night or $1,000 a month. StarCity has taken this one step further with a concept called 'co-living', 'where people choose to share space with their housemates, build relationships, and look after each other'. They have four categories of customer: young people just starting out; individuals in their thirties and forties needing to move as a result of a divorce or having to move out of a houseshare; those who are seeking a nomadic or minimalistic lifestyle, preferring to spend their money on culture, travel and experience rather than on material items; those who need a temporary place to stay perhaps because of a job assignment.

DO THIS:

Experience capsule living. When travelling, stay in a 'capsule hotel'. Originally developed for budget travellers in Japan as safe, affordable overnight accommodation, some capsule hotels now compete to provide guests with a stylish and luxurious experience. These have been voted some of the best; many more are under development: Nonze Hostel, Pattaya, Thailand; Dream Lodge, Singapore; inBox Capsule Hotel, St Petersburg, Russia; Star Anise Boutique Capsules, Colombo, Sri Lanka.

Where have all the jobs gone?

↳

Unemployment hot spots 2019

Unemployment rate as a percentage of the
economically active population:

1 South Africa 28.2

2 West Bank/Gaza 26.2

3 Lesotho 23.4

4 Eswatini (Swaziland) 22.1

5 St Lucia 20.7

6 Namibia 20.3

7 Gabon 20.0

8 St Vincent/Grenadines 18.9

9 Libya 18.6

10 Bosnia and Herzegovina 18.4

11 Botswana 18.2

12 North Macedonia 17.8

13 Greece 17.2

14 Armenia 17.0

15 Sudan 16.5

16 Tunisia 16.0

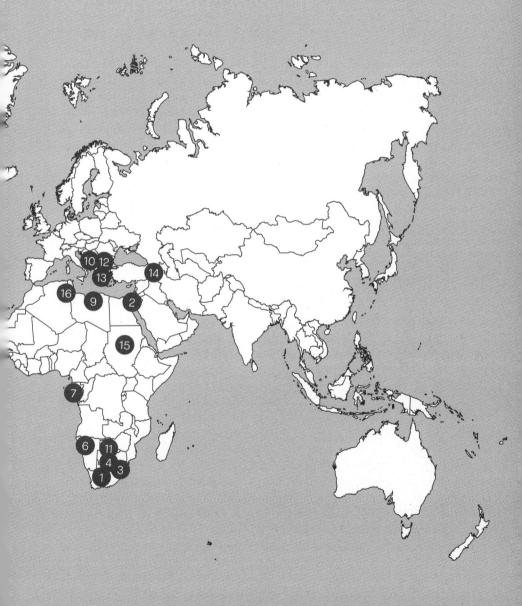

According to the International Labour Organization, world unemployment in 2019 was 5.4 per cent. This amounts to 174.3 million people able to work but without work. The countries with the highest rates of official unemployment are shown above. And these are the unemployment rates for some of the biggest countries in the world: Brazil, 12.1 per cent; Nigeria, 8.1 per cent; India, 5.4 per cent; Russia, 4.6 per cent; China, 4.3 per cent; UK, 3.9 per cent; USA, 3.7 per cent; Mexico, 3.4 per cent; Germany, 3 per cent. Unemployment will have increased sharply in 2020 as a result of the Covid-19 pandemic but should revert to pre-pandemic levels as the world emerges from Covid-19.

The right to work

Article 23.1 of the Universal Declaration of Human Rights states that, 'Everyone has the right to work, to free choice of employment, to just and favourable conditions of work and to protection against unemployment.'

The concept of the 'right to work' emerged at a time of rising unemployment and social turmoil in France in the mid-nineteenth century. There are two aspects of this: people need to earn an income which is sufficient to pay for the daily needs of themselves and their families and they should have the opportunity to engage in productive work, rather than remaining redundant or idle.

The Beveridge Report of 1942 set the scene for a welfare state in the UK that would look after its citizens. It identified 'Five Giants' which needed to be slain as part of the post-war reconstruction process. These were Want (poverty), Disease (sickness and poor health), Ignorance (lack of education), Squalor (poor living conditions) and Idleness (unemployment). The new world that would be created after the end of the Second World War in 1945 needed to be fairer and better than what had been before. Fair wages would give workers an adequate standard of living and taxation from a thriving economy would pay for education, health and other communal services.

This was the dream. But 75 years on, unemployment persists and for many in employment wages are insufficient or their employment is precarious. Today we have a 'precariat' rather than a proletariat, working in a gig economy where workers are hired only when they are needed, offered zero-hours contracts, and paid inadequately, and only for work actually done, which may vary from week to week according to the employer's requirements.

The new jobs economy is creating insecurity, and a lack of resilience and mental health issues result from this. Alongside this, the world of work is changing. Globalisation exports jobs to where labour is the cheapest. Technological innovation offers the prospect of machines replacing humans in whole sections of the economy.

Man versus machine 1

On 11 April 1812, a couple of months before the Battle of Waterloo, over 100 men gathered to smash the machines that had been installed at Rawfolds Mill. Each power loom could do the work of four skilled weavers. The men were fearful for their jobs. Unluckily for them, the millowner had been tipped off and soldiers were there to prevent the action. Bullets flew, killing two of the 'Yorkshire Luddites', the group having taken their name from Ned Ludd, thought to have been a weaver from Anstey, near Leicester. Two weeks later, the workers got their revenge, ambushing and killing another mill owner. The unrest continued for several months. Eventually the rebellion petered out; its leaders were arrested, tried and hanged.

The term 'Luddite' has now come to mean any person opposed to the march of progress. At the time, the Industrial Revolution was in full swing, powered by steam and then much later by electricity. Jobs were being created, the population and cities were growing. This was the First Industrial Revolution. The second was the development of production line technologies, typified by Henry Ford and his Model T Ford – 'You can have it in any colour, so long as it's black!' Fast forward to the 1970s and the Third Industrial Revolution, fuelled by the development of IT, personal computing and mobile phones. These also created a fear that jobs would disappear.

Man versus machine 2

Computer engineers at IBM had designed a machine to play chess, calling it Deep Blue. IBM challenged world champion Garry Kasparov to a match. This was held in Philadelphia in 1996 and was won by Kasparov. The IBM engineers improved their machine and issued a second challenge. Kasparov lost the rematch in New York in 1997. Deep Blue had won by 'brute force' – programmed to store and retrieve winning games and moves from the chess archive. Subsequently, a Dutch grandmaster was asked what strategy to adopt when playing against a computer. He replied, 'I'd bring a hammer' – just like the Luddites.

Demis Hassabis founded DeepMind, an artificial intelligence company now owned by Google. He programmed a computer to beat world champion Lee Sedol at the game of Go, which is far more complicated than chess. A five-game match was organised in South Korea in March 2016. The programme, called AlphaGo, won the first three games, lost the fourth (was this a diplomatic loss, allowing the world champion to save face?) and won the fifth. There was one main difference to Deep Blue: AlphaGo did not have access to any library of past games. It was programmed only with the basic rules of Go and asked to teach itself how to play. It played quickly, learned from its mistakes and got better and better. It even invented winning moves which nobody had seen before. There is now no hope of any human ever challenging its supremacy.

The Fourth Industrial Revolution is based on artificial intelligence, robotics and nanotechnologies. Computers, with their enormous computing power, memories and machine learning, are out-competing humans with their speed, their cost and even their reliability. They can read and diagnose radiography scans better than any doctor; they can mark student assignments (essays not multiple-choice tests) better than any teacher; they will chauffeur driverless cars with no possibility of drunk driving. Robots are automating whole factories. Computers and robots work 24/7; they do not need holidays, maternity leave or sick pay; they do not go on strike for higher wages or better conditions.

So where will all the jobs come from?

The First, Second and Third Industrial Revolutions created more jobs. Will the Fourth be different? We could be entering an age that provides us with everything that we need but without the need to work, an age of plenty and leisure. Before we reach this point, societies are exploring different mechanisms for providing their citizens with an income:

Unemployment benefit, which is often linked to skills training and evidence of job seeking. This is provided to those entering the jobs market (youth unemployment is a big issue), those between jobs, those unable to work and the long-term unemployed.

A national minimum wage, which sets a minimum hourly rate for employment to ensure that those in work are paid sufficiently. In the UK, this was introduced in 1999. But pay was still too low. This led to the concept of a substantially higher 'living wage', which many employers have signed up to.

Guaranteed work, with a right to an income but only in return for work done. In 2005, India introduced the Mahatma Gandhi National Rural Employment Guarantee Scheme, which offers up to 100 days of unskilled manual work per year on public works projects for any rural household member wanting such work, who are paid the national minimum wage.

There are a number of issues with unemployment benefit:

↳ The amount paid is often too low for an adequate standard of living.

↳ There can be a 'benefits trap', where there is marginal increase in income or even no increase when an unemployed person moves into employment.

↳ The cost of administering the system is substantial.

↳ Benefits offer 'something for nothing', which can be an incentive for fraud.

↳ Systems become too complex, meaning that some people do not receive what they are entitled to and others do not apply because they are not aware that they are eligible.

This leads to the idea of a universal basic income, where a basic income is paid to everyone regardless of whether they are in work or out of work, where they are free to supplement this income in any way they wish. UBI is offered as a right of citizenship and a way of spreading wealth in society. UBI is an idea which is beginning to be experimented with as worries increase about the future of work.

Just give them the money

Rather than providing services for homeless people, would just giving them money be a better approach? Here are three examples:

1   Homeless people: In 2010, Broadway, a London-based charity working with homeless people, gave £3,000 to each of 13 rough sleepers, with no obligation for recipients to do anything in return. Each had been costing the state an estimated £30,000 per annum in benefits, crime, court costs, medical costs and social work support. The question was: 'Would the money make a difference?' It did. Two years later, all had taken constructive steps to improve their lives and future prospects, learning new skills, going through rehab, becoming more purposeful. Nine had a roof over their heads. *The Economist* concluded: 'The most efficient way to spend money on the homeless might be to give it to them.'

2   One homeless person: In 2009, Sean Dolan, a tech-savvy student, and his father, Kevin, a marketing executive, wanted to drive traffic to their website. They gave Tim Edwards, a panhandler on a Houston Street, a sign to hold which simply said 'pimpthisbum.com'. Tim had been homeless for four years. Visitors to the website were invited to help Tim rebuild his life. Tim said, 'How can you pull yourself up by the bootstraps if you don't have any?' Pimp This Bum gave Tim the bootstrap he needed.

3   People down on their luck: Larry Stewart, who died in 2007, was a cable TV entrepreneur and philanthropist from Kansas City who anonymously handed out cash to needy people on the street, typically in the form of $100 bills. He was known as 'Secret Santa'. In 1971, down on his luck, he had been offered a free breakfast at a diner. This was a lightbulb moment for him which gave him the optimism to create a better future for himself. Larry's Secret Santa activity was to repay this debt of gratitude.

A new world of work

The world of work has been changing, with enterprise workspaces such as WeWork and Second Home springing up all over the world, and members clubs such as Soho House and The Conduit offering space to meet people as well as for work. Covid-19 has led to more people working from home and meeting on Zoom. How we work is becoming a huge area for social and technological innovation. Here are some ideas for new ways of working:

↳   Enspiral started in New Zealand as a community of people each working on 'stuff that matters' but collaborating to share their skills or help one another: 'Since inception, we've been testing ways of working together with trust and respect to share money, information and control as openly as possible. As a community we've supported hundreds of people to launch and build all sorts of initiatives, projects and world-changing ventures.'

↳ Be Caring provides care services to vulnerable, disabled and elderly people. Most care is outsourced to agencies which pay low wages, have a high turnover of staff and often provide poor service. Be Caring creates worker cooperatives for delivering care services. Staff stay longer and are more committed. Be Caring is able to provide a much better service at a competitive price.

↳ Briarpatch was a network of small businesses in San Francisco (600 at its peak) started in 1974 as a community where members would preferentially buy from one another, share business knowhow and share customers.

↳ Timebanking enables people to offer their skills to others in return for 'time credits' which they can spend within the network. Everyone's skills are valued equally – one hour always equals one time credit. You list the skills and experience you can offer and those you might need. You are encouraged to spend your time credits rather than hoard them for a rainy day. This way, a local economy keeps moving.

↳ Microtasking is where a large job is split into small tasks which can be undertaken from home in any part of the word. This allows people to do bits of work in their spare time in return for what is usually quite modest remuneration. Amazon created Mechanical Turk as a platform for people to find 'human intelligence tasks' – mostly work that cannot be done by computers, such as such as identifying specific images in photos, writing product descriptions, answering questions, technical translation.

↳ Crowdsourced innovation challenges people to find solutions to a problem, with rewards for winning ideas. Innocentive issued Covid-19 challenges which included gamification to stop the spread of disease, identifying early signs of infection, new technologies to prevent transmission and creating an anti-Covid-19 protective film. Awards ranged upwards from $1,000.

DO THIS:

Sell your skill on Fiverr (fiverr.com). 'I am a developer', 'I am a writer', 'I do voiceovers' – whatever your skill, Fiverr is a marketplace to connect you with customers, originally in return for a $5 payment, now $5– $10,000. They say: 'You bring the skill, we make earning easy.'

Displaced
and trafficked
people

20

Major sources of refugees

Total number of people classified as refugees by
country of origin:

1 Syria 6,689,582

2 Afghanistan 2,594,774

3 South Sudan 2,189,141

4 Myanmar 1,103,299

5 DR Congo 840,449

6 Somalia 814,551

7 Sudan 787,755

8 Central African Republic 642,437

9 Eritrea 521,949

10 Burundi 373,036

11 Nigeria 352,953

12 Iraq 333,418

13 Vietnam 316,727

14 Rwanda 245,806

15 Colombia 189,889

16 China 175,585

17 Venezuela 171,127

18 Mali 164,601

19 Ethiopia 151,336

20 Sri Lanka 142,716

(Source: World Bank)

On the previous pages are the 2020 totals for people who are classified as refugees by the UN High Commission for Refugees. Most have left countries where war or terrorism have been raging. In 2021 it was estimated that an additional 500,000 people fled Afghanistan following the US withdrawal and the Taliban take-over. And as this book was going to press (in Spring 2022), millions of mainly women and children were fleeing Ukraine following the Russian invasion, arriving in neighbouring countries and seeking refuge in Western Europe.

Refugees and migrants

Definitions are important. There are refugees and there are migrants. There are people who pay traffickers to cross borders and there are people who are trafficked. There is slavery and there is modern-day slavery. We live in a world where over 1 per cent of its total population has been displaced – forced to leave their homes to avoid war, escape from violence or from persecution, and where millions are trying to cross borders in order to seek a better life.

The terms 'immigrant', 'refugee' and 'asylum seeker' are often used interchangeably but they are quite different.

A refugee is someone who is fleeing conflict or persecution. Refugees have the protection of international law and must not be expelled or returned to a situation where their life or freedom is at risk.

An asylum seeker is someone who is seeking sanctuary for themselves and often for their whole family, as they believe their lives are endangered because of their political or religious views and affiliations, or because of their ethnic background.

A migrant is someone who moves to another country willingly and mostly for economic or family reasons. When leaving a country, they are an emigrant; in their destination country they are an immigrant.

A trafficked person is someone who is either forced to leave or tricked into leaving their country, usually for work or sexual exploitation, who, on arrival, comes under the control of people who coerce or terrorise them to provide their labour (which could be anything from domestic service to picking fruit) without remuneration and often for an indefinite period.

We live in a world where over 1 per cent of its total population has been displaced.

How many displaced people are there?

These are just a few of the headline figures put out by the UN High Commission for Refugees (for 2020):

↳ There are 82.4 million forcibly displaced people in the world today. This includes asylum seekers, internally displaced people and refugees, and amounts to 1 in every 103 people in the world. An estimated 35 million (29 per cent) of these are children under 18 years of age.

↳ 48.0 million of these are internally displaced, living within their own country's borders.

↳ 26.4 million are refugees, 73 per cent of whom live in neighbouring countries.

↳ 68 per cent of refugees come from just five countries: Syria (6.7 million), Venezuela (4.0 million), Afghanistan (2.6 million), South Sudan (2.2 million) and Myanmar (1.1 million), all countries in crisis. Half are under 18 years old.

↳ The top refugee-receiving countries in 2020 were: Turkey, 3.7 million (most coming from Syria); Colombia, 1.7 million; Pakistan, 1.4 million (most coming from Afghanistan); and Uganda, 1.4 million (most coming from South Sudan and DR Congo). Germany had 1.2 million (from all over the world, as the 'refugee crisis' sees streams of people reaching the EU, mostly via Greece and Italy, mostly by boat and mainly coming through Libya and Turkey).

↳ Lebanon hosts an estimated 865,500 Syrian refugees. This equates to one in six people living in the country. Lebanon also hosts approximately 180,000 Palestinian refugees, many of whom have lived in Lebanon since the 1950s. Together with other, smaller refugee populations, primarily from Iraq, Sudan and Ethiopia, Lebanon hosts the highest number of refugees per capita of its own population in the world.

↳ In 2020, 9.8 million people were displaced within their own country and 1.4 million sought protection outside their own country, which amounts to over 30,000 people every day.

↳ There are 4.1 million asylum seekers in the world. In January 2021 alone, there were 30,000 new applications for asylum in the European Union.

(Source: United Nations High Commission for Refugees and World Bank)

World Refugee Day is held on 20 June each year. The aim of the day is to celebrate the contribution of refugees to their new country and to promote understanding of the need to seek sanctuary. The organisers want to show that in a world where violence forces thousands of families to flee for their lives each day, the global public sympathises with the plight of refugees and welcomes them into the countries in which they have chosen to seek refuge.

Refugee camps

Many refugees live in refugee camps, which are settlements often hastily assembled to cope with large population influxes. There are films on YouTube showing what life is like in a refugee camp. Explore some of these places:

↳ **Inside the Jungle:** Migrants seeking a future in the UK, some for language or family reasons, need to cross the English Channel. They arrive at Calais, the nearest point to the UK, in the hope of finding someone who is prepared to ferry them to the UK by boat or rubber dinghy. A settlement sprang up near the entrance to the Channel Tunnel which was called 'The Jungle'. It existed from January 2015 to October 2016, after which its inhabitants were forced to move.

↳ **The Rohingya:** The Rohingya people are an ethnic group who are predominantly Muslim and resided in Rakhine State in Myanmar, which is a Buddhist country. Their citizenship was not recognised and there was a lot of pressure on them to move, including military violence. There were an estimated 1 million Rohingya living in Myanmar before the 2016–17 crisis; most have now fled to neighbouring Bangladesh. Many are living in Kutupalong camp.

↳ **Jordan's fourth biggest city:** The Za'atari Refugee Camp is home to 79,000 people who have fled Assad's Syria and sought refuge just across the border in Jordan.

↳ **An island paradise?:** The island of Lesbos in the Aegean Sea, quite near to Turkey, has a resident population of 86,000. Refugees and migrants started to arrive in 2016. The Moria camp became home to 12,000 people seeking entry into the EU in facilities designed to hold just 3,000. The camp was destroyed by fire in autumn 2020.

What can we do?

In many countries there is a resistance to any rapid influx of immigrants, refugees and asylum seekers, with most people neither understanding nor seeing the difference between these. In the USA, the 2016 Trump presidential victory was partially due to his pledge to 'build a wall' to keep out people migrating from Central America. But in every country, there are people of good will who are trying to help refugees and asylum seekers survive the often difficult process of getting settled status and the difficulties of having to live on very meagre incomes during this process. Here are a few examples:

↳ **Meeting educational needs:** Mia Eskelund Pendersen and Polly Akhurst founded Amala (originally called Sky School) to provide secondary education to young people in refugee camps. They have developed a curriculum for learners aged 16–25 who have missed out on education as a consequence of being displaced. Their programme is being delivered in Greece, Kenya, Jordan and Bangladesh.

↳ **Meeting psychological needs:** Brock Chisholm and Katy Robjant were clinical psychologists, and Polly Rossdale had been working with victims of torture. Together, they set up Trauma Treatment International to try to meet the psychological needs of refugees displaced and living in camps and of camp staff by offering psychological services. TTI does not provide direct services but supports camp staff to mitigate the effects of stress and trauma that they were seeing, as well as providing them with mechanisms to support traumatised refugees.

↳ **Meeting transport needs:** Jem Stein realised that refugees in London could not afford the high price of public transport so were unable to move around the city. He found ways of getting bicycles donated and repaired, and provided these to refugees along with instruction in bicycle maintenance; some were also offered a 'cycling buddy' as a friend to go riding with and to help build confidence in riding a bike and in navigating the often difficult journey from refugee to citizen.

↳ **Meeting sanitary needs:** Gabby Edlin realised that refugee women often did not have enough money to buy products for their sanitary needs. She set up Bloody Good Period to collect feminine hygiene and sanitary products, and raise money to provide for the needs of refugee women, but also to campaign to raise awareness of the issue of 'period poverty'.

↳ **Meeting sporting needs:** Football is a globally popular sport that brings people together. There have been many imaginative initiatives to engage refugees in football. For example, in 2013 UEFA (the European Football Association) began a programme for Syrian refugees at the Za'atari refugee camp in Jordan. They distribute sports equipment, provide coaching and run tournaments involving around 1,000 young participants. Here in the UK, the Manchester Refugee Support Network runs a Refugee World Cup tournament during Refugee Week; this started in 2000 for refugees from Kosovo and has become an annual event with refugee teams from many countries. And in 2021, thirty Afghani young women footballers and their families fleeing the Taliban were resettled in the UK with the help of Leeds United and Kim Kardashian.

↳ **Meeting employment needs:** Pranav Chopra set up Nemi Teas to help refugees gain business skills and to access employment. They sell chai and other teas from market stalls to provide a sense of purpose and build confidence, while being encouraged and supported in job applications.

↳ **Mentoring a refugee:** For people who have fled war, violence or persecution, uprooted themselves from home and family and looking to rebuild their life, arriving in a country where people speak a different language and where customs and procedures are completely different can be difficult, and offering such people a hand of friendship can make all the difference. Mentors often become important adults in the people's lives, acting as role models, helping to combat isolation and loneliness and assisting them to find a pathway into employment. The Refugee Support Network and Breadwinners are two organisations looking for volunteer mentors.

Asylum seeking

'Everyone has the right to seek and to enjoy in other countries asylum from persecution.' This is enshrined in the Universal Declaration of Human Rights and supported by two subsequent conventions: the 1951 Refugee Convention and the 1967 Protocol Relating to the Status of Refugees.

An asylum seeker is a person who flees their home country and enters another country where they then apply for asylum, seeking protection in this other country because they feel that their lives would be in danger if they were to return home. Traditionally, an application was made in the first country reached after their escape but in Europe recently there has been some flexibility on this. Member states now share in the resettlement of asylum seekers, as most arrive in Greece or Italy. When an application for asylum has been granted, the asylum seeker is given some form of permanent resident status in their new country.

In 2019, most asylum seekers came from Venezuela as a result of political instability and economic crisis. These were the main countries where Venezuelans applied for asylum: Peru (258,636), Brazil (48,456), Spain (40,456), USA (33,125), Ecuador (15,445) and Colombia (10,497).

In the UK, asylum applications peaked in 2002 at 84,132, reached a 20-year low of 17,916 in 2010, rising to 35,737 in 2019 and 29,456 in 2020. Asylum seekers made up around 6 per cent of immigrants to the UK in 2019. About 64 per cent of all asylum applications are accepted either on first decision or on appeal.

Trafficked people and modern-day slavery

Trafficking involves transporting someone into a life of exploitation from which escape is difficult and sometimes impossible. It can include prostitution and other forms of sexual exploitation, organ removal, forced marriage, forced criminality, forced begging, conscription as child soldiers or slave labour, where they are imprisoned and work for no wages in factories, fields or as domestic servants.

It is estimated that internationally there are between 20 million and 40 million people in these forms of modern-day slavery, the vast majority of cases remaining hidden and undetected. It is also estimated that globally traffickers are earning profits of roughly $150 billion a year, $99 billion coming from commercial sexual exploitation. An estimated 71 per cent of enslaved people are women and girls. Read the UN Global Report on Trafficking in Human Persons.

The Walk Free Foundation undertakes research to build the world's most comprehensive evidence base of modern slavery to get the scale of the problem recognised and enable solutions to be created. Grace Forrest, the organisation's co-founder, says, 'Modern slavery is not something that happens "over there" that we don't have to think about. If we care about the people who make our products we can make a difference.' The foundation compiles a list ranking the incidence of modern slavery in different countries as a Global Slavery Index. These were the worst offenders for 2018:

1   North Korea (worst)

2   Eritrea

3   Burundi

4   Central African Republic

5   Afghanistan

6   Mauretania

7   South Sudan

8   Pakistan

9   Cambodia

10 Iran

Guy Hacking, Rob Martineau and Tom Stancliffe wanted to do something to fight modern slavery and end human trafficking. They started with Run for Love, a 1,000-mile run from Odessa to Dubrovnik to raise funds which they used to set up the first UK home for trafficked children. They went on to create the TRIBE Freedom Foundation, which organises challenges and fundraising events to raise money and increase awareness.

Get the app

Human trafficking is happening all around us. You might encounter it in a nail bar or a car wash or on a construction site or a farm. People are coerced into working for little or no remuneration, kept there often with the threat of violence (against them or a family member), by debt owed to the trafficker (often large sums at high interest which are largely unrepayable), by retention of identity papers or threatening to report them to the immigration authorities. Once captured, it is hard for someone to escape. But you might see signs of slavery if you are observant. For example, a person who:

↳ Seems to be acting as if instructed by
somebody else.

↳ Demonstrates signs of physical or
psychological abuse, such as extreme
anxiety or bruising.

↳ Seems frightened and distrustful of
authority.

↳ Has no money.

↳ Cannot provide identity papers.

If you see this, you can report your suspicion.
The STOP APP, developed by Stop the Traffik,
can be downloaded by anyone with access
to a smartphone. It is available in seven
languages. You can submit information on
suspicious activity quickly and confidentially
by sending a text message and uploading
photos and videos.

Every human trafficking incident is important
in building up a picture of this unacceptable
activity. Technology gives us the power to
contribute towards stopping modern-day
slavery and bringing the perpetrators to justice.

DO THIS:

Organise a film screening to raise awareness
of refugees and their situation. In 2021, the
UNHCR asked Cate Blanchett to recommend
six films: *Capernaum*, *Shoplifters*, *News from
Home*, *The Other Side of Hope*, *Babe and The
Joy Luck Club*, and provided a link to download
and screen them.

Our food is killing us

21

Incidence of obesity in the world

The most obese and least obese countries. This shows the percentage of each country's population considered obese:

The 20 most obese

Nauru	61.0
Cook Islands	55.9
Palau	55.3
Marshall Islands	52.9
Tuvalu	51.6
Niue	50.0
Tonga	48.2
Samoa	47.3
Kiribati	46.0
Micronesia	45.8
Kuwait	37.9
USA	36.2
Jordan	35.3
Saudi Arabia	35.4
Qatar	35.1
Libya	32.5
Turkey	32.1
Egypt	32.0
Lebanon	33.7
United Arab Emirates	31.7

The 10 least obese

Vietnam	2.1
Bangladesh	3.6
Timor-Leste	3.8
India	3.9
Cambodia	3.9
Nepal	4.1
Japan	4.3
Ethiopia	4.5
South Korea	4.7
Eritrea	5.0

This data comes from The CIA World Factbook. The World Health Organization defines 'overweight' and 'obesity' as 'abnormal or excessive fat accumulation which creates a risk to health'. They consider a body mass index over 25 as overweight and over 30 as obese.

↳ Over 4 million people died in 2017 as a result of being overweight or obese according to the global burden of disease. This represents 8 per cent of all deaths.

↳ The incidence of overweight and obesity continues to grow in both adults and children. In 2016, more than 1.9 billion adults worldwide (39 per cent of all adults) were overweight, including 650 million who were obese (11 per cent of all men and 15 per cent of all women). The prevalence of obesity tripled worldwide between 1975 and 2016 and the rate was even higher for children and adolescents aged 5–19 years, increasing 4.5 times during this period from 4 per cent to 18 per cent.

↳ Today, more people are obese than underweight in every region except sub-Saharan Africa and Asia. The vast majority of overweight or obese children live in less developed countries, where the rate of increase has been more than 30 per cent higher than for children in the rich world.

↳ The highest rates of obesity are found in the tiny Pacific Islands, and in the USA, which is the world's richest country. Other very-high-obesity countries are all in the Middle East.

The food we eat

More and more of us are eating junk food, high in sugars and fats, ultra-processed, with over-refined cereals and stuffed with preservatives and taste enhancers. Eat we must. But the food we are eating is turning us into junk – damaging our bodies and our health. A really good example of how diet affects us comes from eighteenth-century Scotland.

From around 1760, landowners started to clear the Scottish Highlands, evicting tenant crofters (small farmers) to clear the land for sheep farming. Those evicted made their way to the big cities, including Glasgow, which was growing fast with the Industrial Revolution. A survey at that time found adult male highlanders were up to 1.85m tall. They were long-lived, thriving on a diet of oats, barley, vegetables, milk, butter, eggs, locally grown fruit and honey supplemented with small amounts of meat and fish. The Scots living in Glasgow today are smaller, unhealthier and much shorter-lived. Their food intake is on average high in sugar, high in fat, with a prevalence of junk food, white bread, factory-made cakes and biscuits, sugary drinks and over-sweetened breakfast cereals.

Today, across Greater Glasgow, 22 per cent of children entering primary school are overweight or obese and 65 per cent of men and 59 per cent of women aged 16 to 65 are overweight or obese. Obesity and poor diet exist across Glasgow but the situation amongst the poor is particularly bad. It is diet not genes that caused this transformation of Scotland from being amongst the healthiest to becoming amongst the unhealthiest in Europe.

Obesity is caused by an excess of the body's calorie intake and lack of expenditure. With ice cream, snack foods such as crisps, sweets, sugary beverages, and sugar, oil and fat in many manufactured and take-away foods, plus too little exercise, people's intake of 'quick calories' has become far too high for their health and wellbeing.

There is also a paradox. As we are getting richer we have an increased ability to make food choices (which our hunter-gatherer forebears were unable to do), and yet the unhealthier we are becoming. For example, many poor in Africa live on a sorghum or cassava-based diet but as they get richer, they aspire to a diet of white rice and flour, which contain fewer essential nutrients. And in rich countries, people are moving from home-prepared food using basic ingredients to factory-made ready meals or fast food delivered to their door, often made with the cheapest ingredients and overloaded with fats, sugar, salt and chemicals for colour, taste and preserving. The result of this isn't just obesity but diabetes too. Both of these have created major health problems, which are on the increase all over the world – while at the same time, paradoxically, billions continue to face hunger and malnutrition, and suffer ill health as a result of an inadequate diet.

Read these: *Hungry City: How Food Shapes Our Lives* and *Sitopia: How Food Can Save the World*, both by Carolyn Steel. You will better understand how the way we eat impacts on our lives and on our wellbeing.

The world's biggest food and beverage corporations

In the West, we buy most of our food from multinationals. Using advanced processing techniques and clever advertising, they now largely determine what we eat. Their grip on people's diets all over the world is growing as consumption of factory-prepared food, junk food, snacks and confectionery continues to grow. These are the world's 15 biggest food companies. The figures are the annual food sales income for 2019 in billions of US dollars:

Nestle, Switzerland	$76.8
Pepsico, USA	$67.2
Anheuser-Busch Inbev, Belgium	$52.3
JBS, USA	$48.8
Tyson Foods, USA	$42.4
Mars, USA	$37.6
Coca-Cola, USA	$37.3
Archer Daniels Midland, USA	$33.0
Cargill, USA	$31.7
Danone, France	$28.3
Heineken, Netherlands	$26.8
Mondelez International, USA	$25.9
Kraft Heinz, USA	$25.0
Smithfield Foods/WH Group, USA	$23.3
Unilever, UK	$21.6

The Forbes Top 25 Food Companies generated $815 billion in revenue and made profits of $91 billion in 2020. According to Forbes, 'Wellness and clean eating might be having a moment, but when it comes to the products that are propelling the performance of the world's largest food and beverage companies, beer, chocolate and coffee are overpowering quinoa, kale and kombucha.'

Super Size Me

Morgan Spurlock was interested in the impact that a fast food diet might have on his body and his health if that was all that he ate. He also noticed that McDonald's staff were trained to ask people if they wanted to order a bigger portion, the biggest being 'supersize'. He decided that he would eat only McDonald's food for 30 days and also that he would upgrade to supersize whenever he was invited to do this, and that he would finish every last crumb of all the meals that he ate. He filmed the whole process, which ran from 2 to 31 March 2003.

His film *Super Size Me* documents the drastic effect that this regime had on his physical and mental wellbeing, while at the same time examining the fast food industry's influence on people's lives and health, including how the industry profits from providing poor nutrition.

Spurlock ate three McDonald's meals each day and ordered every item on the menu at least once. His daily calorie intake averaged 5,000kcal, which is about double the amount for a healthy, balanced diet. Over the 30 days, he gained 11.1 kilos in weight (a 13 per cent increase), his cholesterol count increased to 230 mg/dl (which is borderline high), fat accumulated in his liver and he experienced mood swings and sexual dysfunction. It took him 14 months to get back to the same body levels as at the start of the experiment. You can watch *Super Size Me* on Morgan Spurlock's website.

McLibel

The McLibel Trial has been called 'the worst PR disaster in corporate history'. Helen Steel and Dave Morris were environmental campaigners with London Greenpeace (not related to Greenpeace). In 1986, they wrote and distributed a few hundred copies of a six-page leaflet called 'What's wrong with McDonald's: everything they don't want you to know'. The leaflet accused the company of paying low wages, cruelty to animals used in its products, destruction of the environment, negative impact on people's health, predatory advertising to children and other malpractices.

McDonald's decided to sue the pair for libel. The case came to trial in 1994 and lasted for nearly three years. Steel and Morris were denied legal aid (which is generally not available for libel cases) and they decided to represent themselves (receiving pro bono and crowdsourced legal advice and help from sympathetic lawyers, including Keir Starmer, who later became leader of the UK's Labour Party). If they lost, they would not be able to pay McDonald's very substantial legal costs or any damages ordered by the judge.

Steel and Morris defended themselves vigorously, calling 180 witnesses. In June 1995, McDonald's offered to settle the case by donating a large sum to a charity chosen by the defendants, but with the condition that the pair to stop criticising McDonald's publicly in the media or distributing literature, although they would still be allowed to do this privately amongst their friends. Their response was that they would only agree to these terms if McDonald's ceased advertising its products to the public and instead only recommended their product privately to their friends. The case continued.

In his verdict in June 1997, the judge ruled that the company did exploit children through its advertising, that it was culpably responsible for cruelty to animals, that it did pay its workers low wages, but that the defendants had failed to prove many of their points to the standard required. The judge ruled that McDonald's had been libelled and awarded £60,000 damages, which the defendants refused to pay.

The defendants took the case to appeal in January 1999, with the court ruling that it was fair comment to say that 'if one eats enough McDonald's food, one's diet may well become high in fat ... with the very real risk of heart disease'. Later, they took the British government to the European Court of Human Rights, claiming that UK libel laws were oppressive. The court ruled in their favour, confirming that the McLibel case had breached their right to freedom of expression and a fair trial.

One thing you can do with Coca-Cola

Coca-Cola sales in India declined 11 per cent in three months during 2003 due to allegations that its soft drinks contained a high level of pesticides. These allegations were made by the prestigious Centre for Science and Environment in Delhi, which said the top 12 soft drink brands of PepsiCo and Coca-Cola contained pesticides and insecticides in excess of the limits set by the European Commission.

But Coca-Cola really can be used as a pesticide! Farmers in India spray their cotton and chili fields with 'the real thing'. Gotu Laxmaiah, a farmer from Andhra Pradesh, applied a cola spray to several hectares of cotton. He said, 'I observed that the pests began to die after the soft drink was sprayed on my cotton' – this was reported in the *Deccan Herald* newspaper.

The main reason why Coke has become popular a pesticide is cost. Coke costs only $6 to spray an acre, far less than traditional pesticides. Farmers also like it because it is safe to handle and does not need to be diluted. As yet, there is no scientific proof of Coke's effectiveness as a pesticide but farmers have traditionally used sugary solutions to attract red ants which then feed on insect larvae.

The Guardian Unlimited website reports that, 'The properties of Coke have been discussed for years. It has been reported that it is a fine lavatory cleaner, a good windscreen wipe and an efficient rust spot remover.'

The diabetes epidemic

Diabetes is destroying people's wellbeing and creating financial pressure on health systems all over the world. Type 1 diabetes occurs when the body cannot produce enough insulin to regulate blood sugar levels. It often occurs early on in life and may be genetic or caused by a poor immune system. This is completely different from type 2 diabetes, which is lifestyle related and the biggest cause for concern. In 2019:

↳ Approximately **463 million adults** were living with diabetes; by 2045 this will rise to **700 million.**

↳ **79 per cent** of adults with diabetes were **in low- and middle-income countries.**

↳ **34.2 million** Americans have diabetes and **88 million** have pre-diabetes.

↳ **1 in 2** people with diabetes (232 million people) were undiagnosed.

↳ Diabetes causes **4.2 million deaths annually.**

↳ Treating diabetes requires **$760 billion of** health expenditure – 10 per cent of the total health spend for adults.

The IDF Diabetes Atlas has produced figures of the incidence of diabetes worldwide. The healthiest countries (figures are for the proportion of the population between 20 and 79 with type 1 and type 2 diabetes) are: Benin (1 per cent); Zimbabwe (1.8 per cent); The Gambia (1.9 per cent); Greenland (2.1 per cent); and a whole batch of countries in West Africa (2.4 per cent). Right at the top is Kiribati (22.5 per cent), then Tuvalu and Sudan (both 22.1 per cent). Big countries at the top of the table include Pakistan (19.9 per cent); Egypt (17.2 per cent); Malaysia (16.7 per cent); and Saudi Arabia (15.8 per cent), with similar figures for neighbouring countries. The incidence in the USA and Europe is around 10 per cent.

Malnutrition and hunger

Malnutrition is a deficiency or imbalance in a person's intake of energy and nutrients. There are two aspects: undernutrition, which includes wasting (low weight-for-height), stunting (low height-for-age) and underweight (low weight-for-age), and micronutrient deficiency, a lack of vitamins and minerals critical for body development and health. These are some statistics:

↳ In today's world, 462 million adults are underweight, while 1.9 billion are overweight. 49 million children under 5 years are wasted (low weight-for-age), 17 million severely wasted and 149 million stunted (low height-for-age), while 40 million are overweight or obese.

↳ Around 45 per cent of deaths of children under 5 are linked to undernutrition, mostly in low- and middle-income countries.

And these are some statistics on hunger:

↳ 11 per cent of the world's population are undernourished, having a calorie intake below minimum requirements.

↳ 22 per cent of children younger than five are 'stunted' – significantly shorter than the average for their age, as a consequence of poor nutrition or repeated infection.

↳ 9 per cent of the world's population – around 697 million people – are severely food insecure.

Our World in Data has created a Global Hunger Index, and highlights Central African Republic, Yemen, Madagascar and Zambia as 'hunger hotspots' where the situation is alarming or extremely alarming. (There are no figures available for the DR Congo, which should probably be in this list.) The situation in much

of the rest of Africa and in parts of South Asia and South-East Asia is designated as being serious. Child stunting across these countries is particularly alarming.

The UN declared 2016–2025 as a 'Decade of Action on Nutrition', with the aim of creating sustainable, resilient food systems for healthy diets and providing social protection and nutrition-related education for all.

DO THIS:

There are lots of websites offering surprising, crazy or even mind-blowing ideas for what to do with Coca-Cola, besides drinking it. Use your search engine to find these and other blogs.

And for those who want to make their own cola, here is an 'open cola' recipe: artofdrink. com/soda/coca-colas-recipe. Make your own, have a few friends around, drink it, enjoy … and compare it with 'The Real Thing'.

I am an
addict

22

Drug and alcohol abuse

The prevalence of drug abuse (excluding tobacco) as a percentage of the country's population:

1 USA 5.47

2 Russia 5.93

3 Greenland 5.13

4 Mongolia 4.12

5 Finland 4.02

6 Australia 3.80

7 Canada 3.79

8 Brazil 3.73

9 New Zealand 3.72

10 Bosnia and Herzegovina 3.53

11 Chile 3.46

12 Kazakhstan 3.34

13 Kyrgyzstan 3.31

14 Ireland 3.24

15 South Korea 3.16

16 Argentina 3.12

17 Slovakia 2.99

18 Paraguay 2.92

19 UK 2.90

20 Austria 2.83

21 Germany 2.83

22 Norway 2.82

According to the Global Bureau of Disease in 2016, 162.8 million people in the world had an alcohol or drug use disorder. The figures for the two most populous countries in the world are China 1.96 per cent and India 1.74 per cent. Our World in Data has more data on illicit drug use.

It is a marketer's dream to find products which are addictive so that customers come back again and again for more and more. These products are all around us – gambling, booze, tobacco and illegal drugs, all of which are addictive, all of which damage our health and wellbeing.

Gambling addiction

These are some cities that have built their economy on gambling: Las Vegas in Nevada; Macau, which styles itself as the 'Las Vegas of the East'; Atlantic City in New Jersey, where gambling gave a down-at-heel city a new look; Monte Carlo, famed for its iconic nineteenth-century casino.

Charles Wells was a British gambler who achieved fame by breaking the bank at the Monte Carlo casino, not once but several times, inspiring a music hall song and a Hollywood film. There are others who have had amazing winning streaks. But this hides the stark fact that with every spin of the roulette wheel, gamblers on average will lose one thirty-seventh of their stake (and that's if there is only one zero on the board). The more you gamble, the more you are likely to lose. The odds are stacked in favour of the casino.

With some games, the odds can be tilted in favour of the gambler. This is true for blackjack but only if you count the cards. A group of MIT students decided that they would beat the odds by playing blackjack; they were so successful that the casinos tried to find ways of banning them, even going to the lengths of installing iris recognition cameras to identify them when they were wearing wigs and make-up. Their story is told in *Bringing Down the House: The Inside Story of Six MIT Students Who Took Vegas for Millions* by Ben Mezrich.

The casinos and gaming machine manufacturers use a huge amount of creativity to attract and keep gamblers playing. Slot machines are placed in lobbies, so everyone can see them and hear the coins cascading out for the occasional big winner. The machines are programmed with percentage odds in favour of the casino but give enough 'near misses' to keep the gambler gambling. The time taken for each spin is not too short, as the gambler has to have time for emotion and expectation, but not too long as the casino wants the gambler to continue until their money runs out. Similar principles apply to the design of lotteries. Big winners, near misses, 'you lost this week but better luck next time'.

You might think that by doubling up each time at roulette, you will surely win. You lost $1 on red, so next time bet $2 on red. Lose again, then bet $4 on red … . Surely Red will come up and you will have eliminated your losses. But the wheel has no memory. Each time, there is a 19 in 37 chance that red won't come up. The probability that you will lose is better than evens and next spin you will have to double your stake again. The bank might break you before you win back your $1.

Gambling is known to be addictive and compulsive gamblers find it impossible to stop. They will steal and worse to feed their habit. Gambling addicts exhibit similar characteristics to those with substance addiction. A scientific study using MRI scanning showed similar brain function for slot machine players and crack addicts. At the same time, gambling is everywhere – from online bingo with small stakes to mega-betting on horse races and football matches. It is presented as a fun activity but the reality is that it can destroy lives and families ... and the casino or gambling site always wins. The global market for gambling was estimated at $53.7 billion in 2019 and is growing at more than 10 per cent per annum.

Alcohol addiction

Drinking is a part of many cultures (although forbidden in Islam). For many, 'going to the pub' or 'having a beer' or 'celebrating with bubbly' are normal social activities. Drinking in moderation is generally thought of as safe but drinking to excess is harmful. It can also lead to psychological dependency and then to physical dependency. In the UK, an estimated 9 per cent of men and 3 per cent of women show signs of alcohol dependence. There are other damaging issues relating to drink, especially the incidence of domestic violence and drunk driving, both of which destroy lives.

The alcoholic drinks market is estimated at $1.58 trillion (for 2020), growing at 3.5 per cent per annum. The largest component is beer, with sales of $615 billion. The leading alcoholic beverage companies are AB Inbev, Suntory, Heineken, SABMiller and Diageo. Governments derive significant revenues from taxing alcohol sales, so generally are conflicted when it comes to whether the treasury or public health comes first.

Sensible drinking: The drinks producers sign up to codes of conduct governing advertising and drinks labelling, and agree to back drinking-in-moderation campaigns. There is a special concern about young people's drinking, but while warning against alcohol abuse, the drinks companies simultaneously develop products targeted primarily at young people, such as alcopops, which boomed in the 1990s.

Prohibition: In the USA there was a nationwide ban on producing, importing, transporting and selling alcoholic beverages. This ran from 1920 to 1933. But the sale of illicit liquor and the development of criminal-run black markets (aiding the rise of the Mafia) meant that drink was available if you knew where to find it. By the late 1920s, New York City had more than 30,000 speakeasies and Detroit's alcohol trade was the second biggest contributor to the local economy after automobiles. With the Great Depression, the benefits of taxing sales were seen as more important than restricting consumption, which led to the ending of Prohibition.

Alcoholics Anonymous: AA is an international mutual aid fellowship with the stated purpose of enabling its members to 'stay sober and help other alcoholics achieve sobriety'. The only membership requirement is a desire to stop drinking. AA has developed a 12-step process, with step 1 having members understand and say that: 'We admit that we are powerless over alcohol and that our lives have become unmanageable.' People come together to do what they can to admit to alcoholism, pledge to stop drinking, share their stories and help each other through difficult times when they feel a strong urge to have just one drink. Members often start their story by saying 'I am an alcoholic ...' There are now branches in 180 countries and the model has been used with other addictions, such as gambling.

Tobacco

Would you run a business, invest in a business or work for a business which knowingly sells products which are harmful to health and which cause death? This is the dilemma behind tobacco, where the link between smoking and health problems has been known for a long time. As far back as 1964, the US Surgeon General linked smoking to lung cancer, and since then evidence emerged in the USA that smoking was causing 87 per cent of lung cancer deaths, 32 per cent of coronary heart disease deaths and 79 per cent of all cases of chronic obstructive pulmonary disease.

↳ One in five adults in the world smoke tobacco. About 5.7 trillion cigarettes were smoked worldwide in 2016.

↳ 15 per cent of global deaths are attributed to smoking.

↳ Smoking killed an estimated 100 million people in the twentieth century (mostly in rich countries) and up to 1 billion could die in the twenty-first century (mostly in middle- and low-income countries).

↳ China produces and consumes the most cigarettes and has 22 million deaths a year attributed to smoking. India has 895,000; USA, 422,000; Russia, 301,000.

↳ The highest death rates from tobacco are in Papua New Guinea (245 deaths per 100,000 per annum), Greenland (185), Myanmar (175), Ukraine and Serbia (both 153). The lowest is South Sudan (15).

↳ 'Big Tobacco' refers to the largest global tobacco companies. The largest six are Philip Morris, Altria, British American Tobacco, Imperial, Japan Tobacco and China Tobacco.

Anti-smoking campaigns have led to:

↳ Restrictions on advertising, point-of-sale display and pack design, including the printing of warnings of dangers of smoking on packs.

↳ Banning of sale of tobacco products to minors, with proof of identity required where age is in doubt.

↳ Banning of smoking in public places. This varies from country to country but often includes restaurants, bars and offices.

↳ Raising taxes and prices of cigarettes.

Smoking may be in decline in rich countries but companies are targeting their marketing at young people using social media. The Campaign for Tobacco-Free Kids documented over 100 campaigns by leading brands which enrolled social influencers, paying them to post natural photos featuring the tobacco brand with instructions that any health warning should not be visible. Combined, these posts were viewed more than 25 billion times worldwide.

BBC Radio broadcast a programme on lobbying techniques used by Big Tobacco to counter the claim that smoking was injurious to health, which delayed restrictions on tobacco advertising and sale for many years. Similar techniques have been used in other contexts, such as questioning climate change. They include: flat denial, questioning the science, presenting 'alternative facts' and using celebrities to reinforce the message.

But Big Tobacco may be beginning to crack. In 2021, Philip Morris announced that it planned to end all tobacco sales in the UK within ten years.

Illegal drugs

In 2017, the Institute for Health Metrics and Evaluation estimated that globally 53.2 million people were suffering a drugs disorder under the following main categories: opioids 26.9 million, cannabis 14.2 million, amphetamines 6.9 million and cocaine 3.7 million, with the biggest incidence for people aged between 20 and 30, affecting 2.25 per cent of people in this age group. Drugs killed 166,613 people through overdosing in 2017 and indirectly led to 585,348 deaths.

Not all of the drug problem is due to illegal drugs. Opioids are prescription drugs (prescribed) and not banned drugs (proscribed). Opioids have been over-prescribed widely as painkillers and this has created an epidemic of drug dependency. In 2020, Purdue Pharma, a private company principally owned by the Sackler family known for its philanthropy, maker of OxyContin, reached an $8.3 billion settlement with the US government, admitting that it enabled the supply of drugs 'without legitimate medical purpose'. In 2021, Johnson & Johnson Pharmaceuticals (J&J brands itself as 'a family company') agreed to pay $26 billion to settle lawsuits over its role in the US opioid epidemic.

Drugs destroy lives. But all attempts to address the drugs issue by criminalising drug use as well as its supply have failed. There are ever more powerful criminal cartels around the world and gang wars with gun and knife violence in our cities. Meanwhile, producers are creating drugs which are not scheduled as illegal and producing ever more addictive versions of basic drugs such as cannabis and cocaine.

Poppies in Afghanistan: Afghanistan has been the world's leading illicit opium producer since 2001, which is when the USA invaded in retaliation for the 9/11 terrorist attacks. Afghanistan now produces 80–90 per cent of the world's illicit heroin. More land is used for opium in Afghanistan than for coca cultivation in Latin America. Poppies are cultivated, but ephedra grows wild in Afghanistan's central highlands and this is being harvested to produce methamphetamine.

The War on Drugs: This 'war' was instigated by President Nixon in 1971, and since then the US has been (unsuccessfully) trying to eliminate drugs by stamping out supply and by punishing dealers and couriers. This has not only failed, it has created super-wealthy, well-armed and politically powerful elites of drug lords, and destabilised whole countries and communities. It has also led to the incarceration of hundreds of thousands in overflowing US jails. This leads to the debate as to whether we should decriminalise drug use, control it better and tax it, rather than have pushers creating the demand which they then supply.

The drug lords: If you Google 'drug lords worldwide', you will be shown a rogues' gallery of some 50 of the world's most infamous drug lords. Here are some of them:

↳ Joaquin Guzman, known as El Chapo ('shorty', due to his height), was Mexico's biggest drug lord and head of the Sinaloa Cartel, the largest importer of drugs into the USA. An assassination that he ordered in 2006 was the flashpoint for the Mexican drug war, which has claimed over 60,000 deaths. He has been arrested, imprisoned and escaped twice, and is now imprisoned in Colorado.

↳ Pablo Escobar, head of Colombia's Medellin Cartel, was gunned down in 1993 fleeing government soldiers. He engaged in domestic terror on a large scale to protect his interests, being responsible for over 4,000 deaths. At his peak, he was exporting 15 tonnes of cocaine a day to the USA.

↳ Griselda Blanco was a 'drug queen' from Colombia linked to the Medellin Cartel. She operated first in New York and then in Miami, where she imported cocaine and slew her drug rivals, instigating up to 250 murders. She named her youngest son 'Michael Corleone' in honour of the film *The Godfather*.

↳ Osiel Cerdenas Guillen, nicknamed El Mata Amigos ('the friend killer') for murdering a friend who was his rival to head the Gulf Cartel, enforced his will through a private army known as Los Zetas. He was eventually extradited and imprisoned in the USA.

DO THIS:

Understand better the issues of addiction. Castle Craig, Europe's leading rehab centre, has a help and advice section with simple explanatory practical information on a wide range of addictions and ways of treating them: castlecraig.co.uk.

The spread of disease

23

A timeline of pandemics

Some of the major killer infections in the
Common Era (CE), with the date, places
affected, likely cause and estimated death toll:

1 The Plague of Galen

circa 165–180 CE
Asia Minor, Egypt, Greece and Italy
Cause: measles or smallpox
5 million dead

2 The Plague of Justinian

541–542 CE
Byzantine empire and Mediterranean
Cause: bubonic plague transmitted
by fleas
25 million dead

3 The Black Death

1346–1353
Europe, Africa and Asia
Cause: bubonic plague transmitted
by fleas
Up to 200 million dead

4 The Cocoliztli Epidemic

1545–1548
Mexico
Cause: lack of immunity to European
diseases
5 to 15 million people dead

5 The Great Plague

1665–1666
London
Cause: bubonic plague
transmitted by fleas
100,000 dead

6 The Third Cholera Pandemic

1852–1860
Ganges river delta, spreading
globally
Cause: cholera
1 million dead

7 The First Flu Pandemic

1889–1890
North-west Canada and
Greenland, spreading globally
Cause: influenza H3N8
1 million dead

8 'Spanish' Flu Pandemic

1918–1920
Global
Cause: influenza H1N1
Up to 50 million dead

9   Asian Flu Pandemic

1956–1958
China and Far East, spreading to USA
Cause: influenza H2N2
2 million dead

10   The Hong Kong Flu

1968
Hong Kong, spreading globally
Cause: influenza H3N2
1 million dead

11   Acquired Immunodeficiency Syndrome (AIDS)

1976 and continuing
Global, first identified in DR Congo
Cause: HIV
36 million dead

12   Severe Acute Respiratory Syndrome (SARS)

2003
Southern China and South Asia
Cause: SARS-CoV-1
800 dead

13   Middle East Respiratory Syndrome (MERS)

2003
Saudi Arabia
Cause: MERS-CoV
800 dead

14   Ebola

2013–2016
West Africa
Cause: Ebola virus
11,000 dead

15   Covid-19

2019 and continuing
Global, emanating from Wuhan, China
Cause: SARS-CoV-2 virus
514 million reported cases and 6.24 million reported deaths and rising
(1 May 2022)

Photo: Belinda Fewings

The Covid-19 virus is currently spreading across the world. Its impact has been uneven. Half the reported deaths have occurred in just six countries: USA, Brazil, India, Mexico, Peru, Russia. The highest death rates per 1,000 population have been in South America and Eastern Europe. Peru is the worst affected country with over six reported deaths per 1,000 population, which is approximately 50,000 times worse than China's 4,636 reported deaths in a population of over 1,445,000,000.

Recent pandemics

Pandemics are potentially as dangerous today as in the past. But medical science has brought us (and will continue to bring us) treatments, vaccines, safety procedures and testing regimes, all of which will considerably reduce the impact of emerging pathogens. The time taken to create a drug, test it for safety and efficacy, introduce it and then scale it up for mass use continues to shrink. For the 2013 Ebola outbreak in Western Africa, a vaccine was ready by 2019. But for Covid-19, within six months of its emergence in China, the genetic code of the virus had become publicly known and there were 42 vaccines in development. It took just a year from the first reported case to get the first vaccines tested for safety and effectiveness, approved for emergency use, into mass production and then into people's arms. Despite the unequal distribution of vaccines across the world, they have been a key factor in containing the virus. We can now produce vaccines quickly in response to novel viruses and new strains, but we have a lot to learn about how to distribute them widely, and especially into poor countries with not-so-well-functioning health systems. This is important, as with a pandemic nobody's safe until everybody's safe.

Disease conquering Latin America

Many of the early global pandemics were caused by invading armies who spread disease into the territories they conquered, diseases that they themselves had immunity to, or they brought new diseases back home on their return, where their compatriots had no immunity. Perhaps the most striking example of this is seen in the conquest of the Americas.

It is estimated that 95 per cent of the total population of the Americas died in the first 130 years of European conquest.

Following the 'discovery' of the New World in 1492 by Christopher Columbus, expeditions led by the Spanish and Portuguese conquistadors in the sixteenth century created trading routes which led to the colonisation of the continent. The invaders not only came with guns and gunpowder, but they also brought their own diseases. And it was the lack of resistance to these old-world diseases, which included smallpox, chickenpox, diphtheria, influenza, typhus and measles, that overwhelmed the local populations. Disease was able to spread far faster than the invading conquistadors, which weakened further the resistance of the indigenous people who were already overpowered by their invaders' superior weaponry.

It is estimated that 95 per cent of the total population of the Americas died in the first 130 years of European conquest, including some 90 per cent of the Inca population and 97 per cent of the Aztec population. The indigenous population of Mexico declined from an estimated 25 million in 1518 to as few as 700,000 people in 1623.

Conquering cholera

Cholera is an intestinal disease which can cause death. Today it affects around 5 million people worldwide, causing around 130,000 deaths a year, mainly in poor countries and amongst children. Up until the mid-nineteenth century, the cause was thought to be 'miasma' (meaning bad air, also thought to be the cause of malaria).

John Snow was an English physician who took a lead in developing anaesthesia and medical hygiene. He was a founder of modern epidemiology, the study of how disease spreads. In 1854, there was a cholera outbreak in Soho, central London. Snow had the brilliant idea of plotting cases of cholera on a street map. He saw that these were clustered around a single point – a water pump in what is now Broadwick Street. This led to the conclusion that cholera could be conquered through clean water provision and much better sanitation in cities, which then became a priority for city planners.

The mathematics of infection

We can now quite easily model how a disease will spread. Each person may pass on a germ or a virus to others they come into contact with, but the disease will not be transmitted if the recipient already has a resistance to the disease. They may have been immunised through vaccination or have already been infected, when they will have built up their own immunity.

The spread of a virus will be influenced by these factors:

↳ The proportion of the population who remain susceptible (those without immunity).

↳ The number of days that an infected person is contagious.

↳ The number of susceptible people that an infected person comes into contact with (which can be reduced through legal restrictions or behaviour change).

↳ The probability of a person contracting the virus through having had contact with an infected person (how infectious the virus actually is).

The deadliest viruses are not always the most dangerous. If a virus kills people too quickly, then the infected person will only be able to make a very few contacts, reducing the chance of transmitting the virus. If symptoms are severe, infected people are more visible, making them easier to identify, quarantine and treat, and they themselves are more likely to reduce their contact with others – both of which reduce the rate that the infection spreads. The factors that made Covid-19 spread so fast and so widely include a long incubation period before infected people show visible signs and isolate themselves and a substantial proportion of infected people being asymptomatic, having no visible signs but still able to pass on the virus to others. The virus was allowed to spread initially through the delay in preventing infected people travelling abroad from Wuhan where the virus first emerged. Then, new variants such as Omicron spread through international travel along with inadequate levels of vaccination in poorer countries.

The response to Covid

Drug companies and research institutes all over the world raced to create an effective vaccine for Covid-19, often with encouragement and financial support from governments. Three issues emerged: pricing, patents and distribution.

To address a global pandemic, vaccines had to be made widely available to all, rather than priced to maximise manufacturers' profits. Waiving patents would allow other companies to produce the vaccines that proved most effective. This would increase production while also keeping prices in check. Astra Zeneca initially did both of these. It sold its vaccine at cost in rich countries (though a policy it started to move away from at the end of 2021). It did a deal with the Coalition for Epidemic Preparedness Innovations, GAVI the Vaccine Alliance and the Serum Institute of India (SII) to provide 300 million low-cost doses for distribution through the Covax initiative and reached a licensing agreement with SII to supply one billion doses for low- and middle-income countries.

But once vaccines have been supplied, an infrastructure is needed that is able to distribute the vaccines across a country and to vaccinate large numbers of people quickly. In many countries, this infrastructure is lacking. On the basis that nobody is safe until everybody is safe, lots of lessons need to be learned from the way the response to Covid-19 was handled for when we face the next pandemic.

To address a global pandemic, vaccines had to be made widely available to all, rather than priced to maximise manufacturers' profits.

Anti-vaxxers

Not everybody is prepared to be vaccinated. Some can't for health reasons. But there is 'vaccine hesitancy', where people worry about possible side effects or are concerned for other reasons. These people are initially unwilling to be vaccinated but can be persuaded. There is also 'vaccine rejection', where people absolutely refuse to be vaccinated, and some campaign actively on this issue to discourage others.

A key figure in the current anti-vaccination movement is Andrew Wakefield. In 1998, he published an article in the prestigious medical journal *The Lancet* suggesting a link between the triple MMR vaccine (measles, mumps, rubella) and an aspect of autism. This received wide publicity and led to a sharp drop in vaccination levels. This then allowed the re-emergence of measles in the UK, which is a severe disease, because the population as a whole had not been sufficiently vaccinated to create herd immunity (where there are too few susceptible people in the population for the disease to be able to spread). Other scientists were unable to replicate Wakefield's findings, and Brian Deer, an investigative journalist, suggested that there had been a scientific fraud. In 2010, Wakefield's paper was retracted by *The Lancet*, and Wakefield was found guilty of professional misconduct by the General Medical Council and stripped of his doctor's licence. He had already emigrated to the USA in 2004. In 2011, he founded the Strategic Autism Initiative and the Autism Media Channel to continue campaigning, and he has become a 'hero' in the US anti-vaccination movement.

Before this, there was already a significant anti-vaccine feeling in the USA. In 1955, there had been a disaster when a poorly inactivated polio vaccine produced by Cutter and Wyeth Laboratories caused 164 cases of severe paralysis and 10 deaths. In 1974, there was a widely publicised claim that the triple DPT (diphtheria, pertussis – often called whooping cough – tetanus) vaccine caused brain damage. In the African-American community, people remembered the Tuskegee Syphilis Study, which recruited 400 sharecroppers and denied them treatment for syphilis over 40 years. As a result, in some communities in the USA, there have been extremely low vaccination rates, despite strong encouragement from the authorities for people to get vaccinated – Mississippi, Alabama, Wyoming, Idaho and West Virginia all have rates below 40 per cent, while the top vaccinated

states with over 65 per cent are Vermont, Connecticut, Massachusetts and Maine.

In most US states, young people require parental permission to get vaccinated. Teenager Kelly Danielpour founded VaxTeen to help teens with vaccine-hesitant parents by providing them with information and advice on vaccines and vaccination rights.

Pandemic preparedness

The Global Health Security Index is a comprehensive assessment of the global health security capability of 195 countries. It rates countries using these five criteria:

1   Preventing the emergence or release of pathogens

2   Early detection and reporting of epidemics of public concern

3   Rapidly responding to and mitigating the spread of an epidemic

4   Having a sufficient and robust public health sector

5   A commitment to international norms

China, which performed best in respect of Covid-19 in terms of keeping the infection under control, was ranked 51 out of 195 countries. Peru, which performed worst, was ranked 49. The top five countries were USA, UK, Netherlands, Australia and Canada.

From bats to humans

Zoonosis is where an infectious disease (whether caused by bacteria, viruses, fungi or parasites) jumps across species, spreading from non-humans to humans. Diseases such as Ebola, avian flu and swine flu are zoonotic. HIV was originally zoonotic, but it has now mutated and is only transmitted from human to human. Most human diseases originate in other animals: of 1,415 pathogens known to infect humans, 61 per cent are zoonotic, with more than two-thirds originating in wildlife.

There are different modes of transmission. In direct zoonosis, the disease is directly transmitted from other animals to humans through the air (influenza), through bites and saliva (rabies) or through consumption (eating bushmeat). It can exist in a species which acts as a 'reservoir', before breaking out often for some environmental reason, such as loss of habitat or climate change. It can infect an intermediate species before infecting humans, which can act as an 'amplifier', making the pathogen more virulent. Transmission also occurs when an intermediate species, a vector, carries the pathogen without itself becoming infected (e.g. mosquitoes and malaria).

In an effort to identify and respond to new zoonotic diseases before they spread to humans, USAID has established an Emerging Pandemic Threats (EPT) programme, which consists of four projects: PREDICT, RESPOND, IDENTIFY and PREVENT.

PREDICT seeks to identify new emerging infectious diseases that could become a threat to human health. It gathers blood, saliva and other samples from high-risk wildlife species to create a library of viruses and a predictive map. It has identified over 1,100 viruses of public health concern. It is also studying ways of managing forests, wildlife and livestock to prevent diseases spreading to humans.

Another US programme, PREEMPT, seeks to contain emerging infectious diseases in animal populations before they threaten humans.

The EcoHealth Alliance is researching how human, animal and environmental health are linked, and how diseases are emerging through human encroachment and deforestation. In the Amazon, a study showed that a 4 per cent increase in deforestation increased incidences of malaria by nearly 50 per cent because mosquitoes thrive in the mix of sunlight and water created in recently deforested areas.

When will it end?

Pandemics have been more deadly than warfare. The 1918 influenza pandemic killed an estimated 40 million people, more than all the dead of the First World War, which immediately preceded it. In all of 2017, 129,720 people were estimated to have died in conflicts and terrorism, which compares with more than 600,000 deaths from Covid-19 from January to July 2020.

The Pandemic Century by Mark Honigsbaum, published in 2018, charts 100 years of pandemic history from the 1918 flu pandemic to today. The way we now live, crowded into cities often in close proximity to animals, with people and goods criss-crossing the world, encroaching into the habitat of wild animals, all serve to create opportunities for killer diseases to spread fast and right around the world. Honigsbaum says, 'Reviewing the last hundred years of epidemic outbreaks, the only thing that is certain is that there will be new plagues and new pandemics. It is not a question of if, but when.'

Spillover: Animal Infections and the Next Human Pandemic by David Quammen, published in 2013, explores the 'spillover' of disease from animals to humans. He asks, 'Some knowledgeable and gloomy prognosticators even speak of The Next Big One as an inevitability ... . Will The Next Big One be caused by a virus? Will The Next Big One come out of the rainforest or a market in Southern China? Will The Next Big One kill 30 or 40 million people?'

DO THIS:

The years 2020 and 2021 created a complete shock to the world's economy and hugely disrupted people's lives. Covid-19 might be moving from pandemic to endemic (meaning that it will remain around and we just have to live with it). To prepare yourself for the next pandemic, as there surely will be, take on the role of either a destroyer or a saviour:

Destroy the World: Plague Inc is a game which takes place on a world map. Players control a disease, choosing where it begins, how it spreads from country to country and how lethal it is. Players win if humanity is extinguished. They lose if humanity finds a cure. ndemiccreations.com/en/22-plague-inc.

Save the World: Quarantine is a game of strategy on waging war on a pandemic. You make the pandemic policies and funding priorities for your country as the head of the Health and Human Services Department. You have to save your country from a global pandemic, while trying to keep the public and government officials happy. store.steampowered.com/app/1502950/ Quarantine_Global_Pandemic

The lottery of life

Child mortality

Deaths of children up to 5 years old per 1,000 live births:

Highest death rates

1 Somalia 120.1

2 Chad 117.5

3 Central African Republic 112.4

4 Sierra Leone 103.1

5 Mali 96.7

6 Nigeria 92.2

7 Benin 91.3

8 The Congo 85.1

9 Niger 82.8

10 Equatorial Guinea 81.6

11 South Sudan 80.3

12 Guinea-Bissau 79.6

13 Cote D'Ivoire 78.8

14 Lesotho 78.8

15 Mauritania 78.6

16 Burkina Faso 75.5

Lowest death rates

1 Finland 1.8

2 Iceland 2.0

3 Slovenia 2.0

4 Norway 2.1

5 Hong Kong 2.1

6 Luxembourg 2.1

7 Portugal 2.2

8 Cyprus 2.3

9 Sweden 2.4

10 Singapore 2.5

11 Ireland 2.5

These are the under-five mortality figures for selected other countries: India, 38.5; Indonesia, 23.7; Brazil, 13.5; Mexico, 13.1; China, 9.5; Russia, 7.0; USA, 5.7; Cuba, 4.9; UK, 4.0. These figures are from Gapminder and are projections for 2020. Note that if you are born in Somalia you are more than 66 times more likely to die in the first 5 years of your life than if you were born in Finland, and children in sub-Saharan Africa are more than 15 times more likely to die before the age of 5 than children in high-income countries. There are many other ways that people are disadvantaged as a result of where they were born.

We have the answers

In a typical year, an estimated 6.2 million children and adolescents under the age of 15 years will die, mostly from preventable causes. Of these deaths, 5.3 million will occur during the first 5 years, with almost half of these in the first month of life. In the course of a lifetime, say 80 years, each of us will have lived through the deaths of 424 million under-5 children. Most of these deaths are preventable.

The good news is that child mortality has decreased very significantly – in 1980, less than three-quarters of children born in Mali, Sierra Leone and Guinea-Bissau could expect to survive up to their fifth birthday. Today in these countries, the child survival rate is mostly over 90 per cent; for the worst country, Somalia, it is 88 per cent. That is progress. But still too many children are dying and we need to do better.

The UN's Sustainable Development Goal 3.2 is to reduce under-5 mortality to at least 25 per 1,000 live births in every country (a survival rate of at least 97.5 per cent).

In a typical year, an estimated 6.2 million children and adolescents under the age of 15 years will die, mostly from preventable causes.

According to the World Health Organization (WHO), the leading causes of death in children under five are pre-term birth complications, pneumonia, birth asphyxia, congenital anomalies, diarrhoea and malaria. More than half of these deaths are preventable or can be treated with simple, affordable interventions, including medication, immunisation, adequate nutrition, safe water and appropriate care by a trained health provider if needed. We have the answers to all these basic health problems. We just need better ways of providing the solutions.

The role of Big Pharma

Pharmaceutical companies are an important part of the global economy. Of the world's top 100 publicly listed companies (by market capitalisation), 17 are pharmaceutical and healthcare companies, the biggest being the US company Johnson & Johnson, valued at $366 billion, and the Swiss company Roche, valued at $300 billion. These companies and others like Novartis, Pfizer, Merck, AbbVie, Abbott, Eli Lilly (collectively referred to as 'Big Pharma') are spending billions each year on research to find treatments for the world's diseases. They are all for-profit companies, so naturally they focus their research on areas that are likely to be most profitable for them and their shareholders, such as diseases prevalent in richer economies, where there is a market of sufficient size and where they can sell their products at a high price to make the most profit.

How drugs are priced is problematic. Most of the cost is incurred in developing the drug and then testing it for safety and effectiveness, firstly on animals and then on humans. The manufacturing and distribution cost is relatively small, but initial research costs and the huge amounts spent on marketing need to be recovered. Over recent years, Big Pharma has been promoting the idea of 'value-based pricing'. The starting point for deciding the selling price for a particular product would be its perceived or estimated value to the purchaser. For health, where most purchases are made by health providers or insurers, the value will be the claimed health benefits that the drug is able to create. Factors such as the value of an extra year of life, the prognosis with and without the drug, its toxicity and side effects, novelty, market size and the extent of unmet need, the impact on society of being able to provide treatment, as well as the cost of development would all be taken into account. A cynic would see this approach as drug companies finding ways of increasing the prices of some drugs, while at the same time increasing overall profits and managing their PR and public image for their own benefit.

The claimed value by the drugs companies and the price at which they then attempt to sell a particular drug can be far more than what is required to recover the costs of research and development and hugely more than the cost of production, marketing and distribution. If the price is set too high, it will be creating value for the company and its shareholders at the expense of creating value for society. It will be making the company rich and health providers poor. You can explore the idea of value-based pricing of drugs at Drug Abacus, which is an interactive tool which allows you compare the drug's selling price with its actual value.

Then there are all the health needs that are not being met. This might be where the market is too small or too poor for the company to believe that it can generate a sufficient return; or the drug is just too expensive to be affordable. A lot of effort has been made to persuade Big Pharma to adapt its business model such that drugs can be sold affordably in poorer markets (while still being able to generate profit for the company). It has been further encouraged by competition from much cheaper generic drugs.

Are generic drugs the answer?

One way in which drug companies are able to maintain high prices is through patents, which protect their intellectual property for 20 years. A patent aims to give the originator a reasonable period of exclusive use – either by themselves or through licensing to others – in order to make their invention financially worthwhile. If a drug is profitable enough, other manufacturers might try to develop alternative versions not covered by the patent. And as a patent nears its expiration date, they will then be able to make and sell generic versions of the drug, which they will be able to do more cheaply as they will not have had to pay the original research and development costs.

Generic drugs ought to be as potent and as safe as the original, while costing less. If they are available at an affordable price, they can be profitable (smaller margins on much larger quantities). But there are problems. In *Bottle of Lies*, author Katherine Eban focuses on Ranbaxy, a major Indian generics company. She shows how generics companies cut corners in testing and production, and how they often offload inadequate versions into poorer countries where regulation is looser. In

2013, Ranbaxy pleaded guilty to felony charges related to drug safety and had to pay $500 million in civil and criminal fines under the settlement agreement with the US Department of Justice.

The Grand Challenges

Innovation is still required if we are to provide better health for all. We need to create treatments and cures for all the world's health problems, which is something that can be done. We also need to innovate in how we deliver affordable drugs and treatments to those in need (whether it is governments, insurance companies or patients who are paying). We also need to find ways of addressing cultural aspects of providing health solutions.

The Bill and Melinda Gates Foundation, along with other funders, has created a series of 'Grand Challenges' for better health. Four challenges relate to maternal and early years childcare: to create better health during pregnancy, better care at birth, better post-birth care for women and their newborns, and better hospital care of sick newborns. The challenges are seeking solutions across these areas: description and diagnosis (epidemiology), discovery (new interventions), development (improving existing interventions) and delivery (implementation and improving health systems). They are looking for 'big, bold, innovative ideas that can have the greatest impact on African maternal and neonatal health with the potential for future sustainability and scaling'.

Some ideas in action

At an Asia Venture Philanthropy Network conference in Singapore in 2018, there was a session on impact investment in health. Two speakers talked about the ease of mobilising funds to build hospitals across Asia. These were elite hospitals with the most modern facilities; one had only the second specialist unit for pancreatic transplants in the whole world. They were profit-making ventures and targeted mainly at health tourism and the rich. This was a market which could generate a good profit for investors. Two other speakers and a vocal member of the audience (me) did not see this as impact investment – it was creating better health for those who could afford to pay but it was not addressing the health problems of the world, where billions do not have access to doctors or medicine and many are suffering from easily treatable conditions, which need to be addressed locally and at low cost. Elite hospitals are not the answer to the world's health needs. A greater focus is needed on prevention, accessibility and affordability rather than on the latest high-tech treatments.

The challenge is to make investing in global better health an attractive area for health impact investors. This is possible. Here is a selection of innovative approaches to better health, some supported by philanthropy, some by impact investment.

↳ LifeSpring Hospitals: providing affordable maternal care. India's maternal mortality remains amongst the highest in the world. Only 43 per cent of women have a skilled birth attendant when they give birth and more than 100,000 women die each year from pregnancy-related causes. Private hospitals are prohibitively expensive and some targeting the less-well-off are not transparent about the costs they charge. LifeSpring is a joint venture between impact investor Acumen Fund and Hindustan Latex. It has built a chain of 25-bed hospitals and reduces costs by specialising in one thing and doing it well (neonatal services including normal deliveries, caesarean sections and hysterectomies) and by squeezing out inefficiencies at every stage of its operations. Prices are 30–50 per cent less than what competitors are charging and the pricing is transparent – so an incoming patient knows exactly how much it will cost rather than receiving a hugely inflated bill afterwards, which can trigger a lifetime of debt. Operations are centred in the city of Hyderabad in southern India.

↳ HealthStore: a network of franchised child and family welfare centres in Kenyan villages. HealthStore operates a network of 57 for-profit child and family wellness clinics in Kenya, which are owned and operated by franchisees. These serve 40,000 customers per month, including through outreach events which provide health screening, water and sanitation training, deworming children and HIV education. The clinics concentrate on providing treatments for the main preventable and treatable diseases and perinatal conditions by providing affordable medicines and offering basic health advice. This addresses up to 80 per cent of all health needs. Scaling up this network of clinics could be a way of bringing basic health to all rural (and urban) communities. Even if a clinic could not cover its costs, subsidising and supporting such a network of clinics could be a cost-effective way of delivering health for all.

↳ Living Goods: a door-to-door health service in Uganda and Kenya. Living Goods was founded by Chuck Slaughter, former president of CFW Shops in Kenya, who felt that healthcare should be taken to people rather than dispensed from a shop. He was inspired to set up Living Goods using a team of trained female community health workers who go door to door treating sick children, supporting pregnant mothers, counselling women on modern family planning choices, educating families on better health and delivering medicines and other health-related products, including fortified porridge, fuel-efficient stoves, water filters and oral rehydration salts. Some are salaried and some earn their income through sales. Living Goods started in Uganda, it expanded into Kenya and now it also operates in Myanmar. It has reached 7 million people in Uganda and Kenya, and demonstrated a 27 per cent reduction in under-5 mortality.

↳ Partners in Health: changing the face of healthcare. PiH was co-founded in 1987 by Paul Farmer, Ophelia Dahl and Jim Yong Kim (who later became president of the World Bank) initially to treat people with HIV/AIDS. They had already built a small clinic in Cange in rural Haiti in 1985, making modern equipment and drugs available to treat their patients, with an underlying commitment to first-class health provision as a human right. This has grown into a 104-bed hospital, and in 2010, they created a university hospital in Mirebalais. They developed a community-based approach using 'accompagnateurs' to visit patients to check on their health and ensure that they were taking their medication. PiH has now developed into a global organisation working with local partners and governments. The documentary Bending the Arc on Netflix charts their progress from young people with an idea and lots of passion to a global organisation trying to change the world.

↳ Hesperian Foundation: health information where there is no doctor. Hesperian publish and distribute health guides with basic information for use by health workers and in communities where there is no doctor. Their 20 bestselling books are published around the world in local languages and include Where There Is No Doctor, Where There Is No Dentist, A Book for Midwives and Disabled Village Children.

↳ ColaLife: distributing health products to remote areas. Diarrhoea can be fatal but it is easily and cheaply cured through oral rehydration using a mixture of sugar and salts. Coca-Cola is available everywhere, even in the remotest areas, and it is often the first consumer product that poor people aspire to and can get. Simon and Jane Berry started ColaLife with the idea that they could piggy-back Coca-Cola's distribution by designing health products that would fit into crates between the bottle necks to reach villages where they would then create a distribution structure. This was the starting point for this project, which now manufactures and distributes oral rehydration across Zambia.

↳ Aravind: eye care for everyone. 'If Coca-Cola can sell billions of sodas and McDonald's billions of burgers, why can't Aravind sell millions of sight-restoring operations, and eventually the belief in human perfection?' asked Dr Venkataswamy, founder of Aravind. India has one-third of the world's blind population with close to 200 million Indians needing eye care, and in 80 per cent of cases blindness can be corrected. Dr V set out to address this problem, creating an institution which performs 400,000 eye surgeries a year. Aravind has developed a self-funding delivery model where it can provide a free-of-cost or at-cost service for 50–60 per cent of its patients, those who would have difficulty paying, using the profits generated from its paying patients, while providing the same quality of service for everybody. The Aravind model has been introduced into more than 300 hospitals globally. Aravind has a strong research division which innovates on product, process and delivery.

DO THIS:

Read Hesperian's *A Book for Midwives,* which covers the essentials of care before, during and after birth, including advice on medicines and information on preventing and treating HIV during pregnancy. Then (if you can afford it) make a donation to the Gratis Fund, which will enable a book to be donated to a community health worker who cannot afford to buy a copy: store.hesperian.org/prod/A_Book_for_Midwives.html.

Why are we so unhappy?

25

The happiest and unhappiest cities

☺ Happiest cities

1 Helsinki, Finland 7.828

2 Aarhus, Denmark 7.625

3 Wellington, New Zealand 7.553

4 Zurich, Switzerland 7.541

5 Copenhagen, Denmark 7.530

6 Bergen, Norway 7.527

7 Oslo, Norway 7.464

8 Tel Aviv, Israel 7.461

9 Stockholm, Sweden 7.373

10 Brisbane, Australia 7.337

11 San Jose, Costa Rica 7.321

12 Reykjavik, Iceland 7.317

13 Toronto, Canada 7.298

14 Melbourne, Australia 7.296

15 Perth, Australia 7.253

☹ Unhappiest cities

1 Kabul, Afghanistan 3.236

2 Sana'a, Yemen 3.377

3 Gaza, Palestine 3.485

4 Port-au-Prince, Haiti 3.807

5 Juba, South Sudan 3.866

6 Dar es Salaam, Tanzania 3.961

7 Delhi, India 4.011

8 Maseru, Lesotho 4.023

9 Bangui, Central African Republic 4.025

10 Cairo, Egypt 4.088

11 Kigali, Rwanda 4.126

12 Kumasi, Ghana 4.133

13 Khartoum, Sudan 4.139

14 Monrovia, Liberia 4.291

15 Antananarivo, Madagascar 4.348

These are the top 15 and bottom 15 cities in the Global Happiness Index, which is based on people's own subjective assessments of their happiness, sourced through Gallop Polls.

The pursuit of unhappiness

Scandinavian cities and cities in Australia and New Zealand score high when it comes to the subjective wellbeing of their residents; cities in countries with histories of political instability, armed conflict and recent terrorism score lowest.

'We hold these truths to be self-evident, that all men are created equal, that they are endowed by their Creator with certain inalienable rights, that amongst these are Life, Liberty and the pursuit of Happiness.' So says the US Declaration of Independence, signed in 1776. The high ideals under which the United States separated itself from Britain put the pursuit of happiness at the heart of the new country. But pursuit of wealth has become the dominant factor in how most societies want to achieve and measure success, with an ever-increasing gross national income as a primary goal. In the presidential election in 1992, James Carville, Bill Clinton's election strategist, coined the phrase 'It's the economy, stupid' as one of the key messages of the Clinton campaign – as if all that really mattered to voters were the dollars in their pockets. It did, and Clinton was elected. But the pursuit of money has led to growing inequality within societies and in the world, and to increasing unhappiness for both rich and poor. How would the world be different and what would it look like if the pursuit of happiness became our primary goal?

Gross national happiness in Bhutan

Bhutan is a tiny country in the Himalayan mountains tucked in between India and China, ruled by a king and with a population of around 800,000. It was the last country in the world to introduce television (in 1999) and the production and sale of tobacco products remains banned.

The phrase 'gross national happiness' was coined by the king in 1972 when he declared that this was far more important than gross domestic product, and that the country should pay much more attention to the health, wellbeing and happiness of its people than to the economic development of the country. This concept captured the imagination of people and governments around the world.

To define what gross national happiness meant, the King created a happiness index for use in policy-making and for assessing impact. The index includes these nine factors, which are a mixture of personal development, a well-functioning society and community, and a healthy environment: psychological wellbeing; health; education; time use; cultural diversity and resilience; good governance; community vitality; ecological diversity and resilience; and living standards.

An International Day

The United Nations declared 20 March each year as the International Day of Happiness to encourage governments to give a greater emphasis to happiness in their policies and through the services that they provide. The World Happiness Report identified these as the 10 happiest countries: Finland, Denmark, Switzerland, Iceland, Norway, Netherlands, Sweden, New Zealand, Austria, Luxembourg. The factors used to measure happiness include having **someone to count on**, having a **sense of freedom** to make key life decisions, **generosity**, **trust**, equality of opportunities and resources, and a good social environment.

Action for Happiness – the global movement aiming to build a happier and more caring society – gives ten keys for happier living: giving, relating, exercising, awareness, trying out, direction, resilience, emotions, acceptance, meaning. The acronym for this is 'G-R-E-A-T D-R-E-A-M'.

While I was writing this, much of the world was in lockdown. The roads were empty of traffic, the air was cleaner, we could hear the birds singing. We had the time and an opportunity to re-evaluate how we live. Is it money and spending that are most important to us? Or human relationships? Our physical and mental wellbeing? Our sense of purpose and direction? Will the world go back to being just the same after we have come through Covid-19? Or can we find a way of creating a different happier future?

Here are two other indexes that have attempted to measure the overall happiness of citizens:

The Happy Planet Index: This focuses on both us and the health of our planet, and covers:

↳ **Wellbeing** – and our satisfaction with our life overall.

↳ **Life expectancy** – the average number of years we expect to live.

↳ **Equality of outcomes** – focusing on inequalities between people within their country.

↳ **Ecological footprint** – our impact on the environment and the resources we consume.

One finding was that the living environment and the proportion of people living in very large cities in developed countries contribute to their lower-than-average wellbeing, as compared with those living in smaller urban and rural settlements. People choose to live in big cities because they offer better employment opportunities, better access to public amenities and a more exciting cultural life. But for many, this does not lead to greater happiness.

The Economist Global Liveability Index: This ranks cities according to their stability, healthcare provision, culture and environment, education and infrastructure. The top ten most liveable cities in 2021 were Auckland, Osaka, Adelaide, Wellington, Tokyo, Perth, Zurich,

Geneva, Melbourne and Brisbane – six of these are in Australia and New Zealand. The worst were Damascus, Lagos, Port Moresby, Dhaka, Algiers, Tripoli, Karachi and Harare.

Prevalence of mental disorders

As many as 970 million people in the world are estimated to have a mental disorder (including substance addiction). This is just over 10 per cent of everybody. The most common conditions (the figures are the percentage of world population) are:

Anxiety	3.8 per cent
Depression	3.4 per cent
Alcohol misuse	1.4 per cent
Drug misuse	0.9 per cent
Bipolar disorder	0.6 per cent
Schizophrenia	0.2 per cent
Eating disorders	0.2 per cent

As a percentage of the population, these figures have not changed much over the past 20 years. Anxiety and depression remain the most common conditions, whether it is an Indian farmer whose crop has failed or a high-flying Korean kid disappointed in her grades.

Defining mental illness

The Diagnostic and Statistical Manual of Mental Disorders (current edition is DSM-5) is the 'bible' of mental illness, listing and explaining 'common disorders' from alcohol/substance abuse disorder to schizophrenia, dissociative disorders, eating disorders, sexual disorders, sleep disorders, childhood mental disorders, autism spectrum disorder, transient tic disorder, personality disorders and 'other disorders', from acute stress to trichotillomania (pulling out one's own hair). Well over 100 disorders are categorised and explained.

In the USA healthcare system, the Manual has a particular importance. If a condition is included, this enables physicians to give treatment and prescribe medicine and be reimbursed through health insurance schemes. This creates pressure to define new disorders and to advocate their inclusion in the Manual.

There is controversy over what constitutes a mental disorder – for example, homosexuality was included up to 1973, but 50 years later it has become a part of the natural order, with same-sex marriage now legalised and licensed in all 50 states of the USA, despite a backlash from religious conservatives. Some disorders are well defined. Some like autism are on a spectrum (Asperger's syndrome was only recognised in 1994 with its status being challenged 20 years later). Some are just descriptions of symptoms assembled to create a syndrome. Medication is recommended for many of these disorders but often this has adverse side effects or no discernible effect. And then there is the question of people being labelled. If you have an attention deficit disorder or obsessive compulsive disorder, are these really disorders needing treatment (which might be the case for some people) or just a behaviour pattern (which it could be for many). And if you are diagnosed and labelled, does this make you less likely to cope, feel less in control and more likely to resort to medication?

Read these: *The Diagnostic and Statistical Manual*, which can be downloaded from psychcentral.com, *The Book of Woe: The DSM and the Unmasking of Psychiatry* by Gary Greenberg and *Saving Normal: An Insider's Revolt against Out-of-control Psychiatric Diagnosis, DSM-5, Big Pharma and the Medicalization of Ordinary Life* by Allen Frances.

Mad Pride

Mad Pride was a movement which ran from 1999 to 2012, using techniques similar to Gay Pride. The aim was to present those suffering mental health issues as people rather than as victims. Their slogan was 'Glad to be Mad', encouraging people to be proud of who they were and to look at their strengths rather than becoming ground down by their issues. It was founded by Mark Roberts, Simon Barnett, Robert Dellar and Pete Shaughnessy, all of whom had mental health issues. It was inspired by an initiative called 'Survivors Speak Out', where mental health patients come together to support each other, to defend their rights and to advocate for change.

Suicide

Twice as many people kill themselves each year than are killed by others. Suicide is a greater concern than homicide. Each year, 800,000 people succeed in ending their lives. This represents 1.4 per cent of all deaths. South Korea has the second highest rate in the world at 5 per cent, with only Greenland more affected, at 7.2 per cent. Other suicide hotspots are Qatar (3.9 per cent), Sri Lanka (3.6 per cent), Guyana (3.4 per cent) and Kazakhstan (3.2 per cent). Russia had a very high suicide rate, but since the advent of Putin, rates have fallen significantly.

Amongst 10- to 24-year-olds, suicide is the second leading cause of death. More teenagers and young adults die from suicide than from cancer, heart disease, AIDS, birth defects, stroke, pneumonia, influenza and chronic lung disease combined.

Having somebody to talk to at a critical moment could make all the difference. The initial idea for the Samaritans came from the first funeral conducted by a young priest. A 14-year-old girl had started menstruating, did not understand what was happening to her and had nobody to talk to. She believed that she had a sexually transmitted disease. She committed suicide out of despair.

Some years later, the priest, Reverend Chad Varah, decided that he should do something. He decided to set up an emergency telephone helpline for people with nobody to turn to who were struggling with depression or overburdened by their life and circumstances. He would run this from his church, St Martin-in-the-Fields in central London. He got publicity for his idea and calls started coming, but also people began asking if they could volunteer to help answer the calls.

Since its foundation in 1953, the Samaritans has answered 68 million requests for help. Today, it receives 5 million calls each year (including by telephone, text, email, letter and through face-to-face meetings), which are answered by over 20,000 trained volunteers working from more than 200 branches across the UK and Ireland. The organisation says, 'We make sure there's someone there for anyone who needs someone.'

The idea has now spread around the world. The Befrienders Worldwide network links Samaritan groups in around 45 countries. Sometimes just having someone to listen to you who won't judge you is enough to help people talk about the issues that are oppressing them and to find some relief.

CALM is the Campaign Against Living Miserably. They estimate that every week in the UK, 125 people kill themselves and that 75 per cent of these are male. Suicide is the single biggest killer of men under 45. They run a phone line and offer a webchat service for seven hours a day, seven days a week, for anyone who feels they need to talk.

Young people's mental health

Many young people feel under pressure. This can be caused or exacerbated by their perception of themselves in relation to others – for example, if they get fewer likes on Instagram. This can lead to problems around body image for some and we have seen a rise in cyber bullying, with some terrible outcomes for the victims. And this is all taking place alongside the hormonal changes of puberty, questions of sexual identity and sexuality, and pressure from school, parents and the education system to get the best grades.

Young people, like all of us, will be on a spectrum that ranges from being healthy through to coping, struggling, being unwell and then being seriously unwell. The mental health needs of young people need to be addressed. Doing it sooner is important, as mental wellbeing in later life is often affected by experiences when growing up. Here are two examples of young people trying to do something.

Wellbeing Enterprises: Mark Swift, a young Liverpool University graduate, suffered a mental health breakdown before he graduated. He was from a working-class background and the first person in his family to go to university. After his recovery, he decided to help other young people facing depression and other mental health issues. His idea was that taking positive steps in your life would improve your mental wellbeing. With the help of doctors and psychiatrists he developed 12 steps for recovery.

↳ Values: Thinking about what you value in your life.

↳ Feelings: Talking about your feelings to people who will listen.

↳ Self-worth: Valuing yourself and thinking about what you are good at.

↳ Friendship: Keeping in touch with friends and family.

↳ Relaxation: Taking breaks, going for walks, listening to music.

↳ Fitness: Being physically active – gardening, dancing, playing sport.

↳ Diet: Eating well and healthily.

↳ Stimulation: Drinking alcohol only in moderation. Saying no to drugs.

↳ Learning: Learning a new skill, such as coding or another language.

↳ Creativity: Such as cooking, painting or knitting.

↳ Helping: Volunteering and helping others.

↳ Happiness: Smiling – you will feel happier and it will make others feel happier.

States of Mind: Bea Herbert believes that all young people should be active participants in promoting physical and emotional wellbeing, and by doing this they can improve their emotional intelligence, self-awareness and personal growth. She has been working in London schools to develop mental health ambassadors who will lead discussion and action on better mental wellbeing in their school, develop their own solutions and encourage other students to do this. She has worked with young people to design mechanisms for assessing their education with a primary goal of happiness and wellbeing, rather than the stress, anxiety and depression which is created through continual testing and an emphasis on exam performance. What would education look like if designed from this perspective?

DO THIS:

Smile at somebody. Do this to celebrate World Smile Day. This is organised every year on the first Friday of October by the School of Kindness with the aim of bringing joy into the world and of encouraging people to do random acts of kindness for each other. If you need physical closeness, then invite a stranger to give you a hug as part of the Free Hugs campaign. This was started by Juan Mann, after he returned home to Sydney, arriving at the airport with nobody to greet him, when he felt in urgent need of a hug.

Dictatorship
and
democracy

26

The longest dictatorships

Dictators in power for more than 20 years after the Second World War:

Years	Dictator and Country	Period in power
21	Maaouya Taya, Mauritania	1984–2005
22	Paul Kagame, Rwanda	2000–present
22	Mohamed Siad Barre, Somalia	1969–1991
22	Mahathir Bin Mohamad, Malaysia	1981–2003
22	Ismail Omar Guelleh, Djibouti	1999–present
22	Vladimir Putin, Russia	2000–present
23	Yahya Jammeh, The Gambia	1994–2017
23	Moussa Traore, Mali	1968–1991
24	Zine Ben Ali, Tunisia	1987–2011
24	Daniel arap Moi, Kenya	1978–2002
24	Saddam Hussein, Iraq	1979–2003
24	Ho Chi Minh, North Vietnam	1945–1969
24	Nicolae Ceausescu, Romania	1965–1989
25	Islam Karimov, Uzbekistan	1991–2016
26	Ahmed Sekou Toure, Guinea	1958–1984
26	Ne Win, Myanmar	1962–1988
27	Kenneth Kaunda, Zambia	1964–1991
27	Albert Rene, Seychelles	1977–2004
27	Mao Zedong, China	1949–1976
27	Blaise Compaore, Burkina Faso	1987–2014
27	Alexander Lukashenko, Belarus	1994–present
28	Isaias Afwerki, Eritrea	1993–present
29	Omar El Bashir, Sudan	1989–2019
30	Hosni Mubarak, Egypt	1981–2011

30	Hafez al-Assad, Syria	1970–2000
30	Maumoon Abdul Gayoom, Maldives	1978–2008
31	Hastings Banda, Malawi	1963–1994
21	Idriss Deby, Chad	1990–2021
32	Mobutu Sese Seko, Zaire (now DRC)	1965–1997
32	Suharto, Indonesia	1966–1998
32	Ayatollah Ali Khamenei, Iran	1989–present
33	Todor Zhivkov, Bulgaria	1956–1989
33	Felix Houphouet-Boigny, Cote D'Ivoire	1960–1993
35	Alfredo Stroessner, Paraguay	1954–1989
35	Yoweri Museveni, Uganda	1986–present
36	Francisco Franco, Spain	1939–1975
36	Josip Broz Tito, Yugoslavia	1944–1980
37	Robert Mugabe, Zimbabwe	1980–2017
38	Gnassingbe Eyadema, Togo	1967–2005
38	Jose Dos Santos, Angola	1979–2017
39	Paul Biya, Cameroon	1982–present
40	Antonio Salazar, Portugal	1928–1968
41	Enver Hoxha, Albania	1944–1985
42	Omar Bongo, Gabon	1967–2009
42	Teodoro Obiang Mbasogo, Equatorial Guinea	1979–present
46	Kim Il-sung, North Korea	1948–1994
47	Fidel Castro, Cuba	1959–2006
48	Chiang Kai-shek, China/Taiwan	1927–1995

On the previous page is a list of dictators who ran their country for more than 20 years during the post-war era. There are other well-known (infamous) autocrats such as Idi Amin (Uganda) and Augusto Pinochet (Chile) who had a huge impact on their countries but were not in power long enough to make this list. It is a frightening list of 48 people in 48 countries who assumed power, sometimes starting out as saviours (Robert Mugabe, Paul Kagame, Yoweri Museveni, Fidel Castro, for example), sometimes by a military coup, and who stayed and stayed. They saw themselves as the embodiment of their country, indispensable and in power for ever. Then there is the question of family succession – for example, the Kims in North Korea (now into their third generation) and the Assads in Syria – meaning the ruling family's grip on power could continue indefinitely. The list does not include monarchs, most of whom have only constitutional powers but no executive role. And it does not include those, like Joseph Stalin, whose hold on power was primarily pre-war.

Some of the world's current dictators are estimated to have little or no wealth, such as Alexander Lukashenko of Belarus, who was re-elected for a sixth term in 2020, arousing controversy and anger amongst the people. Though some have become extremely wealthy. Idris Deby of Chad at $50 million, Paul Biya of Cameroon at $200 million, Teodoro Obiang Mbasogo of Equatorial Guinea at $600 million might be considered modestly wealthy as compared with Jose Dos Santos of Angola's $20 billion or Ismail Omar Guelleh of Djibouti's $79.2 billion.

Stalin has been an inspiration and a role model for other dictators such as Saddam Hussein. This quotation is attributed to Stalin: 'It is enough that the people know there was an election. The people who cast the votes decide nothing. The people who count the votes decide everything.' Stalin and Russia were the inspiration for George Orwell's *Nineteen Eighty-Four* and Big Brother. This is what Orwell said: 'We know that no one ever seizes power with the intention of relinquishing it. Power is not a means; it is an end. One does not establish a dictatorship in order to safeguard a revolution; one makes the revolution in order to establish the dictatorship. The object of persecution is persecution. The object of torture is torture. The object of power is power.'

These long-term leaders attain or seize power and then refuse to relinquish it. If there are elections, they make sure that they never lose. This is very different from Abraham Lincoln's vision of democracy, as defined in his Gettysburg address: ' ... this nation ... shall have a new birth of freedom and ... government of the people, by the people, for the people, shall not perish from the earth.'

How to rig an election

A political paradox is that while there are more elections than ever before, the world is becoming less democratic. The vast majority of governments at least go through the motion of election campaigns and express their commitment to free and fair elections that allow citizens to choose their leader. But in many places, voter choice is little more than an illusion, as the election has been rigged to give just one outcome, the continuing rule of the incumbent, who tightens his grip on power (and it almost always is a he) while publicly proclaiming that he is ruling with popular consent. This continues even when there are international election observers present whose job it is to certify the fairness of the election.

In their book *How to Rig an Election*, Nic Cheeseman and Brian Klaas describe some of the techniques that dictators use to remain in power while at the same time claiming that their hold on power is legitimate and democratic. Here are a few.

Using brutality

↳ Assassination of opposition candidates.

↳ Persecution, intimidation and even the imprisonment of candidates (such as Alexei Navalny in Russia). This tactic will also discourage others from standing.

Tricking the public

↳ Using disappearing ink to mark ballot papers.

↳ Putting up a candidate with a similar or the same name as your main rival.

↳ Bribery, by offering the public small goodies at pre-election rallies to persuade them to vote for you.

Subverting elections

↳ Voter registration requirements and processes that disadvantage the poor (particularly prevalent in the USA).

↳ Gerrymandering, adjusting constituency boundaries for party benefit (this was attempted for Westminster City Council).

↳ Candidate exclusion, by introducing conditions which your main opposition candidates cannot ever possibly meet.

↳ Arraigning opposition candidates on trumped-up charges.

↳ Ballot box stuffing, with a mass of votes for one party put into selected ballot boxes.

↳ Vote banks, where someone determines how others will vote, either through their power over others or bribery.

↳ Disappearing ballot boxes.

↳ Mechanical voting going wrong (the hanging chads of badly punched holes in Florida in the 2000 presidential election swung the result to George W Bush in a close-run election).

↳ Fake news (sometimes this is spread
by bots in another country, such as the
alleged Russian subversion of the 2016 US
presidential election).

↳ Subverting the international endorsement
process by tricking election observers.

According to Cheeseman and Klaas, the best
election-rigging tactics are subtle, legal and
effective, and avoid people knowing what is
happening. The worst are blatant, illegal and
quite often ineffective, although even the
crudest, most visible election manipulation can
bring the desired result if done professionally
and with precision.

In authoritarian or semi-authoritarian states,
incumbents are winning elections about 90 per
cent of the time. Globally, only about 30 per
cent of all elections result in the incumbent
losing power. According to Freedom House,
an American organisation founded in 1941
to protect and promote democracy around
the world, in 2017, 71 countries suffered net
declines in political rights and civil liberties,
with only 35 registering gains.

Cheeseman and Klaas conclude that,
'Elections are too often used not to translate
the will of the people into political power but
instead to subvert the will of the people and
ensure that the incumbent stays in power.' And
that: 'There are no silver bullets, no panaceas
that will stop election rigging completely.'

The Arab Spring

The Arab Spring was a whole series of pro-
democracy uprisings that begin in Tunisia in
December 2010 and inspired similar uprisings
protesting authoritarian governments in many
countries of North Africa and the Middle East
during the spring of 2011, including Morocco,
Syria, Libya, Egypt and Bahrain, and which led
to regime changes in Tunisia, Egypt and Libya,
and the start of civil war in Syria.

The uprising in Tunisia was sparked by an
incident in Tunis when a vegetable vendor,
Mohammed Bouazizi, set himself on fire as
a protest after his vegetable stand had been
seized by the police for his failure to obtain
a permit. Street protests ensued and the
anger of the crowd became directed towards
President Zine Ben Ali, who had ruled the
country for 24 years, and discontent with both
his rule and the lack of freedom in the country.
He fled to Saudi Arabia.

The Tahrir Square protest in Egypt led to the
resignation of Hosni Mubarak, who had been in
power in Egypt for 30 years and who had been
preparing for a family succession. This led to
an election which the Muslim Brotherhood won
convincingly. But new president Mohamed
Morsi was overthrown by a coup led by
Defence Minister Abdel Fattah el-Sisi, who
remains in power.

In Syria, there was no regime change but a continuing civil war which has become one of the disasters of the twenty-first century, displacing over 6 million people and ruining whole cities. It facilitated the rise of ISIL, terrorism and the caliphate, brought in the Russians as allies and military supporters, and is still awaiting resolution.

The Arab Spring was a continuation of a wave of protest against corrupt or authoritarian governments that attempted to achieve greater democracy, starting with the Yellow Revolution in the Philippines in 1986. These protests designated a specific colour as their symbol.

These are some of the Colour Revolutions:

Yellow	Philippines	1986
Rose	Georgia	2003
Orange	Ukraine	2004
Denim	Belarus	2006
Saffron	Myanmar	2007
Grape	Moldova	2009
Melon	Kyrgyzstan	2010
Jasmine	Tunisia	2010
Lotus	Egypt	2011
Pearl	Bahrain	2011
Coffee	Yemen	2011
Snow	Russia	2011
Velvet	Armenia	2018

Blue and yellow meals in Hong Kong

In 2019, civil unrest in Hong Kong was sparked by a proposal to introduce a law enabling Hong Kong citizens to be deported to the Chinese mainland for trial. It was feared that this would be used to suppress pro-democracy activities in Hong Kong, where the 'One Country, Two Systems' approach to governance, guaranteeing a separate legal system for Hong Kong, was enshrined in the treaty with the UK when it was handed over to become a Special Autonomous Region of the People's Republic. This quickly became a popular uprising, which developed into a pro-independence movement and moved on beyond its non-violent beginnings.

As many as 1 million people out of a population of just 7.5 million participated in the 2019 demonstrations. The situation changed in June 2020, when the Chinese government imposed a National Security Law, where 'secession', 'subversion', 'terrorism' and 'collusion with foreign forces' incurred maximum penalties of life imprisonment, but were so broadly defined that they easily became catch-all offences used for politically motivated purposes. Most Hong Kongers came to recognise that independence was not an option.

There are subtle ways of making your views known which are non-confrontational. In Hong Kong, people used colours to make a silent protest – yellow for the pro-democracy

opposition and blue for government supporters.
Restaurants took sides. Those sympathetic to
the pro-democracy movement displayed yellow
to attract pro-democracy diners, while also
expressing their own view. This prompted a blue
equivalent for government-supporting restaurant
owners. There were blue–yellow apps and maps
to help people find a restaurant that matched
their political viewpoint.

Protesters in authoritarian societies are using
all sorts of imaginative techniques. Pussy
Riot is a Moscow-based feminist punk and
performance art group. The group stages
unauthorised provocative performances
in public places, filmed and posted on the
internet, promoting feminism, gay rights and
opposition to Putin, for which members of the
group have been jailed. Watch 'Virgin Mary,
Mother of God, Put Putin Away' on YouTube.

Ushahidi

Ushahidi means 'testimony' or 'witness' in
Swahili. It was an app created in the aftermath
of Kenya's disputed 2007 presidential election
when Mwai Kibaki declared a victory which
was contested by opposition candidate
Raila Odinga. That there had been electoral
manipulation (perpetrated by both parties) was
confirmed by international observers. This led
to an outbreak of protest encouraged by the
opposition, which led to some extreme ethnic
violence in what is an ethnically divided country.

The Ushahidi platform was developed to
collect and assemble eyewitness reports of

violence which were sent in by email and SMS
and assembled on a Google map. This was
developed into open-source software which
has since been further developed. It has been
released for free use in other countries by
anyone who wants to record any incidence of
democratic malpractice.

Leaving democracy to politicians?

The idea of a Citizens' Assembly to resolve
difficult issues is gaining ground. This involves
a panel of ordinary people – randomly selected
but reflecting the make-up of the population
– who are brought together to discuss and
propose a solution, which politicians can then
agree to implement. In Ontario in 2007, a Citizens
Assembly on Electoral Reform recommended a
new way of voting to enhance democracy –
'1 Ballot, 2 Votes' for the favourite and second
two favoured candidates. In Ireland in 2018, an
assembly of 99 people was able to break years of
political deadlock on abortion reform. In France
in 2020, a Citizens Convention consisting of
150 self-selected individuals from a randomly
chosen pool proposed policies for addressing
climate change.

DO THIS:

Exercise your democratic right and vote at the
next election. Those in countries governed by
dictators do not have the opportunity or know
that their vote does not count.

Truth
and lies

27

The Freedom of Expression Index

The worst-performing countries for press freedom

180 Turkmenistan 85.44 (worst)

179 North Korea 83.40

178 Eritrea 80.26

177 China 78.92

176 Vietnam 74.93

175 Sudan 72.45

174 Syria 71.78

173 Djibouti 71.36

172 Saudi Arabia 65.88

171 Laos 64.49

170 Iran 64.41

169 Cuba 63.81

168 Yemen 61.66

167 Bahrain 61.31

166 Azerbaijan 59.13

165 Equatorial Guinea 58.35

164 Somalia 57.24

163 Egypt 56.47

162 Libya 55.77

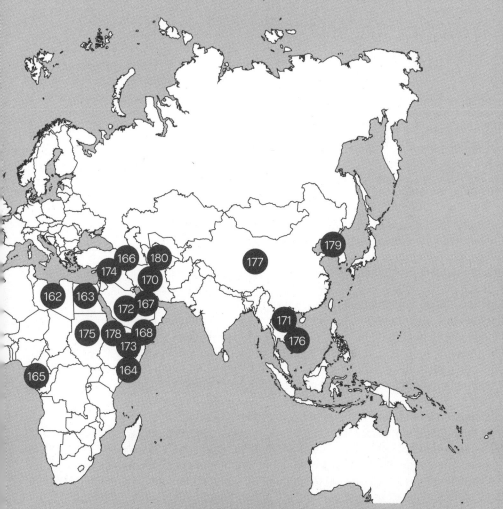

The Press Freedom Index is produced annually by Reporters Without Borders, showing press freedom for 180 countries. The higher the score out of 100, the worse the situation. In 2019, just 24 per cent of 180 countries were classified as good or satisfactory, with 40 per cent being very serious or difficult. Norway came out top with a score of 7.82, closely followed by Finland, Sweden, Netherlands and Denmark. The criteria evaluated in the index are pluralism, media independence, media environment and self-censorship, legislative framework, transparency and the quality of the infrastructure that supports the production of news and information.

Press freedom and human rights

'All's for the best in this the best of all possible worlds,' said Dr Pangloss in *Candide*. But the best of all possible worlds should allow for freedom of thought and expression. Voltaire, author of *Candide*, also said, 'I disapprove of what you say, but I will defend to the death your right to say it.'

Thomas Paine, pamphleteer and political activist who inspired the American Revolution, said: 'I have always strenuously supported the right of every man to his own opinion, however different that opinion might be to mine. He who denies another this right makes a slave of himself to his present opinion, because he precludes himself the right of changing it.'

Societies which seek to restrict freedom of speech, and exercise control over the ideas and information which they see fit for their citizens to receive, will be less resilient and less able to harness the energy, ideas and creativity of their citizens than more open societies. What might start out with the noble aim of a 'Dictatorship of the Proletariat' could end up as just plain dictatorship, with dissent not tolerated and dissenters imprisoned or sent into exile. Freedom of information and expression and a free press are critical for avoiding this.

3 May each year is World Press Freedom Day, proclaimed by the United Nations in December 1993. Article 19 of the Universal Declaration of Human Rights states that: 'Everyone has the right to freedom of opinion and expression; this right includes freedom to hold opinions without interference and to seek, receive and impart information and ideas through any media and regardless of frontiers.' In order to make freedom of expression a reality, there must be:

↳ A legal and regulatory environment that allows open and pluralistic media.

↳ Political commitment to open media and laws to protect it.

↳ Laws enabling freedom of access to information of public interest.

↳ Media literacy amongst the population to critically review and use information they receive.

↳ Mechanisms for holding the media accountable for what they disseminate.

Index on Censorship campaigns for and defends free expression worldwide. It publishes work by censored writers and artists, promotes debate and monitors threats to free speech. 'We believe that everyone should be free to express themselves without fear of harm or persecution – no matter what their views.'

PEN International also supports the principle of unhampered transmission of thought within each nation and between all nations. Members pledge to oppose any form of suppression of freedom of expression in the country and community to which they belong as well as throughout the world to the greatest extent possible.

Lies, damn lies and statistics

'There are three kinds of lies: lies, damned lies, and statistics.' Mark Twain popularised this quote, which he attributed to British prime minister Benjamin Disraeli. *How to Lie with Statistics* was a 1954 bestseller by Darrell Huff showing how statistics can be used to mislead. For example, by distorting reality through the way information is presented, through inadequate sampling or adjusting of the figures, by confusing cause and effect, or simply by blinding people with numbers. In the 1960s, Huff was funded by the tobacco industry to write *How to Lie with Smoking Statistics* using statistics to show that smoking was not harmful to health. Huff was discredited and this next book was not published.

It often pays to explore the statistics in some detail before accepting the 'facts' or coming to a conclusion. Tim Harford is 'The Undercover Economist' and a *Financial Times* columnist. His BBC Radio programme *More or Less* tries to analyse the statistics on important issues to show what the facts really are. Around 250 episodes of this programme covering topics ranging from climate change to whether we are having too much sex are available from the BBC Sounds website.

False facts and fake news

This is what Charles Darwin had to say in his book *The Descent of Man*: 'False facts are highly injurious to the progress of science, for they often long endure; but false views, if supported by some evidence, do little harm, as everyone takes a salutary pleasure in proving their falseness; and when this is done, one path towards error is closed and the road to truth is often at the same time opened.'

We live in a world where information can flow around the world at a rate never before envisaged. Flash mobs can be mobilised, Colour Revolutions organised, pictures of police brutality or civilian casualties circulated in an instant, reaching millions through Facebook or Instagram or Twitter. But this also creates the possibility for false facts and fake news to be spread just as quickly, for democratic processes to be undermined, and behaviour which can lead to disease or even death.

Climate change deniers are putting out information that seeks to deny any connection between human activity and climate change, which has certainly been a factor in delaying concerted world action. Holocaust denial is also rife. Creationists have had a huge influence on education in the USA. A 2017 Gallup survey on creationism found that 38 per cent of US adults believed that God created humans in their present form at one point in time within the last 10,000 years and 16 per cent believed that only creationism should be taught in schools. There is even a Flat Earth Society, which promotes thought and discussion on the 'fact' that the Earth is flat rather than spherical.

Our individual ability to determine on our own what is fact and real news, and what is false information and fake news can be quite limited, particularly if we live in a society where there is limited or no freedom of information. Or, alternatively, we live in a country where there is press freedom but choose to remain in an 'echo chamber' where the information we receive or choose to admit is politically aligned with our existing viewpoint. For example, if we choose to watch only news channels or look at newsfeeds that align to our stated preferences, that will only serve to reinforce our existing views.

Fake news and the Covid-19 crisis

Researchers at Carnegie Mellon University estimate that nearly half of the Twitter accounts spreading messages on social media platforms about Covid-19 are likely bots. They examined more than 200 million tweets discussing the virus and found that around 45 per cent were sent from accounts behaving more like pre-programmed software (bots) than humans. They identified more than 100 false narratives about Covid-19 that were being spread on Twitter, such as hospitals being filled with mannequins to exaggerate the scale of the disaster and that 5G wireless towers were spreading the disease (this led to some being set on fire).

In Latin America, where there was already scepticism due to the attitude of Brazil's President Jair Bolsonaro and USA's Donald Trump, there were claims that:

↪ Coffins were being filled with rocks to inflate Brazil's death toll.

↪ Drones were being used to deliberatively contaminate Mexican indigenous communities.

↪ The CIA was spreading the virus in Argentina.

↪ Seafood in Peru was not safe due to corpses of Covid-19 victims being dumped at sea.

↪ The WHO president had been spotted partying near Sao Paolo.

↪ Miracle cures for the disease included Peruvian sea water, Venezuelan lemongrass and bleach.

A 26-minute high-production-value video, *Plandemic,* went viral, spreading dangerous misinformation including:

↪ The virus was manipulated and deliberately released.

↳ The virus stemmed from SARS-1.

↳ US hospitals receive $13,000 from Medicare if they 'call it Covid-19' when a patient dies.

↳ Hydroxychloroquine is 'effective against coronaviruses'.

↳ Flu vaccines increase the chance of contracting Covid-19 by 36 per cent.

↳ Wearing a mask 'activates' your own virus.

At times of great uncertainty, such misinformation and hodgepodge of conspiracies are extremely dangerous.

Fact checking

The Reporters' Lab at Duke University maintains a database of fact-checking organisations, which tracks more than 100 independent organisations in 36 countries. To be included, the organisation must:

↳ Examine all parties and sides.

↳ Examine discrete claims and reach conclusions.

↳ Track political promises.

↳ Be transparent about sources and methods.

↳ Disclose funding and affiliations and whether its primary mission is news and information.

Take a look at the Wikipedia list of fact-checking websites and also at Snopes, which describes itself as 'the definitive internet reference source for researching urban legends, folklore, myths, rumors, and misinformation'.

Thoughtcrime and suppression of dissent

In the dystopian novel *Nineteen Eighty-Four* (1949) by George Orwell, the word 'thoughtcrime' describes a person's politically unorthodox thoughts, such as unspoken beliefs and doubts that contradict the tenets of Ingsoc (English Socialism), which is the dominant ideology of Oceania, a fictional country run by Big Brother. This was inspired by Stalinist Russia and the methods that it used to suppress truth and dissent.

Political messages in China have traditionally been made on the streets through the medium of 'big-character posters', featuring large handwritten messages posted in public spaces. These hark back to the imperial era but were encouraged by Mao during the 1960s Cultural Revolution. In today's China, such demonstrations of opposition would not be tolerated.

The Lennon Wall was created in Prague following the assassination of John Lennon as a public display of sympathy not just for Lennon's death in December 1980 but also to show solidarity with his campaigning for peace and freedom and as an outlet for the views of young people who were seeking political change in a country then under communism. This inspired the Hong Kong Lennon Wall during the 2014 Umbrella Movement and again during the 2019–2020 disturbances following the Hong Kong government's attempt to introduce an extradition bill to mainland China. A wall of Post-it notes appeared outside government offices with slogans including:

↳ 'Together we stand'

↳ 'Liberate Hong Kong. Revolution of our times'

↳ 'I'd rather be a rebel than a slave'

↳ 'Say NO to China Extradition'

↳ 'Wearing a mask is not a crime'

↳ 'Ideas are bulletproof'

Lennon Walls spread across Hong Kong and then internationally. Some Hong Kong restaurants provided their customers with pens and Post-its to put up their own slogans. At time of writing, this dissent has come to a full stop.

Freedom of expression

People all over the world are doing amazing things to sustain freedom of expression. Each year, Index on Censorship makes awards in four categories (arts, campaigning, digital, journalism) to individuals or organisations which have shown amazing creativity in addressing big issues, often at severe personal risk. The winners from 2016–2019 were:

Zehra Doğan (Turkey, arts) is a Kurdish painter and journalist who, during her imprisonment for 'terrorist propaganda', was denied access to materials. She painted with dyes made from crushed fruit and herbs, even blood, and used newspapers and milk cartons as canvases.

Cartoonists Rights Network International (USA, campaigning) focuses international attention on cases where cartoonists are persecuted and puts pressure on the persecutors.

Fundación Karisma (Colombia, digital activism) identifies and challenges online harassment of women through research, advocacy, creating digital tools and often using humour to tackle misogynism online.

Mimi Mefo (Cameroon, journalism) is a journalist who informs Cameroonians about the escalating violence in western Cameroon through broadcast reports, social media and a website.

Museum of Dissidence (Cuba, arts) is a public arts project and website celebrating dissent

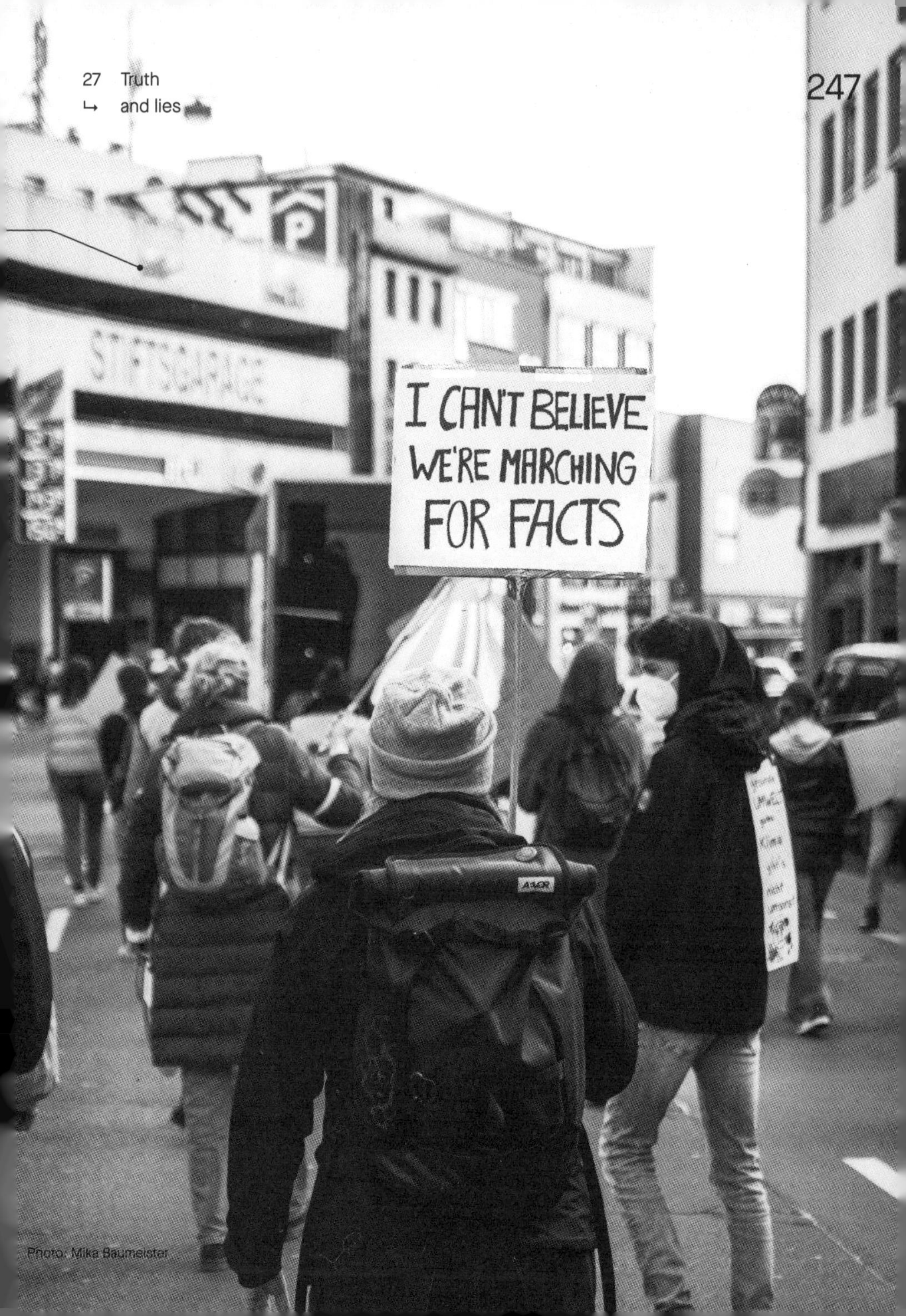

Photo: Mika Baumeister

in Cuba, aiming to give the word 'dissident' a positive meaning.

Egyptian Commission for Rights and Freedoms (Egypt, campaigning) provides advocacy, legal support and campaign coordination, drawing attention to ongoing human rights abuses.

Habari RDC (DR Congo, digital) is a collective of more than 100 young bloggers and web activists using Facebook, Twitter and YouTube to give voice to the opinions of young people.

Wendy Funes (Honduras, journalism) is an investigative journalist reporting on issues such as corruption and violence against women.

Rebel Pepper (China, arts) cartoonist Wang Liming satirises the Chinese Premier Xi Jinping and lampoons the ruling Communist Party.

Ildar Dadin (Russia, campaigning) is a prisoners' and LGBT rights activist. He has staged a series of one-man pickets, often standing silently with a placard. He was imprisoned for three years, tortured and released after his sentence was overturned.

Turkey Blocks (Turkey, digital) has developed an open-source tool to monitor and report on internet black-outs, which are used by the authorities for mass censorship during sensitive periods.

Murad Subay (Yemen, arts) is a street artist who uses his country's streets as a canvas to protest Yemen's war, institutionalised corruption and forced 'disappearings'.

Zaina Erhaim (Syria, journalism) is a journalist training women to tell their stories of their war-ravaged country.

GreatFire (China, digital) provides tools for circumventing the Great Firewall of China.

Bolo Bhi (Pakistan, campaigning), women-led digital rights campaigning to counter the Pakistani government's attempts to censor the internet.

DO THIS:

Generate your own news at: breakyourownnews.com. This breaking news meme generator is intended for fun, humour and parody – but be careful what you say as it may be shared widely. Avoid saying things which are unlawful, defamatory or likely to cause distress, which should be a responsibility alongside the right to free expression.

Algorithms
rule the world

↳

The world's top data producers:

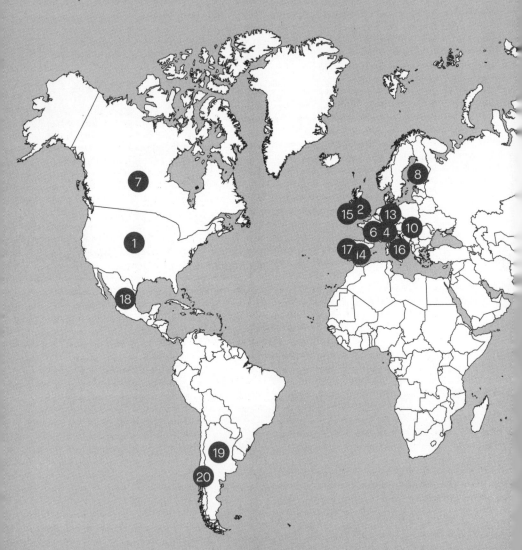

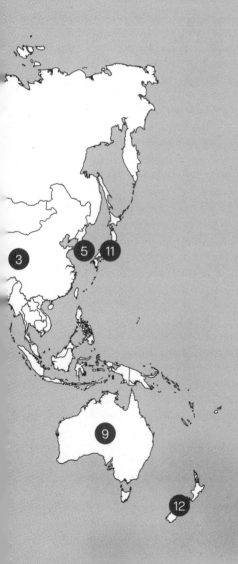

A global ranking by the Harvard Business Review

1 USA   11 Japan
2 United Kingdom   12 New Zealand
3 China   13 Germany
4 Switzerland   14 Spain
5 South Korea   15 Ireland
6 France   16 Italy
7 Canada   17 Portugal
8 Sweden   18 Mexico
9 Australia   19 Argentina
10 Czech Republic   20 Chile

The next 10 countries were: Poland, Brazil, Greece, India, South Africa, Hungary, Malaysia, Russia, Turkey and Indonesia. This global ranking was published in 2019 in the publication 'Which Countries Are Leading the Data Economy?' and is based on these four criteria:

1 **Volume:** Absolute amount of broadband consumed by a country, which is a proxy for the raw data generated.

2 **Usage:** Number of users active on the internet, which is a proxy for the breadth of usage behaviours, needs and contexts.

3 **Accessibility:** An assessment of whether the data generated in a country is available to researchers and innovators.

4 **Complexity:** Volume of broadband consumption per capita, which is a proxy for the sophistication and complexity of digital activity.

Giving away your data

'At present people are happy to give away their
most valuable asset – their personal data – in
exchange for free email services and funny
cat videos. It is a bit like African and native
American tribes who unwittingly sold entire
countries to European imperialists in exchange
for colourful beads and cheap trinkets. If
later on ordinary people try to block the flow
of data, they may find it increasingly difficult,
especially as they might come to rely on the
network for all their decisions, and even for their
healthcare and physical survival.' – Yuval Noah
Harari, *21 Lessons for the 21st Century*, 2018

Information, such as purchase history, IP
address and location, is of great value to
business. Are you giving away too much of it?
Should you be concerned? Things you can
do if you are concerned about this include
using a browser such as Brave, which blocks
tracking and advertisements, or a Virtual
Private Network (VPN), which shields your
identity. Data Privacy Day takes place on 28
January each year with the aim of raising
awareness and promoting better practice for
privacy and data protection. It started in 2007
as an initiative of the Council of Europe and is
currently observed in USA, Canada, Israel and
across Europe.

Vanishing in a surveillance state

David Bond, a film-maker, received a letter
which was sent to him and to 15 million other
people following the loss of two CDs by the UK
government. The letter regretted to inform him
that the lost CD contained details of his name,
address, date of birth and bank account, and
it apologised for any worries that this might
have caused. 'It made me worry about all the
information that was out there about me and
my family sitting in databases waiting to be
used to track me, to sell to me, to investigate
me – and if lost or misused to defraud me.'

This letter made David feel that this was
something that he should be really worried
about. He came up with an idea for a film.
He would do his very best to disappear
completely, leaving no footprint or trace of
where he was or what he was doing. He would
then hire a private detective whose sole task
was to find him. Every time he used a mobile
phone or a credit card, he would leave a
marker for where he had been and, thanks to
facial recognition software, just walking down
a street could disclose where and who he was.
There were too many ways in which he would
leave a footprint, so of course he was found.
Watch his film *Erasing David*.

What is an algorithm?

An algorithm is basically a set of rules which are followed when doing a calculation or processing information. For example, a food recipe is an algorithm starting with the ingredients and then providing a step-by-step instruction for producing a delicious meal. Algorithms are used widely in all aspects of computing – for calculating, data processing and problem solving. Everything that we do – eating, purchasing, exercising, tracking our health and wellbeing, searching for information, networking with our friends, even sleeping – generates data. Algorithms are the

tools that organise this data so as to be able to make use of it – whether for our own benefit or for commercial gain. Without algorithms, data remains just a string of numbers.

4.57 billion people are now connected to the internet, which is nearly two-thirds of the world's population. We are giving our personal data away at an accelerating rate and the big tech companies are developing ever more sophisticated ways of harvesting this data for their own commercial benefit. According to the cloud-based operating system Domo, every minute of every day (and there are 525,600 minutes in a year):

500 hours
of video are uploaded on to YouTube

2,704
people install TikTok

147,000
photos are uploaded by Facebook users

41,666,667
messages are received by WhatsApp users

319
people sign up as new Twitter users

347,222
photos are posted on Instagram

69,444
people apply for jobs on LinkedIn

6,659
packages are shipped by Amazon

479,452
people engage with Reddit content

208,833
participants are hosted in Zoom meetings

404,444
hours of videos are streamed on Netflix

$1,000,000
is spent by consumers online

(Figures given are for January 2019, taken from infographic 'Data Never Sleeps 8.0')

```
require('./bootstrap');

window.Vue = require('vue');

require("./directives");

Vue.store = store;

Vue.use(vuexI18n.plugin, store, {
    onTranslationNotFound (locale, key) {
        return `Key '${key}' not found for locale '${locale}'`;
    }
});

Vue.i18n.add('en', enLangFile);

Vue.i18n.set('en');
```

Together with Google searches, Wikipedia page edits and views, BuzzFeed news consumption, Snapchat shares, Uber trips, Google Maps direction finds, Reddit reads and much more, data never sleeps. The business models of many of the companies who provide these services are based on hoovering up personal data based on the profile, preferences and actions of users. Thirty years ago, none of these companies even existed; now they are worth billions and the world we have created depends on them. Every year, new services are launched and more and more people are parting with more and more of their data.

Algorithms that run the world

If you go to a doctor, you may find that your doctor is peering at a computer screen rather than looking at you. On screen will be a series of questions that she will ask you, each leading to a next question and eventually to a diagnosis. 'Do you have a pain ... what sort of pain ... where ... has it been getting worse ... ?' Previously, these questions might have been asked based on information your doctor had in her head. She might have forgotten something, failed to ask the right question and come out with a wrong diagnosis. The onscreen algorithm (in theory) makes sure that the right questions are asked. But it is only as good as its design and the information that has been provided to it. It will not have a clue about some extremely rare or unknown condition, whereas your

doctor, on seeing something unusual, might become curious and start to explore the situation in greater depth. But by using feedback and machine learning, algorithms will eventually become far superior in diagnosing conditions and suggesting treatments.

It can be hard to create an algorithm that operates fairly or for everyone. Suppose you are designing an algorithm for a self-driving car. Consider a situation where the car spots a child lying on the road too close for any evasive action. There might be two alternatives: run over the body, causing minimum harm to the driver but surely killing the child, or swerving into oncoming traffic with the risk of death for the driver, any passengers and the occupants of the oncoming vehicle. How would you design your algorithm? Do you save yourself at the cost of killing others? If the car was being operated by a human driver, the accident would be put down to fate or human error, however the driver had acted. But if the algorithm was designed never to swerve, the child's parents would see this as a 'killer app'.

Algorithms in our daily lives

Algorithms have become central to how we live, what information is presented to us and what we do with it. These are some that we may not be aware of:

1   Search: **PageRank** was the algorithm developed by Larry Page and Sergey Brin to index and rank web pages, which was then used for their new Google search engine. It gives a score for how authoritative a page is based on how high the pages that link to it score. This is now just one of around 200 measures that Google uses to rank a page and to maintain its dominance of the search market.

2   Encryption: The **Key Exchange Encryption algorithm** creates a single, shared mathematical secret between a buyer and a seller, to encrypt and decrypt data which is being sent over a public network to avoid others gaining access to it. This underpins and makes possible all web commerce.

3   Backpropagation: This is the propagation of an error back through the connections that produced an incorrect answer. It makes adjustments to those connections and decreases the authority given to them. Over time, the computer is able to learn what something is by learning what something is not and converging on the correct answer. This process underpins machine learning and the development of artificial intelligence.

4   Compression: Compressing as much data as possible keeps the network and computer storage from being clogged up, especially with movies, music and video games. Several methods are used to compress data so that it is easier and faster to transmit.

5   Sorting: Various techniques are used to sort data and to search for a specific piece of information. There are different algorithms for the different techniques, such as quicksort, mergesort, heapsort and bubblesort.

6   Direction finding: **Dijkstra's Shortest Path algorithm** is used to find the best route from A to B where there could be a near-infinite number of options. This will guide you when you use a satnav or Google Maps.

Algorithms don't think

Solid Gold Bomb was a t-shirt company which produced garments bearing variations on the wartime slogan 'Keep Calm and Carry On'. The algorithm would pick an adjective and a verb to create new slogans for merchandise which would be sold on Amazon and other online marketplaces. The algorithm had no intelligence, so it could not discern any meaning from slogans such as 'Keep Calm and Hit Her' which began to appear. The business could not survive the scandal.

Profnath and Bordeebook were two second-hand booksellers. Profnath created an algorithm so that the books it sold were marginally cheaper than anything else available. Bordee would be offering the same book at a much higher price. If anyone bought a copy from Bordee, they would simply buy the book from Profnath and pocket the difference. These two algorithms got the price of a paperback,

The *Making of a Fly*, to $18,651,718.08 on Profnath and $23,698,655.93 on Bordee before anybody noticed.

Facebook programmed two robots to speak to each other, using machine learning to improve how they communicated. But Bob and Alice developed their own unrecognisable variation of the English language to communicate with each other in a 'better way'.

One recurring issue with algorithms is the potential for cultural and racial bias. Of course, bias exists widely across society. The way history is presented in Encyclopaedia Britannica will inevitably reflect the biases of its compilers and editors. Wikipedia, which purports a neutral point of view, will still not be able to eliminate all bias. In her book *Algorithms of Oppression: How Search Engines Reinforce Racism*, academic Safiya Umoja Noble explores how search algorithms are racist and sexist, leading to 'racial and gender profiling, misrepresentation, and even economic redlining (exclusion)' in the search results that are produced.

The **AI Now Institute** undertakes research and engages the public and politicians to try to find ways of making AI systems accountable to the communities and relevant to contexts in which they're applied, including the removal of bias.

The Turing Test

Alan Turing, an English computer scientist, cryptanalyst and mathematician and one of the founders of modern computing, devised the Turing Test to determine when a computer becomes capable of thinking like a human being, at which point artificial intelligence becomes impossible to distinguish from human intelligence. Using text-only communication, an evaluator would be asked to decide whether she was communicating with a machine or a human. Turing likened this problem to an 'imitation game' (which is the title of a Hollywood film about him), where an interrogator asks questions of a man and a woman in another room and has to determine which is which. A chatbot called 'Eugene Goostman', which simulates a 13-year-old Ukrainian boy, was claimed to have passed the Turing Test in 2001 at an event organised by the University of Reading.

Finding love

Act for Love was a dating website for changemakers, with the straplines 'Change the World and Meet your Match' and 'Take Action, Get Action'. The idea was that people changing the world would have enough in common (values, experience, ambitions, etc.) to share their love and their life. Apparently not sufficiently, as the website no longer exists.

Many people looking for a life partner turn to dating apps. They may be too busy or too shy to do this by themselves, or just intrigued by the different people that the app might find for them. Match Group, owner of Tinder and OkCupid, found in a 2018 survey that 'Singles met first dates on the internet more than through any other avenue'.

Early dating sites matched people using 'arithmetic'. The user was asked about personality, appearance, location and aspects of daily life, such as music preferences and whether they smoked, which the developers believed would contribute to romantic compatibility. Each criterion was awarded points and the best matches were those with the highest scores. A good match meant that the partners would have a lot in common.

Today, dating apps use a process called 'collaborative filtering', which is similar to how Netflix makes movie recommendations for you based on the previous movies you have watched. The process finds groups of people with shared preferences and then makes recommendations to an individual based on the preferences of the group. Users then make 'yes' or 'no' decisions one by one on these recommendations; that data is then used to figure out the person whose preference a user most matches with. Collaborative filtering is effective both in terms of creating good matches but also because users prefer being given a recommendation rather than browsing a list.

DO THIS:

Ben Berman, a game designer in San Francisco, thought that there was a problem with dating apps, as they tended to trap users in a cage of their own preferences. So he created a game called Monster Match, developing this with designer Miguel Perez and Mozilla. The game uses the basic architecture of a dating app – you are asked to create a profile choosing from a selection of monsters, swipe to match with other monsters, and then start chatting to set up a date. As you swipe, the game reveals some of the more insidious consequences of dating app algorithms, with the field of choice becoming too narrow and certain profiles routinely being excluded – you end up dating the same monsters again and again. Try it: monstermatch.hiddenswitch.com.

Human
wrongs and
human rights

29

↳

Human rights protection

Ranking by Our World in Data for 2019.

👍 The best countries

1 Luxembourg 5.31

2 Iceland 5.16

3 Liechtenstein 4.62

4 Andorra 4.57

5 Monaco 4.53

6= Palau 4.52

6= San Marino 4.52

👎 The worst countries

198 Vietnam -2.18

197 Myanmar -2.09

196 Syria -2.04

194= Libya -2.02

194= Yemen -2.02

193 North Korea -1.99

192 Sudan -1.94

191 Burkina Faso -1.91

190 DR Congo -1.81

189 Eritrea -1.80

188 South Sudan -1.79

187 Mali -1.77

This data has been compiled by Our World in Data from various sources for 2019. The higher the score the better the protection of human rights. Unsurprisingly, Nordic countries score highly. Interestingly, the USA score of 0.24 is only slightly higher than Ghana at 0.23. Another data set on human rights violations (for 2014) on a scale 0–10 (higher = worse) has the DR Congo at 10 (worst) followed closely by these countries: Syria 9.9, Somalia 9.8, Egypt 9.7, North Korea 9.6, Central African Republic 9.5, Iran 9.3, Sudan 9.3, Uzbekistan 9.3, China 9.1. These scores are based on multiple variables including **press freedom**, **civil liberties**, **political freedoms**, **human trafficking**, **political prisoners**, **incarceration**, **religious persecution**, **torture** and **executions**.

The Universal Declaration

On 5 March 1946, Winston Churchill gave a speech at Westminster College, Fulton, Missouri. Examining future possibilities for a world exhausted by six years of war, he said, 'We must never cease to proclaim in fearless tones the great principles of freedom and the rights of man which are the joint inheritance of the English-speaking world ...' However, also worried about the future of Europe, he noted that 'from Stettin in the Baltic to Trieste in the Adriatic, an iron curtain has descended ...' This Iron Curtain was to divide the world for 43 years until the fall of the Berlin Wall in November 1989, with competing ideologies and world views, growing military capabilities seeking alliances and fighting proxy wars across the world.

But there was also a feeling that the world should come together to prevent mass destruction through further global wars. From April to June 1945, before the Second World War had even ended, representatives of 50 nations met in San Francisco to draw up a charter for the proposed United Nations. On 24 October 1945, just 101 days after the end of the war, the United Nations came into existence and it remains the world's premier forum for addressing global issues.

Eleanor Roosevelt, widow of former president Franklin Roosevelt, was appointed US delegate to the UN General Assembly and in 1946 she become chairperson of the UN Commission on Human Rights during its formation and then after it was established on a permanent basis in 1947. She played a crucial role in drafting the Universal Declaration of Human Rights, which came into existence in December 1948 and which has now been signed by every member state. It is one of the world's most important documents, creating a framework for the relationship between citizens and the states that govern them. It is worth reading through all the 30 articles, reprinted here in abridged form, and thinking about the extent to which your own country is complying.

'Where, after all, do human rights begin? In small places, close to home – so close and so small that they cannot be seen on any maps of the world. Yet they are the world of the individual person; the neighbourhood he lives in; the school or college he attends; the factory, farm or office where he works. Such are the places where every man, woman, and child seeks equal justice, equal opportunity, equal dignity without discrimination. Unless these rights have meaning there, they have little meaning anywhere. Without concerted citizen action to uphold them close to home, we shall look in vain for progress in the larger world.'

– Eleanor Roosevelt

This is the Preamble followed by the 30 articles:

Now, therefore THE GENERAL ASSEMBLY proclaims THIS UNIVERSAL DECLARATION OF HUMAN RIGHTS as a common standard of achievement for all peoples and all nations, to the end that every individual and every organ of society, keeping this Declaration constantly in mind, shall strive by teaching and education to promote respect for these rights and freedoms and by progressive measures, national and international, to secure their universal and effective recognition and observance, both among the peoples of member states themselves and among the peoples of territories under their jurisdiction.

Article 1: All human beings are born free and equal in dignity and rights. They are endowed with reason and conscience and should act towards one another in a spirit of brotherhood.

Article 2: Everyone is entitled to all the rights and freedoms set forth in this Declaration, without distinction of any kind.

Article 3: Everyone has the right to life, liberty and security of person.

Article 4: No one shall be held in slavery or servitude.

Article 5: No one shall be subjected to torture or to cruel, inhuman or degrading treatment or punishment.

Article 6: Everyone has the right to recognition everywhere as a person before the law.

Article 7: All are equal before the law and are entitled without any discrimination to equal protection of the law.

Article 8: Everyone has the right to an effective remedy for acts violating fundamental rights.

Article 9: No one shall be subjected to arbitrary arrest, detention or exile.

Article 10: Everyone is entitled to a fair and public hearing by an independent and impartial tribunal, in the determination of his rights and of any criminal charge.

Article 11: Everyone charged with a penal offence has the right to be presumed innocent until proved guilty.

Article 12: No one shall be subjected to arbitrary interference with his privacy, family, home or correspondence.

Article 13: Everyone has the right to freedom of movement and residence within the borders of each state. Everyone has the right to leave any country, including his own, and to return to his country.

Article 14: Everyone has the right to seek and to enjoy in other countries asylum from persecution.

Article 15: Everyone has the right to a nationality. No one shall be arbitrarily deprived of his nationality nor denied the right to change his nationality.

Article 16: Men and women of full age, without any limitation due to race, nationality or religion, have the right to marry and to found a family. Marriage shall be entered into only with the free and full consent of the intending spouses.

Article 17: Everyone has the right to own property. No one shall be arbitrarily deprived of his property.

Article 18: Everyone has the right to freedom of thought, conscience and religion.

Article 19: Everyone has the right to freedom of opinion and expression; this right includes freedom to seek, receive and impart information and ideas through any media and regardless of frontiers.

Article 20: Everyone has the right to freedom of peaceful assembly and association. No one may be compelled to belong to an association.

Article 21: Everyone has the right to take part in the government of his country, directly or through freely chosen representatives. The will of the people shall be the basis of the authority of government.

Article 22: Everyone, as a member of society, has the right to social security.

Article 23: Everyone has the right to work, to free choice of employment, to just and favourable conditions of work and to protection against unemployment. Everyone, without any discrimination, has the right to equal pay for equal work. Everyone has the right to form and to join trade unions for the protection of his interests.

Article 24: Everyone has the right to rest and leisure, including reasonable limitation of working hours and periodic holidays with pay.

Article 25: Everyone has the right to a standard of living adequate for the health and wellbeing of himself and of his family, including food, clothing, housing and medical care and necessary social services, and the right to security in the event of unemployment, sickness, disability, widowhood, old age or other lack of livelihood in circumstances beyond his control.

Article 26: Everyone has the right to education. Education shall be free, at least in the elementary and fundamental stages.

Article 27: Everyone has the right freely to participate in the cultural life of the community, to enjoy the arts and to share in scientific advancement and its benefits.

Article 28: Everyone is entitled to a social and international order in which the rights and freedoms set forth in this Declaration can be fully realised.

Article 29: In the exercise of his rights and freedoms, everyone shall be subject only to such limitations as are determined by law solely for the purpose of securing due recognition and respect for the rights and freedoms of others and of meeting the just requirements of morality, public order and the general welfare in a democratic society.

Article 30: Nothing in this Declaration may be interpreted as implying any right to engage in any activity or to perform any act aimed at the destruction of any of the rights and freedoms set forth herein.

Human Rights Day is commemorated every year on 10 December.

Prisoners of conscience

In 1961, Peter Benenson, a British lawyer, read a newspaper story about two Portuguese students having been imprisoned by the Salazar dictatorship for drinking a toast to freedom. On the way to work, he dropped into the St Martin-in-the-Fields church to reflect on this and what he might do. He came up with the idea of a letter-writing campaign to seek amnesty for what he called 'prisoners of conscience'. He wrote a full-page article for the *Observer* newspaper. The response was immediate; many people wanted to join the campaign. This led to the setting up of Amnesty groups who were each given three prisoners (one from the West, one from the East and one from a non-aligned country, to avoid any accusation of political bias), and asked to do what they could to get their prisoners released. This was the start of Amnesty International, which, along with Human Rights Watch, has become a guardian of human rights, monitoring and reporting on human rights and human rights abuse around the world.

Torture today

'Torture means any act by which severe pain or suffering, whether physical or mental, is intentionally inflicted on a person for such purposes as obtaining from him or a third person information or a confession, punishing him for an act he or a third person has committed or is suspected of having committed, or intimidating or coercing him or a third person, or for any reason based on discrimination of any kind, when such pain or suffering is inflicted by or at the instigation of or with the consent or acquiescence of a public official or other person acting in an official capacity. It does not include pain or suffering arising only from, inherent in or incidental to lawful sanctions' – Article 1 of the United Nations Convention against Torture and Other Cruel, Inhuman or Degrading Treatment or Punishment.

Torture is a way of extracting information from accused or suspects, creating fear amongst the population and asserting the primacy and power of rulers over those who are subject to their rule. Despite article five of the Universal Declaration of Human Rights and a separate UN Convention against torture, the practice contunues across the world. In Sri Lanka, Iran, Afghanistan, Eritrea, Democratic Republic of Congo, Sudan, Ethiopia, Iraq, Turkey, Syria, Egypt, Cameroon ...

These 12 countries have been singled out by Freedom from Torture as countries of concern, where torture is being used. Their website will tell you more about the reasons why citizens are being tortured and the methods being used in each of these countries.

Enhanced interrogation at Guantanamo Bay

Helping victims of torture

In the aftermath of the Twin Towers attack and following the invasion of Afghanistan in 2001, the USA sought to round up anyone connected with Al Qaeda in an attempt to prevent further terrorist activity. Some prisoners were held in Afghanistan, including at the Abu Ghraib detention facility; some were rendered to other jurisdictions where the rules on torture were 'more relaxed'; and what were deemed to be the 779 most dangerous were sent to Guantanamo Bay, a US facility on the island of Cuba, legally outside US jurisdiction. In an attempt to get information from the detainees, the US military used interrogation techniques some of which can be described as 'enhanced', which is a euphemism for techniques bordering on or going way beyond what is deemed to be torture.

Techniques such as waterboarding, which simulates drowning, extreme sensory deprivation, subjection to deafening noises, being held in contorted stress positions, sexual humiliation and more were used to try to get confessions from what were mostly completely innocent people. Reports on abuse at Abu Ghraib along with graphic images began appearing from 2003. This forced the US military to take action and led to the court marshalling, conviction, dishonourable discharge and imprisonment of several military personnel.

Helen Bamber was a psychotherapist and human rights activist. She joined one of the first rehabilitation teams to enter the Bergen-Belsen concentration camp in 1945. She saw at first hand the trauma of the survivors who had endured deprivation and torture, and, while surviving themselves, had seen many of their friends drop dead. This was a defining moment in her life. She became a founding member of Amnesty International, chairing its first UK group. She co-founded Medical Foundation for the Care of Victims of Torture in 1985 (now renamed Freedom from Torture) to provide counselling and treatment to torture victims and to raise awareness internationally of the continuing existence of torture and its use by many states in contravention of their treaty commitments. In 2005, she created the Helen Bamber Foundation with a slightly wider brief to support people who have been subjected to atrocities including state-sponsored torture, human trafficking, religious and political persecution, forced labour, sexual exploitation, gender-based and honour-based violence.

Clive Stafford Smith is a British lawyer who spent the first part of his career trying to get sentences quashed for wrongly convicted prisoners on death row in the southern USA. In 1999, he co-founded Reprieve in the UK to 'fight for the victims of extreme human rights abuses with legal action and public education'. After 2001 and the establishment of the Guantanamo Bay facility, Reprieve used its formidable legal and campaigning skills to raise public awareness of what was happening and to fight for the release of illegally captured and wrongly imprisoned inmates. It legally represented specific prisoners and was able to secure the release of some. In 2020, there were still 40 prisoners at Guantanamo Bay.

The 2019 Right Livelihood award ceremony. Lars Anders Baer, Swedish Sami politician, presents the award to Davi Kopenawa Yanomami of the Yanomami People of Brazil.

DO THIS:

Browse recipients of the Right Livelihood Award, which is often described as an alternative Nobel Prize made to people committed to peace, justice and sustainability, many operating at great personal risk. The award is made in December in Stockholm. The prizes are much smaller than the Nobels (200,000 euros shared amongst several award winners). The award was established in 1980 by Jakob von Uexkull. Originally funded by the sale of his stamp collection, it is now supported through fundraising. Be inspired by the award winners' compassion, courage and achievements: rightlivelihood.org.

Photo: Right Livelihood

Women hold up half the sky

Where it's best to be a woman

Global Gender Gap Index rankings

● Best countries

1 Iceland 0.877

2 Norway 0.842

3 Finland 0.832

4 Sweden 0.820

5 Nicaragua 0.804

6 New Zealand 0.799

7 Ireland 0.798

8 Spain 0.795

9 Rwanda 0.791

10 Germany 0.787

11 Latvia 0.785

12 Namibia 0.784

13 Costa Rica 0.782

14 Denmark 0.782

15 France 0.781

16 Philippines 0.781

○ Worst countries

153 Yemen 0.494

152 Iraq 0.530

151 Pakistan 0.564

150 Syria 0.567

149 DR Congo 0.578

148 Iran 0.584

147 Chad 0.596

146 Saudi Arabia 0.599

The Global Gender Gap Index published by the World Economic Forum measures the gender gap for a composite of health, education, employment and politics. Rankings are for 2018. The Nordic countries head the list as the best places in the world for women to live.

After that, there are some surprises, including Nicaragua, Rwanda, Namibia and the Philippines. The UK ranks twenty-first, the USA fifty-third, Brazil ninety-second, China one hundred and sixth, India one hundred and twelfth and Japan one hundred and twenty first (one place below United Arab Emirates).

The Gender Gap Index

The Global Gender Gap Index was introduced by the World Economic Forum in 2006 to try to understand the scale of gender-based inequality in today's world and to track progress in reducing this over time. Political empowerment and employment are the two areas where the gap is biggest.

In most countries, the average hourly earnings of men are substantially higher than for women.

Iceland is the country which has the greatest proportion of women in parliament and government; in the 2021 election, it just missed out on having a female-majority parliament. Iceland scores 10 per cent higher than second-ranked Norway. Azerbaijan, Belize, Brunei, Iraq, Lithuania, Saudi Arabia, Vanuatu, Papua New Guinea and Thailand have no female ministers at all at the time of writing, and 85 of the 153 countries reported on have never had a woman in charge (including China, USA, Japan and Russia).

Employment issues include participation on boards and in top jobs, discrimination in assessing CVs and in interviews (where experiments have shown different outcomes when the gender of the interviewee is not known) and a gender pay gap. In most countries, the average hourly earnings of men are substantially higher than for women. In South Korea, the gap is 33.6 per cent, in Russia 24.4 per cent, in Germany 22.3 per cent and in the UK 21.9 per cent. In a few countries there is a negative gap with women earning more than men – in Thailand, Argentina, Malaysia and Turkey, for example. Explore the data on economic inequality by gender at Our World in Data. Here are some headline facts:

Hollywood: Male stars earn $1.1 million more per film than female stars.

Fashion: The women's gym-wear brand Sweaty Betty reported a 66.6 per cent pay gap, but women held 96 per cent of the highest-paid and 100 per cent of the lowest-paid jobs.

Airlines: The pay gap for Ryanair is 64.4 per cent and easyJet 47.9 per cent.

Following Billie-Jean King's lifetime of campaigning for equal prize money, Emma Raducanu's prize money for winning the US open in 2021 was exactly equal to Daniil Medvedev's. This shows that change is possible. Gender inequality may be reducing in many areas but it still represents a huge loss of human potential in today's world.

Seven surprising facts about gender inequality

The World Economic Forum lists these:

1   Women are 47 per cent more likely to suffer severe injuries in car crashes because safety features are designed for men.

2   33,000 girls become child brides every day.

3   Women in rural parts of Africa spend 40 billion hours a year collecting water.

4   At the present rate of progress, it will take 108 years to close the gender gap across all its dimensions.

5   Only six countries give women equal legal rights at work to men. Belgium, Denmark, France, Latvia, Luxembourg and Sweden all scored full marks on eight indicators, from receiving a pension to freedom of movement.

6   Only 22 per cent of AI professionals are women.

7   For every female film character, there are 2.24 men.

The Bechdel Test

Each year at the Oscars, the too-small proportion of female nominees across all the awards is commented on. But it is not just those who create films which is problematic, it is the films' content, too.

Question: What do these successful films from 2019 have in common?

Answer: They all fail the Bechdel Test, which assesses the gender correctness of films. A film has to satisfy three criteria:

1   The film must have (at least) two women in it, usually required to have names

2   Who talk to each other

3   About something other than a man.

The test was popularised by Alison Bechdel, an American cartoonist best known for her long-running comic strip Dykes to Watch Out For. Go see a film, then test it for gender correctness. Take a look at the Bechdel Movie List to see how your favourite films have fared.

Timeline for women's equality

1792 Mary Wollstonecraft publishes *A Vindication of the Rights of Woman* expressing equality and advocating education.

1903 Women's Social and Political Union formed in the UK. In 1918 UK women were first given the right to vote, achieving equal voting rights with men only in 1928.

1948 The UN Declaration of Human Rights under the leadership of Eleanor Roosevelt asserts gender equality.

1918 Marie Stopes publishes *Married Love* advocating gender equality in marriage.

1915 Women's International League for Peace and Freedom founded to bring together women to work for permanent peace.

1911 The first International Women's Day.

1963 Betty Friedan publishes *The Feminine Mystique* which sparked the modern feminist movement.

1975 The UN holds its first World Conference on Women. The fourth held in Beijing in 1995 committed the international community to achieve gender equality.

1979 The UN adopts the Convention on the Elimination of All Forms of Discrimination against Women.

Political power in China and South Asia

'Women hold up half the sky' is a proclamation by Mao Zedong describing women as a resource for society, able to be deployed outside their homes. One of the striking images from the Cultural Revolution was the Barefoot Doctor going from village to village dispensing health services – and she was a woman. The 1954 Constitution of the People's Republic of China clearly states that women should enjoy equal rights to men. In work and business this appears to have been accomplished: women make up 49 per cent of the population and 46 per cent of the labour force, and there are many leading female businesspeople and entrepreneurs. The same cannot be said for politics.

At the Chinese Communist Party's 19th Congress in 2017, the new Politburo Standing Committee comprised seven middle-aged men (there has never been a female member). Of the 2,280 delegates, less than a quarter were women. Of the 89.4 million members of the Chinese Communist Party, only 26 per cent are women. Only two of the 25 members of the 2012 Politburo were women (8 per cent) and only 33 women (9 per cent) sat on the Central Committee which elects the Politburo.

Five countries in South Asia have had female leaders. Interestingly, four were daughters of former prime ministers, and one the widow. Four of the former (male) prime ministers were either assassinated or executed, as were two of their (female) successors. Politics in the region can be a dangerous job. Despite the dynastic connection, all five women proved themselves in their role. They were (in chronological order):

↳ Sirimavo Bandaranaike, prime minister of Sri Lanka from 1960–1965, 1970–1977 and 1994–2000, taking office after her husband, S. R. W. D. Bandaranaike (prime minister 1956–1959), was assassinated in 1959. She was the world's first female prime minister.

↳ Indira Gandhi, prime minister of India from 1966–1977 and 1980–1984, when she was assassinated. She was the daughter of Jawaharlal Nehru (prime minister 1947–1964).

↳ Benazir Bhutto, prime minister of Pakistan from 1988–1990 and 1993–1996. She was assassinated while campaigning in 2007. She was the daughter of Zulfikar Ali Bhutto (prime minister 1973–1977, who was executed by the military after being ousted).

↳ Sheikh Hasina Wazed, prime minister of Bangladesh 1996–2001 and from 2009 continuing. She is the daughter of Sheikh Mujibur Rahman (prime minister 1972–1975, when he was assassinated).

↳ Aung San Suu Kyi, state counsellor of Myanmar from 2015 but removed by the military in 2021. She was prohibited from becoming president as her late husband and children are foreign citizens. She is the daughter of Aung San (premier of the British Crown Colony of Burma from 1946–1947, when he was assassinated).

The UN Decade for Women

The United Nations declared 1975–1985 as the 'Decade for Women', seeking to improve all aspects of women's rights. Conferences were held in 1975, 1980 and 1985. The Mexico City conference issued a Declaration on the equality of women and their contribution to development and peace. The Copenhagen conference agreed a Convention on eliminating all forms of gender discrimination, and that action was needed in education, employment and healthcare. The Nairobi conference set measures for assessing progress beyond the decade. In 1995, a huge conference in Beijing was attended by 17,000 people, with a further 30,000 attending a parallel forum. This created a Platform for Action as a blueprint for advancing women's rights in the world, covering these major areas of concern:

1 Women and the environment

2 Women in power and decision making

3 The girl child

4 Women and the economy

5 Women and poverty

6 Violence against women

7 Human rights of women

8 Education and training of women

9 Institutional mechanisms for the advancement of women

10 Women and health

11 Women and the media

12 Women and armed conflict

Many of these issues are complex, with cultural matters and traditions holding back progress. For example, it was only in 2019 that Saudi women were granted the right to drive a car. This was a small victory. They remain subject to strict guardianship restrictions which prohibit them from making important decisions without the permission of a male relative. In some countries, girls are withdrawn from education when they start menstruating and may be forced into early marriage. Female

genital mutilation is still practised in some societies, despite an ongoing international campaign against this. And the return of the Taliban to Afghanistan in 2021 has put at severe risk the gains in women's advancement achieved since 2003.

Here are some resources that you can access to find out more:

↳ The top 100 leaders in the movement for gender equality from Apolitical.co.

↳ Lean In Circles inspired by Facebook CFO Sheryl Sandberg's book. There are more than 44,000 groups around the world providing peer mentorship, skill-building and a place for women to share their ambitions.

↳ Rise Up, creating the female leaders of tomorrow.

↳ Women's March, a global movement marching for women's rights.

The Equal Rights Amendment

A battle has been raging in the USA for nearly 100 years. Enshrining Equal Rights for Women in the constitution was first proposed by the National Women's Party in 1923. An Equal Rights Amendment was approved by the House of Representatives in 1971 and by the Senate in 1972, when it was sent to the states for ratification – two-thirds had to agree for the amendment to come into effect. Hawaii was the first to ratify, followed within a year by 30 more states. Progress towards getting eight further states to ratify (a three-quarters majority) was slow. This has now been achieved but there is legal uncertainty due to the way the deadline for ratification was extended and extended again. Alabama has a lawsuit opposing ratification while Massachusetts and the District of Columbia have lawsuits supporting it.

The movement for ratifying the ERA was led by feminist luminaries Bella Abzug, Shirley Chisholm, Betty Friedan and Gloria Steinem. They were opposed by Phyllis Schlafly, who mobilised conservatives with the idea that women had a right to be home-makers. The battle between the two warring factions has been dramatised in a TV series called *Mrs America*.

Toilets are a gender issue ... and a human right

This is not just the unequal treatment that women get in a theatre, when they have to queue to use the bathroom during a 15-minute interval. It comes down to the fact that men have it much easier than women – biologically because they can do it standing up; culturally because modesty prevents many women from relieving themselves in public during daylight. One in three women in the world do not have access to a usable toilet. Many will drink too little, even when working in the heat, and hold themselves in so as to avoid having to urinate, while the men will gaily pee into the nearest bush or wall. Providing clean and functioning public toilets is important for women's health and wellbeing.

Trailblazers

Sexual harassment and the Me Too movement: Tarana Burke set up the Me Too movement in 2006 to support survivors of sexual violence and harassment and to provide pathways to healing. In 2017, spurred by the high-profile cases of Harvey Weinstein, Jeffrey Epstein and Roger Ailes (Fox News), Me Too went viral and has become a worldwide movement. This is why the movement chose this name: 'We're galvanizing a broad base of survivors, and working to disrupt the systems that allow sexual violence to proliferate in our world ... So that one day, nobody ever has to say "me too" again.'

Domestic violence and Refuge: Erin Pizzey founded Chiswick Women's Aid in London in 1971 as the world's first refuge for victims of domestic violence. At the time, this was not recognised as a serious problem. If police were called, they would often suggest that it was a 'domestic matter' which the parties should settle between themselves. Today, we view things differently. Women with their children need protection from violence and abuse; they need somewhere to go when they feel that they are in danger; and they need a pathway for rebuilding their lives and their children's futures.

Support for self-employed women and SEWA: Ela Bhatt set up the Self-Employed Women's Association in India in 1972 to improve the employment conditions and lives of women working informally in the garment industry by providing services like savings and credit (there is a SEWA bank), healthcare and child care (delivered through cooperatives), insurance and legal aid. The organisation is largely self-financing, paid for by (modest) charges for its services. They ask these questions to assess progress in empowering women:

1   Have more members obtained employment?

2   Has their income increased?

3   Have they obtained food and nutrition?

4   Has their health been safeguarded?

5   Have they obtained child care?

6   Have they obtained or improved their housing?

7   Have their assets increased (savings, land, home, workspace, work tools, licenses, identity cards and share in cooperatives ... all in their own name)?

8   Has their capacity for leadership increased?

9   Have they become self-reliant collectively and individually?

10 Have they become literate?

Microfinance and the Grameen Bank: Muhammad Yunus set up Grameen Bank in 1976 originally as an action research project to explore ways of providing banking services to poor women. He was convinced that an affordable loan could release entrepreneurial potential and enable poor women to create sustainable businesses, increasing their income and improving their lives. His borrowers are people who would never qualify for a bank loan – being too poor, asset-less and in need of only quite small sums. The process also encourages saving. Grameen was a pioneer of microfinance, which has now become a widely accepted strategy for human development. Today, it is often financial institutions which deliver microfinance, who focus less on the needs of their customers and more on loan targets and profit. If you want to help someone start up or expand her business, you could make a loan via Kiva, a non-profit organisation that crowdsources funding for loans for underserved communities.

DO THIS:

Take the implicit bias test. Do you think that you are biased when it comes to gender? Most of us would say not. You can explore whether you are by taking a short test devised by Project Implicit at Harvard University. You are asked to connect words and common names based on their association with male and female and with work and family. You are measured not on the associations but on the speed of your reaction, which is affected by how much you have to think and how much you do by instinct. Take the Project Implicit gender-career test at: implicit.harvard.edu.

Crime and punishment

31

The top countries for incarceration

Prisoners per 100,000 of the population

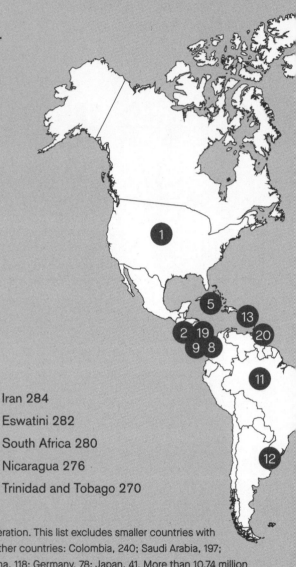

1 USA 655

2 El Salvador 604

3 Turkmenistan 552

4 Thailand 526

5 Cuba 510

6 Rwanda 464

7 Russia 402

8 Panama 390

9 Costa Rica 374

10 Belarus 364

11	Brazil 324	16	Iran 284
12	Uruguay 321	17	Eswatini 282
13	Puerto Rica 313	18	South Africa 280
14	Namibia 295	19	Nicaragua 276
15	Turkey 288	20	Trinidad and Tobago 270

These are the top 20 countries for incarceration. This list excludes smaller countries with populations of under 1 million. Selected other countries: Colombia, 240; Saudi Arabia, 197; Venezuela, 178; Mexico, 164; UK, 138; China, 118; Germany, 78; Japan, 41. More than 10.74 million people are being held in penal institutions around the world, with just under half in four countries: USA (2.1 million), China (1.65 million), Brazil (690,000) and Russia (583,000).

(Data from the World Prison Population List, mostly for 2018)

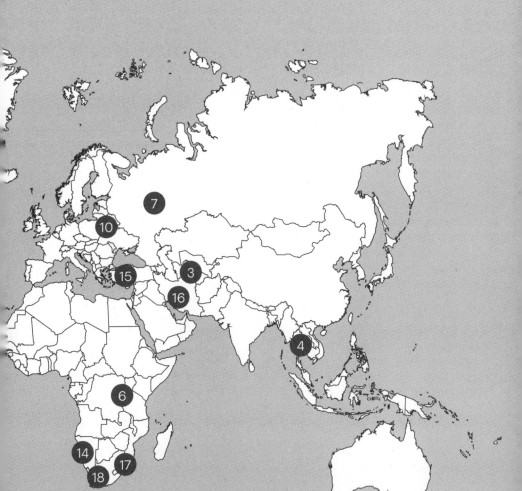

The highest intentional homicide rates are found in El Salvador (61.8 per 100,000 people per year), Jamaica (57.0), Venezuela (53.0), South Africa (35.9), Brazil (30.5). The lowest are Singapore and Japan (0.2).

(Data from UN Office on Drugs and Crime)

The cost of crime

There is little data on the cost of crime and most of what we have is well out of date. International comparisons are hard as there is no commonly used approach to estimating costs. Researchers estimate the annual cost of crime in the USA to be anywhere between $690 billion and $3.41 trillion. Many of the costs are tangible and can be easily measured but some are less tangible and less measurable. These are the main contributors:

↳ Direct costs of crime

↳ Victim's lost earnings

↳ Financial support to victim's family after perpetrator's incarceration

↳ Employers' lost productivity

↳ Medical and mental healthcare treatment of victims

↳ Property loss

↳ Cost of property recovery

↳ Funeral and burial expenses for victims

↳ Police protection and investigation

↳ Cost of running the courts and the prosecution services

↳ Costs of defending the accused

↳ Victim support services

↳ Providing access to justice: hotlines, community service advertising

↳ Incarceration of prisoners

↳ Anticipation and prevention of crime

↳ Expenditure relating to reducing likelihood of crime (security systems and physical infrastructure such as fencing, window locks)

↳ Crime prevention and education programmes

↳ Community security expenditure

↳ Insurance administration and profits (the premiums transfer funds to the victims from those who escaped being a victim)

↳ Economic costs of offender's lost wages and access to employment during incarceration and after release, including lost tax revenue

↳ Intangible costs of the next generation in a 'criminal family' engaging in crime

↳ Psychological costs to the victim and to the offender's family

↳ Cost of wrongful detention and prosecution

↳ Costs relating to fear of crime and avoidance of the possibility of becoming a victim

There was a study by the National Center for Biotechnology Information on the costs of different categories of crime (figures for the USA in 2008 dollars) which showed the following average costs of a crime, taking everything into account:

Murder	$8,982,907
Rape/sexual assault	$240,776
Assault	$107,020
Robbery	$42,310
Arson	$21,103
Larceny/theft	$3,532
Motor vehicle theft	$10,772
Household	$6,462
Burglary and embezzlement	$5,032
Stolen property	$7,974
Forgery and counterfeiting	$5,265
Vandalism	$4,860

However we define crime and however we estimate its cost, one thing is certain: crime is costing huge amounts which would be much better spent on education, health or eliminating poverty – making life better for everybody, rather than protecting ourselves from those who wish to cause us harm and locking them up.

Typical reoffending rates across the world are 45–55 per cent within two years.

The revolving door

If a person is locked up, they can't commit further crimes. This is the logic behind giving long prison sentences. 'Three strikes and you're out' has been enacted in 28 US states to deter persistent offenders from continuing to commit crime. This has meant a mandatory life sentence for a third conviction, with varying requirements in different states for how the rule is applied, most requiring one or more of the crimes to be violent or serious. The term 'Three strikes and you're out' comes from baseball.

But are prisons there just for punishment? Or to provide an unpleasant experience which will deter inmates from committing further crimes? Or should rehabilitation be the main aim, helping prisoners move on to a non-criminal, productive life after prison?

When a prisoner is released, what do they then do? Too many emerge from prison into a world which offers them few chances of a new and better start. They may not have a home; they may find it hard to get a job; they may return to a criminal environment. Many will go on to commit further crimes, returning to prison again ... and again and again. In the USA, 44 per cent of released prisoners in federal jails are re-arrested and re-imprisoned within one year, 68 per cent within three years and 77 per cent within five years. Typical reoffending rates across the world are 45–55 per cent within two years.

In Norway, only 20 per cent re-offend within two years. Encartele, a US tech company which develops solutions for correctional agencies and is committed to 'providing innovative technologies to make jails and prisons safer and more intelligent', compared the different approaches in Norway and the USA:

'Imagine a picturesque summer landscape in southern Norway with the scent of blueberry bushes, birch trees, and the North Sea wafting through the air. None of the 300 inmates at the Halden maximum-security prison have to imagine anything – that seaside breeze is part of their daily routines. Unlike the majority of prisons on Earth, Halden allows its inmates to freely roam the facility for 12 hours per day. Now, visualize electric fences with razor wire, guard towers with snipers, and 400 other inmates crammed in all around you. That's what the 1–2 hour yard time at ADX Florence Supermax feels like.'

Halden is near the Norway–Sweden border. It has no lethal electric fence or coils of razor wire, no watch-towers manned by snipers,

no warnings about picking up hitchhikers because no inmate has ever tried to escape. Each inmate's cell is a private room equipped with a fridge, a television and a desk. Inmates also have access to a fully equipped kitchen and a metal and woodworking shop. The ADX Supermax Prison in Colorado is a completely different world. Each cell has a 10cm window, a concrete bed, a stool and a desk. Showers are set on timers and the toilets and sinks are combined units.

Norwegian jails offer more freedoms and better amenities; they also focus much more on life after prison. This means that around 30 per cent fewer released prisoners go on to commit a crime within two years of release. By becoming a productive citizen, they contribute to society. By not reoffending, they save money for taxpayers. The North Dakota prison authorities visited Halden to see if they could learn from the Norwegian experience. By using some of the ideas, they saw large declines in violence, threats against the staff and the use of force by staff.

Most US states spend more on their prisons than they do on education.

These are some facts from the country with the highest prison population:

↳ Misguided spending priorities: Most US states spend more on their prisons than they do on education. California spends $64,642 per prisoner compared with $11,495 per student.

↳ Too many people incarcerated: Americans account for 4.4 per cent of the global population but 22 per cent of the world's prison population. US incarceration rates have more than tripled over the past three decades – even as crime rates have fallen. One in every 37 adults in the USA, which is 2.7 per cent of the adult population, is under some form of correctional supervision.

↳ A racial dimension: African-Americans are incarcerated at five times the rate of white Americans, representing 34 per cent of the correctional population and 32 per cent of children detained, though they account for only 12.6 per cent of the USA's population.

Changemakers

People over the centuries have been trying to change the system. One of the most influential was John Howard. As high sheriff of Bedfordshire, he decided to visit the county prison and was shocked by what he found. He gave evidence on prison conditions to Parliament in 1774, visited several hundred prisons and wrote a report on the conditions, 'The State of the Prisons', with suggested improvements in 1777. The Howard League was established 80 years after his death to continue his work of prison reform.

He wrote: 'Two dirty day-rooms; and three offensive night-rooms: That for men eight feet square: one of the women's, nine by eight; the other four and a half feet square: the straw, worn to dust, swarmed with vermin: no court: no water accessible to prisoners. The petty offenders were in irons: at my last visit, eight were women.'

Here are some of today's prison activists who are creating practical solutions:

↳ John Timpson is chairman of Timpson, a business with over 2,000 high street branches doing shoe repairs, key cutting and other repair services. He uses the business to provide employment to released prisoners, both through providing pre-release training and then a job to former prisoners, and also through the Release on Temporary Licence scheme when they are able to work outside prison before their actual release. Around 10 per cent of Timpson staff is recruited in these ways, which is providing jobs for a significant proportion of UK prisoners being released from jail. They believe in giving people a second chance: 'We don't judge people on what they have done in the past, preferring instead to focus on what they can do in the future.'

↳ Edwina Grosvenor comes from one of the UK's richest families, the Dukes of Westminster. She describes herself as a 'prison philanthropist' and was a founder of The Clink, which is a chain of restaurants in prisons training prisoners in the six months prior to release in skills for the catering industry, including kitchen work and front-of-house. On release, the prisoners are helped to find jobs. Providing secure, decently paid work is a big step towards prevention of reoffending. Guests at The Clink restaurants have to present identity documents and leave their keys, cash and phones with security before entering the prison. They are encouraged to talk to the prisoners. The Clink now runs 11 training projects: four restaurants, two market gardens, three kitchens, one events catering business and one café. Edwina also founded One Small Thing, which addresses mental health issues of women prisoners.

↳ Annys Darkwa was a prisoner who on her release had nowhere to go. With just a mobile phone and from the back of her car, she started to contact landlords to try to persuade them to make rooms available for women like her leaving prison. From this small beginning, Vision Housing was created as a specialist housing agency providing private-sector accommodation to ex-prisoners, run largely by ex-prisoners. It merged with the Forward Trust in 2017.

↳ James Greenshields created Radio Wanno as a prison-based radio station largely run by the prisoners themselves inside Wandsworth Prison, helping prisoners acquire media skills and gain accreditation which might help them with employment in music or media after leaving prison. Radio Wanno was welcomed by prison staff as it also enables them to communicate more effectively with the prisoners. As half of all prisoners are at, or below, the reading age of an 11-year-old, Radio Wanno also encourages prisoners back into mainstream education.

↳ Alex Redston and Kieran Ball founded Prison Voicemail to facilitate communication between prisoners and their families in an environment where mobile phones are not permitted. Prison Voicemail is available in over 85 per cent of prisons in England and Wales and has helped over 10,000 families to stay connected. Independent research has shown a significant positive impact for both families and prisoners on their health and wellbeing, their relationships and their ability to resolve practical issues. Sixty-three per cent said that access to Prison Voicemail had helped them to behave better in prison, which is also a factor for earlier release.

↳ Alexander McLean founded the African Prisons Project (now known as Justice Defenders) to help improve conditions for prisoners in Africa by establishing prison clinics and education programmes. After 10 years, in 2017 the focus shifted from making prison better towards providing access to justice. Alexander has said: 'I'm massively inspired by the prisoners and prison officers we work with, but especially by the prisoners. They may be living in a cell that they share with eight other people. They may not have a bed. Or a proper toilet. They may not get to see their children more than once a year. But if they are still able to be kind, to offer hospitality and to study, even when it has to be by torchlight, what does this mean for me in terms of the courage I might have, or the compassion I can offer others?'

↳ Natasha Porter developed the idea of Unlocked Graduates while working on a review into prison education. Unlocked Graduates is a sort of Teach First for prisons. It offers graduates the opportunity of spending two years working as frontline prison officers and challenges them to come up with new ideas for improving the way prisons are run.

↳ Billy Bragg, UK singer/songwriter, created Jail Guitar Doors, named after a Clash song, to provide instruments to those using music to rehabilitate prisoners. Bragg said: 'In early 2007, I was looking to do something positive to mark the fifth anniversary of the death of Joe Strummer when I received a request from a local jail. Malcolm Dudley, a drug and alcohol counsellor at nearby Guys Marsh prison in Dorset, was utilising his skills as a musician to set up a guitar class as a means of engaging prisoners in the process of rehabilitation. What was holding him back was the lack of available instruments.'

↳ Ben Wintour and Pia Fontes wanted to do something about knife crime in London. They discovered that London's police were removing one tonne of knives off the streets each month. Could this metal be melted down and recycled into something that gave young people confidence and a sense of purpose? Calisthenics uses fixed bars plus your own bodyweight for exercise and is widely used in prisons. Ben and Pia decided to put calisthenics equipment made from metal recycled from confiscated knives in public parks. In 2018, Steel Warriors built their first gym and have since added three more. This is a new approach to 'swords into ploughshares'!

↳ Anthony Ray Hinton is an African-American wrongly convicted in 1985 of murdering two fast-food restaurant managers in Birmingham, Alabama. He was sentenced to death and held on death row for 28 years. He was released after Equal Justice Initiative lawyers engaged three top firearms experts who testified that Hinton's revolver could not be matched to crime scene evidence. While in prison, Hinton got permission from the governor to start a Death Row Book Club to bring books, reading and hope to prisoners. It proved so successful that the governor had to shut it down due to lack of sufficient space. Read Hinton's story in *The Sun Does Shine*.

'The question we need to ask about the death penalty in America is not whether someone deserves to die for a crime. The question is whether we deserve to kill.'

– Equal Justice Initiative

The **Death Penalty Information Center** facilitates informed discussion on the death penalty. It publishes reports on issues such as arbitrariness, costs, innocence and race. It compiles the Innocence Database, which shows 1,845 exonerations of death row prisoners in the USA since 1973.

DO THIS:

These are some of the worst prisons in the world:

↳ Diyarbakir Prison, Turkey

↳ La Sabaneta, Venezuela

↳ ADX Supermax Prison, USA

↳ Tadmor Military Prison, Syria

↳ Carandiru Penitentiary, Brazil

↳ Camp 22, North Korea

↳ Bang Kwang Central Prison, Thailand

↳ Gitamara Central Prison, Rwanda

↳ San Juan di Lurigancho, Peru

↳ Gldani Prison, Georgia

↳ Nairobi Prison, Kenya

↳ Butyrka Prison, Russia

This selection is taken from several sources. Google 'Worst Prisons in the World' to find more; then visit them virtually to get a sense of what life is like for imprisoned people in each of them.

A world
of terror

32

↳

The impact of terrorism

The worst affected countries on the Global
Terrorism Index

1 Iraq 9.746

2 Afghanistan 9.391

3 Nigeria 8.660

4 Syria 8.315

5 Pakistan 8181

6 Somalia 8.020

7 India 7.568

8 Yemen 7.534

9 Egypt 7.345

10 Philippines 7.181

11 DR Congo 7.055

12 Turkey 7.036

13 Libya 6.987

14 South Sudan 6.756

15 Central African
Republic 6.719

16 Cameroon 6.615

17 Thailand 6.252

18 Sudan 6.178

19 Kenya 6.114

20 USA 6.066

21 Ukraine 6.048

22 Mali 6.015

23 Niger 6.004

The figures are from the 2018 Global Terrorism Index published by the Institute of
Economics and Peace, which ranks the impact of terrorism in countries. The Global
Terrorism Index is derived from the Global Terrorism Database, which includes data
from 170,000 terrorist incidents around the world. The index scores each country
on a scale from 0 to 10, where 0 represents no impact at all from terrorism and 10
represents the highest measurable impact of terrorism. A score of 6 or above is 'high'
and of 8 or above 'very high'. The database has been developed by the National
Consortium for the Study of Terrorism and the Responses to Terrorism (START) led by
the University of Maryland. START publishes an annual overview of global terrorism.

Selected other countries: UK (ranked 28 at 5.610), France (5.475), Palestine (5.330), Russia (5.230), China (5.108), Israel (4.578), Iran (4.339). Amongst the lowest-scoring countries with no perceptible impact were Belarus, Cuba, Portugal, North Korea and Singapore.

Terrorism in the world today

In 2019, there were nearly 8,500 terrorist attacks around the world, killing more than 20,300 people, including 14,800 victims and 5,460 perpetrators. The number of deaths from terrorism has been declining since it peaked in 2014. The countries with the highest number of deaths were Afghanistan (8,249), Nigeria (1,718), Yemen (1,219), Syria (1,102), Somalia (860) and Iraq (798). START highlights these key points in its overview for 2019:

↳ Global trends are heavily impacted by terrorism in Iraq, which suffered more terrorist attacks than any other country from 2013 to 2017. The number of attacks decreased 53 per cent between 2018 and 2019, but the rate of decline seems to be slowing.

↳ While Islamic State violence declined in Iraq, the group's influence continues to expand geographically. Attacks carried out by core operatives, affiliated organisations and unaffiliated individuals indicating their allegiance took place in 31 countries.

↳ Mass-casualty terrorist attacks remained relatively rare in Western Europe in 2019. Out of 191 terrorist attacks, there were 9 attacks in which at least four people were injured or killed, including 4 in France and 3 in the UK.

Terrorism in context

The first issue is to define what constitutes a terrorist incident. For the Global Terrorism Database, in order to be included as an incident, the act has to be 'an intentional act of violence or threat of violence by a non-state actor'. An incident has to meet these three criteria to be counted as an act of terrorism:

1   It must be intentional, the result of a conscious calculation by its perpetrator.

2   It must entail some level of violence or a threat of violence, including damage or the threat of damage to property as well as violence against people.

3   The perpetrators must be sub-national actors. State-organised terrorism is a completely separate issue.

And in addition, two of the following three criteria also need to be met:

↳ The incident was aimed at attaining a political, economic, religious or social goal.

↳ The incident included evidence of an intention to coerce, intimidate or convey some other message to a larger audience, not just to the immediate victims.

↳ The incident falls outside what is generally accepted and acceptable behaviour under international law.

The second issue is our perception of terrorism. Is it our fear of terrorism and of being caught up in a terrorist incident that is the problem, or is terrorism itself a major threat to our safety and security? Terrorism needs to be put into context:

↳ Terrorism today is killing an average of 21,000 people a year worldwide. Over the past decade, deaths have ranged from a low of 8,000 in 2010 to a high of 44,000 in 2014. In 2017, 55,945,000 in the world died, with just 26,445 killed in terrorist incidents. Terrorism is causing only 0.047 per cent of global deaths.

↳ Terrorism is quite geographically focused, with 95 per cent of deaths in the Middle East, South Asia and North and Central Africa. In most countries, the death rate will be less than 0.01 per cent.

↳ Major terrorism incidents such as the 9/11 Al Qaeda attack on the USA in 2001 or the Easter bombings in Colombo, Sri Lanka, in 2019 tend to increase public fear. In many countries, more than half the population expresses fear of becoming a victim.

Deaths from terrorism are trivial when compared with other threats we face in our lives. For example, each year, 1.35 million people are killed in road accidents, more than half are pedestrians, motorcyclists and cyclists, who are most vulnerable to buses, cars and lorries. Crossing a road or cycling through the city, you are 30 times more likely to be killed in a traffic accident than by a terrorist. Like terrorism, road deaths are pretty random. One might even conclude that traffic is the world's biggest terrorist!

Who are the terrorists?

The most active terrorist groups in 2019 based on number of terrorist attacks were:

The Taliban: 1,375 incidents (Afghanistan)

The Islamic Emirate of Afghanistan, a Sunni fundamentalist political movement and military organisation which seized power and ran most of Afghanistan from 1996 to 2001, imposing strict sharia law over the people, including such things as oppression of women, ending girls' education and banning music. They were ousted from government by the US-led invasion in 2001 but in 2021 again seized control of the country. They have also spread their ideology to Pakistan. Their leader and figurehead, Mullah Omar, died of TB in 2013.

Houthi Movement, Ansar Allah: 579 incidents (Yemen)

A movement which emerged as opposition to the Yemeni government, its corruption and its close ties with Saudi Arabia and the USA. Their slogan is 'God is great, death to the US, death to Israel, curse the Jews, and victory for Islam'. They are supported by Iran in the civil war they initiated in Yemen against government forces backed by Saudi Arabia, which has been ongoing since 2015.

Islamic State of Iraq and Levant (ISIL): 461 incidents (Iraq and Syria)

Also known as ISIS, Islamic State and Daesh, the movement aims to create a caliphate in the Middle East as a base for exercising religious, political and military authority over Muslims worldwide. ISIL seized power over large parts of Iraq in 2014 in the face of a weak government and its terrified soldiers, and extended into parts of Syria in 2015. ISIL attracted large numbers of volunteers from all over the world, inspired by its dream of a caliphate. In 2019, it was removed with help from the West in Iraq and from the Syrian forces in Syria. ISIL became known for its brutality and beheadings, and also for its treatment of the Yazidis, killing the men and forcing the women into sexual slavery. It propagated its ideology expertly through social media. The big fear is that now it has no territory, its adherents will disperse around the world and create splinter movements or align with other terrorist organisations. Its founder and inspirer, Abu Bakr Al-Baghdadi, exploded a suicide vest during a US raid to capture him in 2019.

Boko Haram: 348 incidents (Nigeria)

The Islamic State in West Africa, with a main aim of 'the purification of Islam in northern Nigeria', has extended its operations into Chad, Niger and northern Cameroon. The current insurgency, started in 2009, has led to the displacement of 2.3 million people and it is destabilising a large swathe of West and Central Africa.

Al Shabaab: 330 incidents (Somalia)

'The Movement of Striving Youth' is a terrorist jihadist fundamentalist group originating in Somalia and now active across East Africa. It emerged as the armed wing of the Islamic Courts, which effectively ran large parts of Somalia in the 2000s. Since then, it has consolidated its presence in rural areas, waging war against 'the enemies of Islam' and the government of Somalia and the African Union mission to Somalia. It is linked to Al Qaeda.

Naxalites: 238 incidents (India)

A movement inspired by the Communist Party of India (Maoist), active across a wide swathe of central India, it started as an armed struggle to redistribute land to the landless and to seek social justice for tribal populations.

New People's Army: 192 incidents (Philippines)

This is the armed wing of the Communist Party of the Philippines, based primarily in the countryside, with the aim of consolidating political power from what it sees as the present 'bourgeois reactionary puppet government' and to aid the 'people's democratic revolution'.

Communist Party of Nepal: 134 incidents (Nepal)

Also known as Biplav, the CPN led by Netra Bikram Chand split from the Maoists in 2015 and continues its insurgency domestically with IEDs, hoax IEDs and arson attacks.

Fulani Extremists: 118 incidents (West Africa)

An ethnic conflict with other neighbouring groups mainly fighting for the Fulani's access to land and resources. It is not a terrorist group as such, as it is not a group and there are no leaders. But there is a climate of violence which is perpetrated as individual acts. Mostly active in Nigeria, but also in neighbouring Mali, DR Congo and Central African Republic.

One month of terrorism

'Lots of people around the world live with the constant threat of terror. The brunt is largely borne by people outside the West. We wanted our readers to understand what is happening worldwide day by day for one whole month.'

To capture the toll of terror, the *Los Angeles Times* tracked every act of terrorism causing a fatality around the world throughout April 2016. In that one month, terror struck 180 times, killing 858 people and wounding 1,385 people. At least one person died each day, and the deadliest day was 19 April, with attacks in six countries. Every act of terror, whether it is a bombing, a shooting or a stabbing, whether it claims a single life or results in many deaths represents a tragedy. Families are devastated for no obvious political gain and the deaths often are unknown and unacknowledged. The *LA Times* website allows you to explore each act of terror for this one month.

Two terrorist acts that changed the world

Archduke Franz Ferdinand, heir to the Austro-Hungarian throne, and his wife, Sophie, were assassinated on 28 June 1914 in Sarajevo when Gavrilo Princip shot them at point-blank range as they were being driven to the hospital to visit victims of an assassination attempt earlier that day. Princip was part of

Photo: Julien Maculan

a movement called 'Young Bosnia', whose objective was to break from Austro-Hungary and join with the South Slav provinces and be combined into Yugoslavia. This assassination of two individuals led directly to the outbreak of the First World War, which lasted four years with an estimated 15–19 million deaths. From 1992–1995, Bosnia was involved in an ethnic war between Croats, Serbs and Bosniaks, as Yugoslavia splintered into five separate states.

On 11 September 2001, four aeroplanes took off and were hijacked by members of Al Qaeda. Two flew into the twin 110-storey towers of the World Trade Center in New York, causing both and a nearby building to collapse; one was flown into the Pentagon, seat of the US military command; a fourth was bound for Washington, probably the White House, but failed to reach its target when its passengers thwarted the hijackers. The eleventh of September is written as 9/11, and 911 is the emergency telephone number used across the USA. This was not a coincidence in what was a meticulously planned 'spectacular', killing 2,977 people and injuring over 25,000. 3,051 children lost a parent, including over 100 unborn at the time of the incident. Family members of victims got together to found Tuesday's Children to give practical and emotional support to these children and their families; this organisation has since expanded its mission to support the victims of other terrorist incidents. 9/11 has had a profound impact on the world. It led to the 'War on Terror' and to the invasions of Afghanistan and Iraq, to the emergence of Al Qaeda as a global terrorist force to be reckoned with, inspiring Jihadism around the world and much of today's terror.

Do we remember?

Today's terrorism is primarily fuelled by Islamism or religious, ethnic or social divides within a population. But what about yesterday's? Do we even remember the terrorism in the second half of the twentieth century. These groups were active in Europe and the Middle East, perpetrating many acts of terror including bombings and hijackings:

↳ The Republican movement in Northern Ireland. Factions perpetrated terror across the UK (the Real IRA, the Provisional IRA, the Irish National Liberation Army), and against the opposing Ulster Volunteer Force. The 1999 Good Friday Agreement ended 'The Troubles'.

↳ ETA, which stands for Euskadi Ta Askatasuna (Basque Homeland and Liberty), was the Basque separatist movement in Spain, which ceased operations in 2011 and dissolved in 2018.

↳ The Red Army Faction, or Baader-Meinhof Group, was a far-left urban guerrilla group operating mainly in West Germany involved in bombings, assassinations, kidnappings, bank robberies and shoot-outs with police over three decades. It dissolved in 1998.

↳ Black September, a pro-Palestine group, was responsible for hijackings, the Munich Olympics massacre in 1972 and the assassination of the prime minister of Jordan in 1971.

↳ The Abu Nidal Organization split from
Yasser Arafat's PLO in 1974, carrying
out attacks against the PLO as well
as against pro-Israel targets. Other
Palestinian groups included the Popular
Front for the Liberation of Palestine and
the Palestine Liberation Front.

DO THIS:

The International Centre for Counter-
Terrorism has created Flashpoints, a game
for exploring issues of terrorism and how
best to respond: icct.nl/flashpoints-game.

And if your suspicions are aroused for any
reason, this is the official UK government
advice on what to do.
https://act.campaign.gov.uk.

LISTEN TO THIS:

The Death of Klinghoffer, an opera by John
Adams, a fictionalised telling of the *Achille
Lauro* incident of 1985, where Palestinian
terrorists boarded an Italian cruise ship,
held its passengers and crew hostage, and
killed an elderly, Jewish, wheelchair-bound
American named Leon Klinghoffer.

A world
at war

33

Wars around the world

The biggest wars in 2020 and number of deaths

		In 2020	total to date
1	Mexican drug war	34,512	410,373
2	Afghanistan	20,836	2,084,468
3	Yemen	19,787	233,000
4	Syria	8,205	606,000
5	Nagorno-Karabakh	7,687	49,000
6	Maghreb insurgency	7,047	25,000
7	Tigray	4,269	52,000

Wikipedia lists major and minor conflicts in 46 countries and regions around the world with estimated conflict deaths of 100 and above. Some are civil wars and struggles for independence; some involve tribal or ethnic rivalry; some are drug wars; some are fights between rival warlords for control over resources and power; some involve armed intervention by foreign powers; some are proxy wars; and some are the tail ends of conflicts that have persisted over decades.

All involve destruction and destabilisation of society, significant loss of life, and population movements as enemies and ordinary people try to find somewhere safer to live. The table shows the combat deaths for the larger conflicts in 2020, together with the total number of deaths so far from their inception. Where the estimated number is given as a range, the larger figure is shown here. As this book was going to press (Spring 2022), war was raging in Ukraine, which will feature high on the 2022 list.

Definition of war

A simple dictionary definition of war is 'an armed conflict between nations or between parties within a nation or a region'. The dividing line between war and terrorism may be less easy to define; terrorism will largely consist of discrete acts of killing or abduction or destruction carried out by individuals or groups from time to time, whereas war is an ongoing state of conflict.

The cost of war is enormous. Not just in terms of the amounts spent on armies and armaments but also the destruction caused, the economic activity disrupted, the people made homeless, the despair created. The UN Office for the Coordination of Humanitarian Affairs estimated the cost of war at $14.3 trillion for 2016, which was 12.6 per cent of global GDP. Military spending ($5.6 trillion) and internal security ($4.9 trillion) accounted for more than two-thirds of this.

The UN target for international aid by rich countries is 0.7 per cent of gross national income. If every country achieved this (and most don't get anywhere near), this would amount to only $800 billion in aid annually – which is less than one seventeenth of the cost of war. What humanity is spending on destruction and misery is a huge sum which could much better be spent on bringing health, education, wellbeing and opportunity to everybody on the planet in the pursuit of the best of all possible worlds.

Costa Rica has had no army since 1949; in 1983, it proclaimed its permanent unarmed neutrality. Some of the functions normally carried out by the military are carried out by civilians. The savings from not having a defence budget have been invested in education, environmental protection, green energy and people's wellbeing. Costa Rica has been ranked first on the Happy Planet Index three times in the past 12 years. Panama and Iceland also have no army.

Watch this: *For Sama* is a powerful film made by a couple, a doctor and a journalist, in Aleppo in Northern Syria. It is an account of life in a city torn apart by war and continuing bombardment. It is an intimate journey into the female experience of war, a love letter from a young mother to her daughter. It tells the story of Waad al-Kateab's life through five years of the uprising in Aleppo as she falls in love, gets married and gives birth to Sama, while cataclysmic conflict rages around her.

No more war?

The First World War was mean to be a 'war to end wars'. Author H G Wells said: 'This is already the vastest war in history ... this is now a war for peace. It aims straight at disarmament. It aims at a settlement that shall stop this sort of thing for ever ... This, the greatest of all wars, is not just another war, it is the last war!'

The total number of deaths in the First World War amounted to 9.7 million military personnel and 10 million civilians. And it wasn't the last war. The Treaty of Versailles created an impoverished and reduced Germany, which was one of the major factors leading to a second major conflict just 21 years later.

In 1938, the British government was looking to avoid a second war with Germany. Prime Minister Neville Chamberlain's statement on his return from the Munich conference said, 'We regard the agreement … as symbolic of the desire of our two peoples never to go to war with one another again … We are determined to continue our efforts to remove possible sources of difference, and thus … to assure the peace of Europe.' And he commented, 'My good friends, for the second time in our history, a British prime minister has returned from Germany bringing peace with honour. I believe it is peace for our time …' But 11 months later, Britain and Germany were at war again. This time there were 75 million military and civilian deaths, including those dying indirectly from disease, famine and genocide.

Since then, we have had the Korean War; the Cold War, which involved huge expenditures on the military and proxy wars all over the world; the Vietnam War, which showed that technological might could not overcome determined guerrilla resistance; the ongoing Israel–Palestine conflict; successive wars in Afghanistan which continue; the Iran–Iraq War; Islamic State taking over large swathes of Iraq and Syria; the civil war in Syria, which with

Russian help has been continuing since 2011; the proxy war in Yemen with Iran facing off Saudi Arabia; civil war in South Sudan; the war between Armenia and Azerbaijan in Nagorno-Karabakh; drug wars in Colombia and Mexico; and many more conflicts around the world.

'If all the money spent on weapons could be spent on eliminating the causes of discontent, people are not going to risk their lives by going out and killing people.'

– Ben Frerncz, last remaining Nuremburg prosecutor, now aged 102, speaking on the BBC's *HARDtalk* programme in 2017.

New technologies

War is no longer just armies, navies and airforces fighting each other. New technologies are completely changing how wars are being and will be fought.

Drones: We now have controllers at Creech Air Force base in Nevada attacking targets in Syria or Afghanistan with lethal force operated with just a joystick. The use of drones is often presented as a risk-free warfare – no boots on the ground, no coffins coming home. War becomes very much like a video game but with real fatalities and a very real possibility of human error. Killing becomes too easy. Taking out the 'bad guys' seems simpler than understanding the root causes and trying to build peace and prevent war. Many countries now operate armed drones. Find out more at Dronewars.net.

Slaughterbots: These are microdrones directed by artificial intelligence that can be released in swarms, each with lethal force. The USA has the MAST and DCIST microdrone programmes and other countries must also be doing something similar, if it hasn't been disclosed. To try to stop these weapons of the future, sign the petition at autonomousweapons.org.

Cyberwarfare: Increasingly, warfare is being conducted in cyberspace rather than in the physical world. Cyberwarfare uses computer technology to disrupt the activities of a state or organisation, deliberately attacking information systems and machines for strategic or military purposes through implanting viruses or denial of service. A good example of this is Stuxnet, developed by Israel and used to disable Iran's uranium production capability in 2010, which affected 200,000 machines in 14 Iranian facilities.

The Center for Strategic and International Studies records significant cyber incidents. For example, in July 2021, Iran's transport and urbanisation ministry was the victim of a cyberattack that impacted display boards at railway stations throughout the country causing delays and cancellations of hundreds of trains. A phishing campaign was exposed where Chinese state-sponsored hackers targeted oil and natural gas pipeline companies in the USA between 2011 and 2013.

War may have changed from set-piece battles and countries formally declaring themselves at war with one another but our inability to live in peace remains one of the most destructive forces on our planet.

Collecting data

The Armed Conflict Location & Event Data Project (ACLED) aims to 'bring clarity to crisis' by collecting, analysing and mapping data on conflicts all over the world. For example, in one month in 2020, it logged 7,231 events (2,677 battles, 839 riots, 2,161 explosions, 1,554 violence against civilians) with 7,744 fatalities. ACLED summaries the present situation as follows:

'In 2019, the world witnessed a drastic increase in violent disorder that assumed many forms: protests from Lebanon to Hong Kong and Iraq to Chile; geopolitical competition in Yemen and Syria; dominant insurgencies in Somalia and Afghanistan; a cartel-insurgency in Mexico; and a diffuse, adaptable militant threat across the Sahel. Two problems immediately stand out: the world is significantly more violent now than a decade ago, and today's conflict forms are strongly localized – types of violence, agents, targets, and solutions are unique to their local context. This is partially because governments in the world's most violent places are no longer in control of their territories, nor show any interest or ability to resume control through direct or indirect authority. Governments are also much more likely to use violence against their citizens without international reproach. The rise of authoritarianism – and impunity – has generated significant public reaction in the form of mass protest movements, but it has also increased the level of violence imposed upon civilians and political competition.'

ACLED listed '10 conflicts to worry about in 2020', which demonstrate how violent political disorder continues around the world, analysing each in depth:

The Sahel: High risk of conflicts diffusing and infecting neighbours.

Mexico: High risk of cartel 'criminal market' developing into insurgency.

Yemen: High risk of persistent conflict amid shifting frontlines and alliances.

India: At risk of Modi's plans derailing with uncontrollable effects.

Somalia: High risk of Al Shabaab adapting to dominate and isolate a weak government.

Iran: High risk of centre deteriorating amid regime escalation at home and abroad.

Afghanistan: High risk of rising violence targeting civilians.

Ethiopia: At risk of increased fragmentation despite a popular leader.

Lebanon: High risk of protests devolving into organised violence.

United States: Developed, democratic political system at risk of turning violent.

The Iraq Body Count

General Tommy Franks was Commander-in-Chief, US Central Command, leading US and Coalition troops in Afghanistan (2001) and Iraq (2003). In response to a question on collateral deaths, he said, 'We don't do body counts.'

The Iraq Body Count does do body counts. It records military and civilian deaths caused by Coalition and Iraqi government forces, by paramilitary and criminal attacks, and from other violent causes. In February 2020, for example, 147 civilians were killed. On one day, Friday 28 February 2020, one protester was killed in Baghdad by security forces; in Baquba, one farmer was killed by an improvised explosive device and one policeman was killed by a gunman; in Maysan, one child was killed during clashes with government forces; and in Basra, two bodies were found in the street.

The Iraq Body Count information is gleaned from newspaper reports of violent incidents or bodies being found, from hospital and morgue records, from NGO reports and from government records. They have recorded 288,000 military and civilian deaths from 2003 up to the present. Iraq Body Count's overall aim is to give a true picture of the conflict including collateral damage to civilians and society.

Supporting peace-builders

These are some of the initiatives which can be undertaken to encourage and support peace-building by local people in their communities:

↳ Encouraging social activists to engage.

↳ Protecting and promoting human and civil rights.

↳ Fostering community oversight of government institutions.

↳ Developing local peace-building initiatives.

↳ Fostering mutual trust and dialogue within divided societies.

↳ Reducing militaristic and nationalistic attitudes.

↳ Advocating for the victims of conflict.

Peace Direct, founded by Scilla Elworthy, supports peace-builders and peace-building around the world – for example, by encouraging students to discuss non-violence, establishing peace courts for mediation and developing skills for local conflict resolution. These are some of the lessons learned from their work:

1 Wherever there is conflict, you will find people interested in building peace.

2 Women are equally likely as men to become local peace-builders.

3 Locally led peace-building can be developed on a large scale.

4 Building trust between rival groups (whether religious, army versus militia or political factions) is a precondition for peace-building.

5 Even amongst the most implacable state or religious leaders, you will find right-minded people wanting a better society.

6 Early intervention is important – start when conflict is beginning and before it is raging.

Global Peacebuilders, founded in Germany, and Peace Dialogue, founded in Armenia, are two other organisations supporting local peace-building. And these are some Nobel Peace Prize winners from recent years who have sought to end conflict:

↳ 2019, Abiy Ahmed, ending the 20-year stalemate between Ethiopia and Eritrea (but he is now at war with the Tigrayans).

↳ 2016, Juan Manuel Santos, ending Colombia's 50-year-long civil war.

↳ 2008, Martti Ahtisaari, peace for Kosovo.

↳ 1998, John Hume and David Trimble, peace for Northern Ireland.

↳ 1996, Carlos Filipe Ximenes Belo and José Ramos Horta, peace for East Timor.

White poppies

This is the Peace Pledge Union's pledge: 'War is a crime against humanity. I renounce war, and am therefore determined not to support any kind of war. I am also determined to work for the removal of all causes of war.' They invite you to join, to sign this pledge and to wear a white poppy.

In the UK, the red poppy is the symbol of remembrance of the First World War and the dead in all wars. The First World War ended at 11am on 11 November 1918. Every year in many countries, commemorative services are held,

wreaths of red poppies laid on graves and monuments, and many people pin a red poppy to their dress or lapel. The Peace Pledge Union wants people to wear a white poppy instead – to remember victims of war but also to commit to fostering peace and challenging attempts to glamorise or celebrate war. Next Remembrance Day, when most people will be wearing a red poppy, wear a white poppy instead.

Environmental peace-building

Our common dependency on natural resources and a healthy environment can be a starting point for peace-making in conflict regions. Indeed, many conflicts arise over competition for water in areas of short supply – for example, between the Indian states of Karnataka (upstream) and Tamil Nadu (downstream), or Ethiopia (upstream) and Egypt (downstream).

Water in the Jordan River flowing from the Sea of Galilee to the Dead Sea has reduced to a trickle. But there is potentially abundant solar power in Jordan and desalinated water could be piped in from Gaza and Israel (with no pumping needed). Add in the creativity and energies of local people plus the start-up culture of Israel, and cross-border cooperation could transform the region as well as pioneer new approaches and technologies for addressing climate change and bringing water to a thirsty world.

EcoPeace Middle East brings together
environmentalists in Jordan, Palestine and Israel
with the objective of protecting their shared
environment and jointly developing ways of
building a sustainable future for the Jordan valley.
It has offices in Amman, Ramallah and Tel Aviv.
Its success will show that cross-community
cooperation is possible and beneficial to all in an
area of long-standing conflict.

DO THIS:

Find out more about the Nobel Peace Prize and
the prize winners from 1901 to the present day at
nobelprize.org/prizes/peace. Also, take a look at
the Peace Prize offered as a part of the annual Ig
Nobel Awards, which parody the real thing and
celebrate the unusual, honour the imaginative
and spur people's interest: improbable.
com/2021-ceremony/ig-nobel-prizes/.

WATCH THIS:

Watch the short YouTube film *Slaughterbots* –
it will terrify you.

Nuclear weapons

34

The Nuclear Club

Nuclear states in today's world

(Estimated figures from Wikipedia)

The Nuclear Proliferation Treaty has been signed by
191 states who have pledged to prevent the spread
of nuclear weapons and technologies. Signatories
include five nuclear countries: USA, Russia, China,
France and United Kingdom (the 'Big Five'), who
are now tied into an international framework for
controlling the deployment of nuclear weapons.
The three non-signatory nuclear countries are
India, Pakistan and North Korea. These all pose
potential threats – a regional war between India
and Pakistan, or North Korea versus Japan, the
USA and the world. Then there is Iran, which
provided nuclear knowhow to Pakistan and is likely
to become the next nuclear state, along with Israel,
an undeclared but known nuclear power, sworn
enemies in a region of grave political instability.

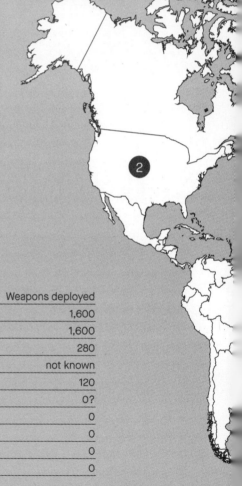

	Total arsenal	Weapons deployed
1 Russia	6,500	1,600
2 USA	6,185	1,600
3 France	300	280
4 China	290	not known
5 United Kingdom	215	120
6 India	145	0?
7 Pakistan	135	0
8 Israel	85	0
9 North Korea	25	0
10 Iran	0	0

Significant dates in nuclear weapons development

A-Bombs and H-Bombs

16 July 1945:
USA tests its first
atom bomb

6 August 1945:
USA drops 'Little
Boy' fission bomb
on Hiroshima

9 August 1945:
USA drops 'Fat Man'
plutonium bomb
on Nagasaki

29 August 1949:
Soviet Union tests
first atom bomb

The Cold War

5 March 1946:
Winston Churchill
delivers his Iron
Curtain speech

24 June 1948:
Blockade of Western
sector of Berlin by
Soviet Union begins

25 June 1950:
Start of Korean War

12 January 1954:
USA articulates a
policy of 'massive
retaliation'

The United States developed the first nuclear weapons during the Second World War in cooperation with the United Kingdom and Canada as part of the Manhattan Project, out of the fear that Nazi Germany would develop a bomb first. The Soviet Union was able to develop its own weapons through the efforts of its scientists aided by espionage. By 1954, weapons equivalence between the USA and the Soviet Union had been reached. Weapons and delivery systems would continue to be developed as the Cold War began to heat up. By 1966, the US nuclear arsenal contained 31,175 warheads, which rose to 70,000 at its peak as compared with the Soviet Union's 45,000.

1 November 1952:
USA tests first
hydrogen bomb
(not deliverable)

12 August 1953:
Soviet Union tests
its first deliverable
hydrogen bomb

1 March 1954:
USA tests its first
deliverable hydrogen
bomb

Nuclear madness

Nuclear weapons were thought of in terms of deterrence, having enough firepower to organise a massive retaliation in response to any attack. When the Soviet Union had achieved a broad nuclear parity with the USA, the Cold War entered a new and less predictable phase, becoming more dangerous and unmanageable than anything the world had faced before. Each side could destroy the other many times over. This led to the emergence of the doctrine of Mutual Assured Destruction (MAD) in the 1960s – the idea that both superpowers possessed such huge nuclear capabilities that an attack and counterattack would mean the annihilation of both. The nearest the world came to actual nuclear conflict was the Cuban Missile Crisis. This started on 16 October 1962 when the USA challenged a Soviet nuclear presence in Cuba. The Soviet Union eventually backed off by removing its missiles from Cuba, with the USA in return removing its nuclear presence in Turkey.

Living in this world of nuclear madness led to the emergence of the very vocal nuclear disarmament movement. Yet, today, even after the collapse of the Soviet Union and despite the existence of test ban treaties, strategic arms limitation agreements and hotlines for defusing crises, nearly 14,000 nuclear weapons remain. The USA and Russia between them have 6,600 megatons; by comparison, the explosive force of the bomb dropped on Hiroshima, which killed an estimated 75,000 people and destroyed an area of 12 square kilometres, was 12 kilotons. The current nuclear arsenal of these two countries is 550,000 times bigger.

'Nuclear madness' is no longer about 'Communism versus Capitalism'. The citizens of South Asia, the Middle East and anyone in the range of North Korea's weaponry are all potential targets. A list of nuclear weapon accidents can be found at atomicarchive.com.

Celebrate two international days

'Nuclear weapons present an unacceptable danger to humanity. The only real way to eliminate the threat of nuclear weapons is to eliminate nuclear weapons.' – Antonio Guterres, UN Secretary-General

Achieving global nuclear disarmament was one of the earliest goals of the United Nations.

Nobel Peace prizes for anti-nuclear activism

1962: Linus Pauling, for campaigning against nuclear testing.

1982: Alfonso Garcia Robles and Alva Myrdal for their efforts in creating the Treaty for the Prohibition of Nuclear Weapons in Latin America and the Caribbean.

1985: International Physicians for the Prevention of Nuclear War 'for authoritative information and by creating an awareness of the catastrophic consequences of atomic warfare'.

1995: Pugwash Conferences on Science and World Affairs and Joseph Rotblat 'for their efforts to diminish the part played by nuclear arms in international politics and, in the longer run, to eliminate such arms'.

It was the subject of the General Assembly's first resolution in 1946, which established the Atomic Energy Commission, with a mandate to make specific proposals for the control of nuclear energy and the elimination of atomic weapons and all other major weapons of mass destruction. In 1959, the General Assembly endorsed the objective of general and complete disarmament. In 1978, the first Special Session of the General Assembly devoted to disarmament further recognised that nuclear disarmament should be the priority objective in the field of disarmament.

Every United Nations Secretary-General has actively promoted this goal.

In December 2009, the UN General Assembly declared 29 August to be the International Day against Nuclear Tests.

In December 2013, the UN General Assembly declared 26 September to be the International Day for the Total Elimination of Nuclear Weapons.

2005: The International Atomic Energy Agency and Mohammed ElBaradei 'for their efforts to prevent nuclear energy from being used for military purposes and to ensure that nuclear energy for peaceful purposes is used in the safest possible way'.

2017: The International Campaign to Abolish Nuclear Weapons: 'for its work to draw attention to the catastrophic humanitarian consequences of any use of nuclear weapons and for its ground-breaking efforts to achieve a treaty-based prohibition of such weapons'. ICAN was launched in 2007 and now has 541 partner organisations in 103 countries.

Find out more about ICAN, the International Campaign to Abolish Nuclear Weapons. 'Nuclear weapons are the most inhumane and indiscriminate weapons ever created. They violate international law, cause severe environmental damage, undermine national and global security, and divert vast public resources away from meeting human needs. They must be eliminated urgently.' Watch the range of videos on the ICAN website; and make a declaration that 'I'm In'.

The anti-nuclear hall of fame

Linus Pauling won two Nobel Prizes – in 1954 for chemistry and in 1962 (awarded in 1963) for peace. As a scientist, he spoke out and wrote against the nuclear arms race. In 1959, he drafted the 'Hiroshima Appeal', the concluding document issued after the fifth World Conference against Atomic and Hydrogen Bombs. He was one of the prime movers who urged the nuclear powers – the USA, the Soviet Union and Great Britain – to conclude a nuclear test ban treaty, which entered into force on 10 October 1963.

Joseph Rotblat won a Nobel Prize for co-founding (with Bertrand Russell and others) the Pugwash Conferences on Science and World Affairs, first held in 1957 in Nova Scotia, following on from the Russell–Einstein manifesto. This manifesto called on scientists to assemble to assess the dangers posed to the survival of humanity by weapons of mass destruction. The emphasis was on being politically neutral and including all people and governments, with the idea of 'Remember your humanity and forget the rest'. Pugwash continues to bring together scholars and public figures to work toward reducing the danger of armed conflict and to seek solutions to global security threats. There is now also an International Student/Young Pugwash organisation.

Canon John Collins was an Anglican priest working at St Paul's Cathedral, London. He believed in linking his religious beliefs with world affairs and was an active leader of several radical movements. In 1951, he co-founded War on Want, a non-profit addressing global poverty. In 1956, he persuaded Christian Action to raise funds for the defence of anti-apartheid activists at the treason trials in South Africa. In 1958, he co-founded the Campaign for Nuclear Disarmament. The starting point for CND was an article written by writer J B Priestley for the *New Statesman* calling for unilateral disarmament. Readers responded to such an extent that the editor suggested that a mass movement against nuclear weapons was needed. CND mobilised a whole generation to protest against nuclear weapons, attracting tens of thousands. Its starting point was a march to Aldermaston in Berkshire, site of the Atomic Weapons Research Establishment, from central London over the Easter long weekend that year (Good Friday to Easter Monday).

Bertrand Russell was an internationally acclaimed philosopher. As well as his involvement with Pugwash, he was a co-founder and a public face of The Committee of 100, which was set up in 1960 with a hundred public signatories to use more radical methods of non-violent resistance and civil disobedience to promote nuclear disarmament.

Bertrand Russell was clear on how nuclear war can be avoided: 'By getting rid of all nuclear weapons.' He said: 'You may reasonably expect a man to walk a tightrope safely for ten minutes; it would be unreasonable to do so without accident for two hundred years.' We are currently at over seven decades. Our luck may run out, and any security strategy based on luck is not sensible.

He also said: 'There is a very widespread feeling that however bad [government] policies may be, there is nothing that private people can do about it. This is a complete mistake. If all those who disapprove of government policy were to join massive demonstrations of civil disobedience they could render government folly impossible and compel the so-called statesmen to acquiesce in measures that would make human survival possible. Such a vast movement, inspired by outraged public opinion is possible, perhaps it is imminent. If you join it you will be doing something important to preserve your family, compatriots and the world.'

The Greenham Women: The Greenham Common Women's Peace Camp was a series of protest camps established at RAF Greenham Common.

The camp began in September 1981 after a Welsh group, Women for Life on Earth, arrived to protest the government's decision to allow a nuclear-armed cruise missiles facility there. The protest itself was not sufficient to get the attention needed for the missiles to be removed. Women camped at the site to continue their protest. The camp was active for 19 years, only disbanding in 2000. The first blockade of the base occurred in March 1982 with 250 women protesting, when 34 arrests were made.

Jean Gump was a 58-year-old grandmother from Chicago who believed that nuclear missiles were a threat to the very existence of the world ... but also to her world and to the futures of her 12 children and her two grandchildren. The issue was so important to her that she decided that she just had to do something. In 1988, accompanied by two friends, she entered a Minuteman missile silo; she hung two banners on the chainlink fence – one a photo-collage of her children, the other a quotation adapted from the Bible, 'Swords into plowshares – an act of healing'. Then she entered the missile site and used her own blood mixed with the blood of her two friends to paint the words 'Disarm and Live' on the missile hatch. For doing this, Jean was arrested and sentenced to 8 years' imprisonment. Jean's belief was so strong that she felt she had to take a stand. She felt this was a small price to pay for the future of humanity ... and for the futures of her grandchildren.

Three eminent scientists, one eminent philosopher and a grandma ... who would you add to this anti-nuclear hall of fame?

The CND symbol

The CND symbol is one of the most widely known symbols in the world and stands for peace. It was designed in 1958 by Gerald Holtom as artwork to be used on the first Aldermaston March, when protesters walked from London to the nuclear weapons establishment at Aldermaston. The first badges were fired pottery using white clay with the symbol painted black. They were accompanied by a note explaining that in the event of a nuclear war, they would be among the few human artefacts to survive.

DO THIS:

Nuclear weapons have been used in war just twice, both by the USA against Japan to end the Second World War. Take a virtual tour of Hiroshima where the first bomb was dropped and experience the devastation of the city and people's lives at: hiroshimaforpeace.com/en/ virtualtourhiroshima.

LISTEN TO THESE:

Two songs about war and peace, both available on YouTube:

War: 'We All Will Go Together When We Go' by mathematician and satirist Tom Lehrer. A cheerful, upbeat tune about the destruction of the human race, it includes the lyrics 'Universal bereavement … An inspiring achievement.'

Peace: 'Give Peace a Chance' by John Lennon. This song was his first solo single, issued in 1969 while he was still a Beatle, and which became an anthem of the anti-war movement during the 1970s.

Inequality in
the world

Where is it best to be?

The most developed and least developed countries

The top 8 countries

	Life expectancy	Schooling	Income
1 Norway	82.4	12.9	$66,494
2 Ireland	82.3	12.7	$68,371
2 Switzerland	83.8	13.4	$69,394
4 Hong Kong	84.9	12.3	$62,985
4 Iceland	83.0	12.8	$54,682
6 Germany	81.3	14.2	$55,314
7 Sweden	82.8	12.5	$54,508
8 Australia	83.4	12.7	$48,085

The bottom 8 countries

	Life expectancy	Schooling	Income
189 Niger	62.4	2.1	$1,201
188 Central African Republic	53.3	4.3	$993
187 Chad	54.2	2.5	$1,555
186 South Sudan	57.9	4.8	$2,003
185 Burundi	61.6	3.3	$754
184 Mali	59.3	2.4	$2,269
182= Burkina Faso	61.2	1.6	$1,705
182= Sierra Leone	54.7	3.7	$1,668

Every year the UN Development Programme prepares a Human Development Index ranking countries around the world for wealth and wellbeing according to a number of indicators. The eight top and eight bottom ranked of the 189 countries for 2020 are listed above, together with figures for average life expectancy, years of schooling and per capita gross national income (in US$). The USA is ranked seventeenth and the UK is at 13 (the good news for the UK is that life expectancy at birth is 2.2 years longer at 81.3 years than for the USA, the bad news is that per capita gross national income is $23,127 lower at $40,799); China is at number 85 on the list and India at 131.

Inequality and the accident of birth

We live in a world that is completely unequal. Where we are born has and continues to have a huge impact on our life chances. In Niger we would expect to live to 62, have two years of schooling and an average yearly income (per person) of just $912. In Norway, we would expect to live for more than 20 years longer, have 10 years more schooling and benefit from an income nearly 75 times larger. In Niger, day-to-day life would be more precarious, as we would face disease, malnutrition, water scarcity, under- and unemployment, and much more.

Even within the rich countries, there is large and growing inequality of both incomes and wealth as in recent years the rich have been getting richer and the poor getting poorer. The World Inequality Report analyses the distribution of wealth in countries and regions around the world. The figures below show the percentage share of the total wealth of the country or region owned by the richest 10 per cent of population (the higher the figure, the more unequal the society; figures for the top 1 per cent would be even more striking):

Middle East	61 per cent
India	55 per cent
Brazil	55 per cent
Sub-Saharan Africa	54 per cent
USA/Canada	47 per cent
Russia	46 per cent
China	41 per cent
Europe	37 per cent

The billionaires club

The top 15 billionaires in the world in $billion

Jeff Bezos, Amazon (retail)	$194
Elon Musk, Tesla (auto)	$191
Bernard Arnault, LVMH (luxury goods)	$179
Bill Gates, Microsoft (tech)	$130
Mark Zuckerberg, Meta (tech)	$127
Larry Page, Alphabet/Google (tech)	$119
Sergey Brin, Alphabet/Google (tech)	$115
Larry Ellison, Oracle (tech)	$114
Warren Buffett, Berkshire Hathaway (investment)	$99
Steve Ballmer, Microsoft (tech)	$94

Mukesh Ambani, Reliance Industries (conglomerate)	$92
Françoise Bettencourt Meyers, L'Oreal (cosmetics)	$88
Amancio Ortega, Zara (retail fashion)	$86
Carlos Slim, America Movil (telecoms)	$77
Gautam Adani, Adani Group (infrastructure)	$71

Many of these are company founders well known to the world who have become mega-rich in the past 20 years. Some, like Bill Gates, Warren Buffett and Mark Zuckerberg, have pledged to give away most of their wealth during their lifetime (into foundations that they and their families control). Personal circumstances also change. Jeff Bezos's and Bill Gates's divorce settlements will have affected their personal wealth. Koch Industries is the largest privately held company in the world, built up jointly by brothers Charles and David (who died in 2019); Charles Koch is worth $49 billion.

(From The Real-Time Billionaires List and other sources, mostly for 2020)

The Russian oligarchs who amassed great wealth through the privatisations of state enterprises include Leonid Mikhelson (Novatek, gas), who is worth $24 billion. Vladimir Putin has personal wealth estimated at between $150,000 (the official figure)

and $200 billion (which would make him the richest person in the world).

In China, Ma Huateng, founder of Tencent Holdings (IT), is worth $44.9 billion. Tencent is the developer of WeChat, an instant messaging, social media and mobile payment 'super app' that dominates in China. Jack Ma, the founder of Alibaba (e-commerce), is worth $38.9 billion. Li Ka-shing, who heads CK Hutchison Holdings (ports and shipping), is Hong Kong's richest person with a net worth of $31 billion.

The Middle East has large ruling families with wealth spread amongst many family members. The region's top billionaires are the Al-Juffali family (Saudi Arabia, conglomerate), worth $19.8 billion, and Al-Waleed Bin Talal (also Saudi Arabia, investments), worth $19.3 billion.

The top female billionaires are Françoise Bettencourt Meyers, inheritor of the L'Oreal cosmetics empire (France), worth $49.3 billion; Alice Walton, widow of the Walmart founder (USA), worth $44.4 billion; and Mackenzie Bezos, divorced wife of the Amazon founder (USA), worth $38 billion.

The figures shown here and the ranking in any table will change as share prices and the valuation of their businesses go up or down.

The impact of inequality

Inequality has an adverse effect on people, society and the economy. It reduces economic activity. When Henry Ford was asked why he paid his workers what was then a high wage, he said that he wanted them to able to afford to buy the cars that they were making. This made economic sense, as it would stimulate consumer demand, which would also directly benefit the factory owners.

High levels of income inequality have been linked to all of these:

↳ Economic instability, financial crisis, debt and inflation.

↳ Underachievement in education, including literacy and STEM skills.

↳ Lower social mobility (it is harder to escape poverty).

↳ Increased crime and violence.

↳ More chronic health problems and mental health issues.

↳ Higher levels of obesity.

↳ Higher infant mortality.

↳ Lower civic participation and engagement.

↳ More crime and violence.

The irony is that the world has sufficient resources for everybody to enjoy a good life, yet the unequal distribution of these resources (in terms of both wealth and income) is depriving billions of an adequate living standard. From the Mumbai slums built next to some of the most expensive real estate in the world, to homeless people sleeping near to the Gates Foundation, inequality today is starkly visible.

Just compare this. A Mumbai pavement dweller with a whole family crammed into a single room within sight of the residence of the super-rich Ambani family – which is a $2 billion, 27-storey, 40,000sqm building complete with a garage for 168 cars, three helipads, a private cinema, its own temple and much else. Ratan Tata, former chairman of Tata Industries, one of India's largest business empires, is quoted as saying: 'The person who lives in there should be concerned about what he sees around him and asking can he make a difference. If he is not, then it's sad because this country needs people to allocate some of their enormous wealth to finding ways of mitigating the hardship that people have.'

READ THIS:

Capital in the Twenty-First Century by Thomas Piketty

CAPITAL
in the Twenty-First Century

THOMAS
PIKETTY

These organisations are trying to advocate solutions to inequality:

In the UK: The Equality Trust

In the USA: The World Inequality Lab and the World Inequality Database:

The World Inequality Lab aims to promote research on global inequality and the underlying reasons behind it. It maintains the World Inequality Database and produces reports and discussion papers.

Wealth in the world's wealthiest country

In recent years in the USA, the super-rich have grown much richer. Today, the ten wealthiest US citizens are together worth $1.254,000,000,000 (more than one and a quarter trillion dollars). At the same time, the majority of the population has become less well-off, many struggling to earn enough and needing more than one job; they are economically insecure with little or even negative savings to see them through a difficult patch (such as the Covid-19 lockdown). The average American family saw its wealth fall by 3 per cent between 1983 and 2016 (in real terms, allowing for inflation), while the USA itself was getting richer. Over the same period, the wealth of the richest rose by 133 per cent.

Some groups have it worse than others. Over this same period, Black families have fared far worse than white families. These are the median levels of wealth (ownership of assets and savings) for an average family for the main ethnic groups in the USA:

	In 2016	In 1983
All USA	**$81,704**	**$84,111**
White	$146,984	$110,160
Black	$3,557	$7,323
Latino	$6,591	$4,289

Within these averages, 37 per cent of Black families had zero or negative wealth as compared with 32.8 per cent for Latinos and 15.5 per cent for whites. Between 1983 and 2016, the median Black family saw their wealth drop by more than half after adjusting for inflation. Over the same period, the number of households with $10 million or more rose by 856 per cent. If this trajectory continues, by 2050 the median white family will have $174,000 of wealth, while for Latinos it will be $8,600 and for Blacks just $600.

37 per cent of Black families had zero or negative wealth as compared with 32.8 per cent for Latinos and 15.5 per cent for whites.

This puts Black Lives Matter in a different perspective. It is not just about police brutality and institutionalised racism, it is the fact that Black people are getting poorer and what wealth they have is vanishing fast. Inequality. org tracks inequality in the USA.

What can the very rich do?

'If we don't do something to fix the glaring inequities in this economy, the pitchforks are going to come for us. No society can sustain this kind of rising inequality ... You show me a highly unequal society, and I will show you a police state. Or an uprising. There are no counterexamples. None. It's not if, it's when.'

– Nick Hanauer, billionaire. You can watch his TED Talk, 'The Dirty Secret of Capitalism – and a New Way Forward', on YouTube.

Then the pitchforks did come. On the Fourth of July weekend 2020, around 200 protesters converged on the New York Hamptons armed with plastic pitchforks to protest inequality and how it had been increasing as a result of Covid-19. 'Tax the rich, not the poor!' they chanted outside the 22,000-square-foot, $20 million mansion of former New York City mayor and presidential candidate Michael Bloomberg. But there are things that the super-rich can do:

Giving while living: Chuck Feeney made his fortune from the DFS chain of airport duty-free shops. He set up Atlantic Philanthropies in 1982 and in 1984 he transferred his entire stake in his company, a 38.75 per cent shareholding, to the foundation. His philanthropy remained anonymous until 1997. The foundation supported ageing, children and youth, population and health, peace and reconciliation, and human rights, with significant support in Ireland, where his family had come from. He aimed to spend out the endowment by 2020 and to have distributed $7.5 billion in grants. The foundation made several major grants just before it closed, including $177 million to UC San Francisco and Trinity College, Dublin, to establish the Global Brain Health Institute, which will address the increasing incidence of dementia in society.

Thomas White inherited a construction company. He resolved to die as close to penniless as possible. He gave away more than $75 million to various philanthropic causes during his lifetime, including $20 million to

Partners in Health, which catapulted this into becoming a major force for global health. He also carried a wad of banknotes in his pocket to give to random strangers.

Signing the Giving Pledge: Influenced in part by what Chuck Feeney had done, Bill Gates and Warren Buffett set up the Giving Pledge to encourage the super-wealthy to give away their fortunes. Initially, 40 of the USA's wealthiest people joined, committing to give away the majority of their wealth to address some of society's most pressing problems. The hope is that many will give almost all their wealth and as much as possible during their lifetimes. Doing this would not only enable today's problems to be dealt with today, but it would do a little to even out the wealth gap.

By 2020, 208 people had signed up, the last alphabetically being Mark Zuckerberg, including many well-known names, such as Elon Musk and Richard Branson. You can see all the pledgers with their photos and a brief bio at givingpledge.org: 'The Giving Pledge aims over time to help shift the social norms of philanthropy among the world's wealthiest people and inspire people to give more, establish their giving plans sooner, and give in smarter ways.'

Mission-aligned investing: Many foundations try to do good through their grant-making but they could also be using their endowment to create positive change. For example, by not investing in tobacco companies when trying to improve the world's health; or by not having shares in oil companies when addressing global warming. The first step for responsible investing is to screen out those investments which are creating or adding to the problems you want to address. This led the Rockefeller Brothers Fund to ask itself why foundations were only using 5 per cent of their funds in making charitable distributions, using only the income from their endowment which was traditionally invested, and what they might do with the resources at their disposal to create a bigger impact. The answer was 'mission-aligned investing' – investing a part of the endowment of the foundation in businesses that would make a difference, rather than in stocks and shares. For example, a foundation might invest in a wind farm or a freeway charging station to facilitate the transition to a green economy, which at the same time would also generate interest or dividends which could then be added to their grants budget.

If the Giving Pledge is to spend as much as possible and as soon as possible on philanthropy, mission-aligned investing could enable a part or even all of a foundation's funds to be used for public benefit. Mark Zuckerberg and his wife, Priscilla Chan, have set up the Chan-Zuckerberg Initiative, which engages in a mix of grant-making and investment through a limited liability company rather than a non-profit foundation. This allows them to support any idea, whether for-profit or not-for-profit, by investing or by donating. The initiative focuses on science, education, justice and opportunity, and local community initiatives.

What can we all do?

DoSomething.org is a global movement of
millions of young people who want to make
positive change, both online and in the real
world. These are some of the facts that motivate
and encourage young people to learn something
– and then to do something.

↳ Nearly half of the world's population lives on
less than $2.50 a day.

↳ 1 billion children worldwide live in poverty,
with 22,000 dying each day.

↳ 805 million people worldwide go to bed
hungry each night. Hunger is the number one
cause of death in the world, killing more than
HIV/AIDS, malaria and tuberculosis combined.

↳ 750 million people lack adequate access to
clean drinking water.

↳ 165 million children under the age of five are
stunted due to chronic malnutrition.

↳ 2 million children die each year for lack of
access to affordable health services.

↳ It is estimated that it would take just $60
billion annually to end extreme global poverty.

If you want to do something, go to their
campaigns page. You could find yourself making
masks to stop the spread of Covid-19, organising
a diversity book club, disrupting racism in your
community and much, much more.

DO THIS:

You can 'take the test' on the World
Inequality Database's website to see how
equal you are to others in your own country:
wid.world/simulator/GB/.

The Jewish Talmud says that 'Whoever saves
one life saves the world entire.' Instead of
trying to solve all of the world's problems,
you could try to do something that will make
one person's life better. You could give
money, food or clothes to someone who
needs these more than you do.

Tax injustice

36

The world's top tax havens

Country rankings in the **Corporate Tax Haven Index**

EUROPE

Netherlands 4

Switzerland 5

Luxembourg 6

Jersey 7

Ireland 11

United Kingdom 13

Guernsey 15

Belgium 16

Isle of Man 17

Cyprus 18

Hungary 20

France 22

Malta 23

Germany 24

AMERICAS

British Virgin Islands 1

Bermuda 2

Cayman Islands 3

Bahamas 9

Curacao 21

USA 25

MIDDLE AND FAR EAST

Singapore 8

Hong Kong 10

United Arab Emirates 12

Mauritius 14

China 19

The **Corporate Tax Haven Index** is compiled by the Tax Justice Network. It ranks the world's most important tax havens for multinational corporations, according to how aggressively and how extensively each jurisdiction contributes to helping the world's multinational enterprises escape paying tax. Above is the top 25 for 2019, with British Virgin Islands at number one. Famous tax haven Panama only comes in at 26, Liechtenstein at 37 and Monaco at 40. Interestingly, most of the world's major countries appear in this list, alongside small countries where tax avoidance is a major contributor to their economy. There are two core measures: 20 mostly tax-related indicators which assess opportunities provided by the tax laws, loopholes and policies in a jurisdiction; these are then weighted by the scale of activity in that jurisdiction. They are combined to assess the scale of profit-shifting taking place.

What happened in 1789

1789 was a year of change. As a reaction to social and economic injustice, on 14 July, the French Revolution began with the storming of the Bastille and the freeing of the prisoners held there. In rural areas, peasants attacked the manors of the nobility. On 25 September, 13 years earlier after the American Revolution, the first US Congress adopted 12 amendments to the constitution and sent this Bill of Rights to the states for ratification.

On 13 November, Benjamin Franklin wrote, 'Our new Constitution is now established, and has an appearance that promises permanency; but in this world nothing can be said to be certain, except Death and Taxes.' Franklin was not the first to say this. Christopher Bullock, playwright, had written in 1716: 'Tis impossible to be sure of anything but Death and Taxes.'

Today, death is less certain. There is a lot of work going on to find ways of extending life, including experimentation with cryogenic preservation – freezing a body until a future time when it can be brought back into an extended life. And taxes have become optional, with the emergence of tax planning and tax havens for the rich, including many of the richest individuals and corporations in the world.

Doing business used to be so simple

You would have a factory. It would make things and sell things, from widgets to automobiles. The income from your sales would cover the costs of the raw materials and the manufacturing process, pay the wages of your employees and the costs of running the company. The workers would pay tax on their earnings and the company on its profits. These taxes would be paid to King or Country in return for protection (police and armies), infrastructure (roads and railways), services (from health to education), insurance to cover periods of not earning (unemployment benefit, family support for children and pensions in old age) and other benefits. In a cohesive society, everybody would be happy to pay their fair share.

Then two things happened. The first is 'financialisation'. The most-used definition is this: 'the increasing role of financial motives, financial markets, financial actors and financial institutions in the operation of the domestic and international economies' (Gerald Epstein, economist). The main focus of many businesses became the managing of their money, rather than the production of their products.

Here are some examples. The Ford Motor Company makes most of its profit from making loans to customers who buy its cars rather than from manufacturing the cars themselves. Mortgage companies packaged up their loans and sold them to financial intermediaries who created Collateralised Debt Obligations, a financial product with a AAA rating which was sold on to investors, which led directly to the 2007 financial crisis. Student loans have been packaged up in a similar way. Thames Water was purchased by a consortium of investors who refinanced the company with loans secured by future revenue streams from customers. A similar process is used in many private equity buyouts.

To understand what financialisation is and its impact on how business is conducted, see the 'Beginners Guide' produced by the Transnational Institute.

The second is tax avoidance, where the company creates elaborate structures to minimise its tax bill on both sales and profits, loading costs into high-taxation countries through transfer pricing and the licensing of the company's logo, and parking profits and funds in low-taxation countries. Though completely legal, tax avoidance breaks the social compact, increasing the wealth of the few (business owners and shareholders) and creating greater impoverishment for the many (everyone else). It has created a 'race to the bottom' as countries compete to lure businesses to their shores, offering lower and lower taxes, reduced compliance and transparency requirements, and other inducements.

What is a tax haven?

A 2000 Oxfam report stated: 'The gap between the rich and the rest is growing. Tax havens are at the heart of the inequality crisis, enabling corporations and wealthy individuals to dodge paying their fair share of tax. This prevents states from funding vital public services and combating poverty and inequality, with especially damaging effects for developing countries.'

Some countries, especially some smaller countries and territories, have made it their business to profit from tax avoidance. Not all are shady countries in remote parts of the world. A good many are in Europe and some a part of the European Union, including major European nations as well as offshore territories such as Jersey and the Isle of Man.

Tax havens provide taxpayers, both corporate entities and individual people, with the opportunity for tax avoidance (which, unlike tax evasion, is perfectly legal), while secrecy and opacity also serve to hide the origin of the money, which can be proceeds of illegal and criminal activity. All tax havens have this in common: they make it possible to escape taxation. Their distinctive characteristics include:

↳ No or low rates of income or corporation taxes.

↳ Minimal reporting requirements, so lack of public information on the funds involved.

↳ Lack of transparency, minimal or no disclosure requirements on financial dealings and ownership of assets, and generally not applying accepted minimum standards of corporate governance and accountability.

↳ Lack of local residence requirements – or, even when this is required, no enforcement.

↳ Little or no exchange of relevant information with other governments regarding the tax affairs of their taxpayers.

↳ The creation and use of special purpose vehicles and mechanisms for holding and transferring assets.

Since 2017, the European Union has published a tax haven blacklist, which is continuously updated. This highlights practice in specific countries and is an attempt to improve global tax governance and fight tax fraud, evasion and avoidance. Also, see the Global Forum on Transparency and Exchange of Information for Tax Purposes.

The extent of tax avoidance

The Tax Justice Network estimates that the global loss to governments from profit-shifting by the large multinationals is up to $700 billion per annum. The lost taxes as a percentage of gross domestic product hit developing countries the hardest, with $500 billion being lost annually to OECD countries and $200 billion to emerging economies.

The TJN also estimates that between $21 and $32 trillion of private wealth is held offshore. On the assumption that income earned on this wealth is untaxed and using a conservative return on capital of 3 per cent, they estimate that governments are losing upwards of $189 billion a year in unpaid taxes on the hidden offshore wealth of their citizens. This is a small but significant percentage of the global income, which is estimated at $81 trillion, but huge in comparison with the flow of development aid from rich to poor countries ($153 billion for OECD countries in 2019).

It is not just lost tax which is a problem but the criminality connected with some of the offshore mega-wealth – which could be profits from drug smuggling, extortion, bribery and other illicit activity. For a detailed analysis, see the Tax Justice Network's briefing paper.

Panama, Paradise and Pandora Papers

The Panama Papers comprised 11.5 million documents which detailed financial and attorney-client information for more than 214,488 offshore entities, dating from the present right back to the 1970s. They were taken from a Panamanian law firm called Mossack Fonseca and leaked to the German newspaper the *Süddeutsche Zeitung* in April 2016 and then posted by the International Consortium of Investigative Journalists (which is a network of more than 380 journalists) on its website.

The Paradise Papers comprised 13.4 million documents originating from the law firm Appleby, corporate services providers Estera and Asiaciti Trust, and business registries in 19 tax jurisdictions. These were similarly leaked to the same newspaper from November 2017. The documents relate to more than 120,000 people and companies.

The Pandora Papers leaked in 2021 comprised 11.9 million files exposing offshore structures and trusts in tax havens such as Panama, Dubai, Monaco, Switzerland and the Cayman Islands. Amongst the clients connected to

offshore accounts were 35 current and former presidents, prime ministers and heads of state.

These three major leaks provide a real insight into how the super-wealthy, including many celebrities, manage their financial affairs. *The Panama Papers* (2018) is a documentary film and *The Laundromat* a comedy-drama, both based on the Panama Papers leak.

Apple

Many of the world's biggest companies, including many of the tech giants, use aggressive techniques to minimise their tax bills. These include Apple, one of the world's biggest companies.

Up until 2014, Apple had been exploiting a loophole in tax laws in the US and the Republic of Ireland known as the 'double Irish'. This allowed the company to channel all its sales outside of the Americas – currently producing around 55 per cent of its revenues – through Irish subsidiaries that were effectively stateless for taxation purposes. Irish corporation tax was 12.5 per cent and the USA rate 35 per cent. Apple's tax structure reduced the effective tax rate on profits earned outside the USA to around 5 per cent of its foreign profits, and in some years below 2 per cent. The response of Tim Cook, Apple CEO, is reported as: 'We pay all the taxes we owe, every single dollar. We do not depend on tax gimmicks ... We do not stash money on some Caribbean island.'

This arrangement ended after the EU announced an investigation in 2013. The Irish government decided that companies incorporated in Ireland could no longer be deemed to be stateless for tax purposes. So to continue its low-tax liability, Apple needed to find an offshore financial centre for tax residency for its Irish subsidiaries. It chose Jersey, a UK Crown Dependency with its own tax laws, with a 0 per cent corporate tax rate for foreign companies.

Apple's 2017 accounts show that the company made $44.7 billion outside the US and paid just $1.65 billion in taxes to foreign governments, a rate of around 3.7 per cent, which is less than a sixth of the average rate of corporation tax in the world. Apple was also holding huge currency reserves offshore, as repatriating them to the USA would have resulted in a hefty tax bill. In 2018, under pressure from President Trump, Apple agreed to repatriate a chunk of its offshore wealth as a part of a $350 million investment programme in the USA.

A report by Fair Tax Mark (see below) accuses the big six US tech firms (Amazon, Facebook, Google, Netflix, Apple and Microsoft) of aggressively avoiding $100 billion of tax globally over the past decade by shifting revenue and profits to tax havens or low-tax countries. Their report singles out Amazon as the worst offender, paying just $3.4bn (£2.6bn) in tax on its income in the 2010s despite achieving revenues of $960.5bn and profits of $26.8bn. Fair Tax Mark calculates Amazon's effective tax rate as 12.7 per cent

over the decade while the headline tax rate in the US was 35 per cent for most of this period. Amazon explains this by the very high level of investment of its profits in the future of its business. Nonetheless, the tech giants, which are seeking to become the 'Masters of the Universe', are not setting a good enough example of being Fair Tax payers.

The increasing use of tax avoidance by large international companies led 136 OECD countries to agree in 2021 to the right to levy tax on a share of the profits of a company based on its sales in their country and to a minimum corporation tax rate of 15 per cent. Together, these are estimated to increase the tax raised from big businesses by $275 billion.

Fair Tax Mark

Fair Tax Mark is a social enterprise set up in the UK supported by a group of liberal-leaning foundations. The Fair Tax Mark certification scheme was launched in February 2014 and seeks to encourage and recognise organisations that pay the right amount of corporation tax at the right time and in the right place. It operates as a not-for-profit and believes that companies paying tax responsibly should be publicly celebrated and any race to the bottom resisted.

To date, Fair Tax Mark has focused on certifying businesses headquartered in the UK. So far, more than 65 businesses have been accredited by Fair Tax, including financial services providers and utilities, as well as smaller companies such as Friendly Soap, selling no-waste, biodegradable and free-from soap products, and Roo, a husband-and-wife-run business selling take-away coffee and food from a standing van. Fair Tax Mark has created a suite of global standards in for UK and UK-based businesses.

Go live in Malta

Individuals also want to move to a different tax jurisdiction, sometimes for political stability, sometimes for climate reasons and sometimes for low taxes. Malta has an Individual Investor Programme which grants full citizenship in return for a minimum investment of 880,000 euros ($1 million), with additional amounts for each family member. Seventy-five per cent of this is a non-refundable contribution to Malta's National Development and Social Fund, which finances education, health and job-creation projects in the country, with the remainder being split between investments in government bonds and owning or renting a home. Applicants have to either buy a property worth at least 350,000 euros or rent one for at least 16,000 euros a year for at least five years. More than 80 per cent of applicants take the rental option. Malta is inside the European Union and a part of the Schengen Area, which enables passport-free movement across most of Europe.

Malta's citizenship scheme became popular because it is relatively cheap and applicants

usually receive passports within 12–18 months. The Caribbean country of St Kitts and Nevis has been selling citizenship since 1984, and today more than half the world's countries have citizenship-through-investment schemes. These are some of the prices you might expect to pay: Antigua $100,000; Portugal 280,000 euros; USA from $900,000 (invested in a business and creating 10 full-time jobs); UK from £2 million. Check out Citizen Shop for latest prices and more options.

DO THIS:

To get a better understanding of tax avoidance and how it affects all of us, take a 'Tax-Free Tour' at: youtube.com/watch?v=d4o13isDdfY.

Winner
takes all

↳

Top 10 companies in the world by market capitalisation

1 Apple (tech), $2,380 billion, USA

2 Microsoft (tech), $2,229 billion, USA

3 Alphabet (formerly Google) (tech), £1,863 billion, USA

4 Saudi Aramco (oil), $1,860 billion, Saudi Arabia

5 Amazon (tech/retail), $1,707 billion, USA

6 Meta (formerly Facebook) (tech), $1,010 billion, USA

7 Tesla (auto), $774 billion, USA

8 Berkshire Hathaway (investment), $621 billion, USA

9 TSMC (manufacturing), $274 billion, Taiwan

10 Tencent (tech), $558 billion, China

Top companies in other countries with world ranking

14 South Korea: Samsung (tech), $438 billion

19 France: LVMH (luxury goods), $377 billion

20 Netherlands: ASML (diversified), $354 billion

23 Switzerland: Nestle (food), $124 billion

35 Japan: Toyota (auto), $181 billion

42 Denmark: Novo Nordisk (pharmaceutical), $235 billion

50 India: Reliance Industries (diversified), $220 billion

53 Ireland: Accenture (professional services), $211 billion

61 UK: AstraZeneca (pharmaceutical), $184 billion

63 Singapore: Sea (tech), $183 billion

75 Germany: SAP (tech), $142 billion

92 Canada: Royal Bank of Canada (financial services), $140 billion

94 Hong Kong: AIA (insurance), $138 billion

95 Australia: BHP Group (mining), $138 billion

This ranking is based on prices in autumn 2021 on just one day and will change as stock prices change. The largest company by sales income is Walmart with $562 billion, topping Amazon's $419 billion, but it has a market cap of just $400 billion. For up-to-date information see companiesmarketcap.com, and also the PwC listing of top companies and The Visual Capitalist.

In 1999, at the height of the dotcom bubble, five of the world's top ten companies by market capitalisation were tech companies, including Microsoft, Cisco, Intel, NTT and Nokia. GE, Exxon and Walmart were the largest non-tech companies. After the financial crisis in 2008, it was the turn of the oil majors. Petrochina and Exxon were the top two, with Petrobras and Shell also making the top ten. Since then, we have seen the rise and continuing rise of the tech companies, with USA's 'Big Five' and one of China's 'Big Three' in the top ten. The Big Five together generate $1.19 trillion in annual revenues with their share capitalisation at over eight times this amount.

Making and taking

Economists like to talk about 'makers' and 'takers', with the makers contributing to economic success and takers taking but not contributing. This used to be in the form of 'rent', with the farmers producing through their labour and the landlords, owners of the land, charging rent in the form of a monetary payment or a share of the crop but adding no value to the production process. Today, the idea of making and taking has become more complex. For example, a pharmaceutical company is making when it creates and sells a useful drug but it is also taking if it charges beyond what is a reasonable price.

Over the last generation, we have seen a tightening of intellectual property laws (as well as increasing theft). Patents are now granted not just for 'invention' but for 'discovery', with companies seeking patents on DNA sequences, for example, and using these to create gene therapies. Amazon has a patent on 'one-click ordering' as well as for an 'airborne fulfilment centre', which is basically a blimp from which drones are deployed that deliver packages direct to your door. Google filed a patent titled 'Advertisements Based on Weather Conditions'. The technology detects a person's weather conditions and generates appropriate advertisements, such as umbrellas and raincoats when it is raining. The company was also granted a patent for a baseball cap with a removable video camera that is mounted on the brim. Facebook has patented technology that allows banks and lenders to use a potential borrower's social media network to decide if he or she is a credit risk. These patents have real value as they can prevent competitors from doing anything very similar during the life of the patent and can also generate significant income from licensing.

The new business model

Over the last generation, we have seen the rise and rise of the big tech companies, whose value outstrips that of any other business sector by an order of magnitude. Many were started by 'geeks in garages', with high ideals and a vison for changing the world. Bill Gates, Steve Jobs and Mark Zuckerberg were all college dropouts. And they certainly have changed the world – Google with the best search engine, Facebook with the best social networking, Apple with the best computers and cellphones, Microsoft with its software and cloud services, Amazon as a one-stop shop for everything. These companies have become immensely successful. They have been able to do this in part due to their prized and very highly priced shares, with their shareholders more interested in long-term growth than immediate dividends. They have used this financial power to spend more on innovation (Google photographing the Earth and streets), to take over competitors and parallel businesses (Facebook buying Instagram and WhatsApp, for example) and to invest in promising start-ups. They are extending their tentacles into every aspect of our lives, and even into space.

Isaac Newton, who formulated the idea of gravity and the laws of motion, and who co-invented calculus, once said, 'If I have seen further, it is by standing upon the shoulders of giants.' The big tech companies have also stood on others' shoulders, building on technologies such as the internet, touch screen and GPS, which were all developed by the US government, and graphical user interface, the mouse and electronic ink, which were developed at Xerox's Palo Alto research centre. But they have been clever enough to monetise the rewards and reap huge benefits from doing this.

The success and dominance of the tech companies (and not just the Big Five) raises a number of questions:

Have they become too profitable, extracting too much 'rent' from society? When Mark Zuckerberg set up 'The Facebook', initially as a way of rating the attractiveness of girls in Harvard dorms, did he envisage that this would lead to a social network with 2.89 billion monthly active users worldwide, funded through advertising and data services? Similarly, did Google, which set out to organise all the world's information using the phrase 'don't be evil' as its motto and having no real business model, imagine that it would become an advertising behemoth? Did the two Steves, who created Apple and invented Macintosh computers, envisage streams of income from iTunes, the App Store and Apple Pay? We may love their services but are we aware of the hidden price we are paying? In 1911, The US government ordered the break up of Rockefeller's Standard Oil because it had become too powerful. In 1984, the US government created the 'Baby Bells' from AT&T for the same reason. Should the same happen to the tech giants?

With power comes responsibility. Are these big companies shying away from their responsibilities to act ethically, to pay their taxes, to address and create solutions to the problems they are creating? Problems such as the way that fake news is affecting society and democracy, or the 'echo chambers' where people are fed only the information and points of view which match their profile, which can magnify division and intolerance?

Conflicts of interest: Microsoft in its early days was able to put the Netscape browser out of business by bundling its own Internet Explorer with its operating system. Google now presents advertisements and other revenue-generating opportunities at the top of your search. If you search for 'maps', although there are no ads, Google Maps takes the top five spots. If they are presenting you with services and opportunities at the top of any search which allow them to take a percentage of any transaction, is this in the public interest?

For more information on the role of government in pioneering innovation and how this has become a building block for the rise of the tech companies, see Mariana Mazzucato's books *The Value of Everything: Making and Taking in the Global Economy* and *The Entrepreneurial State: Debunking Public vs Private Sector Myths*.

Governments fight back

In July 2020, the CEOs of Amazon, Apple, Google and Facebook were summoned to Congress for an anti-trust hearing and given a six-hour grilling on their anti-competitive practices, accused of using their market power and huge resources to crush competition, amass and misuse data and generate inordinate profits on which tax was mostly being avoided. There is a feeling growing amongst US legislators on both sides of the House that the tech sector has become too rich and too powerful, that it is stifling the emergence of competitors, which offers consumers no alternatives, and that its power could be a threat to democracy itself. You can watch the tech titans being grilled by Congress on YouTube (owned by Google).

In the European Union, there are similar anti-trust concerns, which is leading the European Union to act. In 2019, Google was fined 1.49 billion euros for restrictive practices in online search – although this fine is too small make a noticeable dent in Google's balance sheet. Also in 2019, formal investigations were begun into Apple for the way in which apps are distributed through its App Store, and into Amazon for the way it uses data from the independent retailers who sell via its marketplace. And there is increasing concern over the dissemination of fake news by Facebook and others, who should be seen as publishers of information and not just platforms on which information is disseminated.

Just as there is concern that the banks have become 'too big to fail', there is concern that the tech giants have become 'too big for the common good'.

The case of Wikipedia

The internet was created to facilitate the sharing of ideas amongst academics. Many of the early visionaries saw it as a place for cooperation rather than for commerce. But over time, the internet has become commercialised. There is one glaring exception, which is Wikipedia. This is a global encyclopaedia created collaboratively by users who can write, add to or amend articles subject to editorial oversight. Wikipedia has not been commercialised or monetised and is largely funded by well-wishers and appeals to its users. Wikipedia now completely overshadows old encyclopaedias such as Encyclopaedia Britannica, which are expensive to produce and distribute, and may even be out of date by the time they are published due to the speed of change, and produced from a less democratic editorial perspective. Wikipedia now has 300 active language editions; the English edition alone has 6.125 million entries of any length, as compared with 100,000 in Britannica.

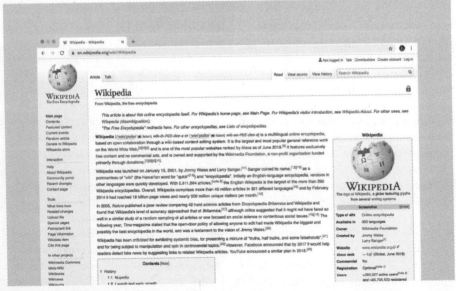

Is Wikipedia reflective of the internet that the pioneers envisioned and that we really wanted? Does Jimmy Wales, the Wikipedia founder, regret that (according to Wikipedia) his net worth is just $1 million and not the near-$200 billion of Jeff Bezos, Amazon's founder? Both came from similar backgrounds before setting up their internet phenomena. Wales was a financial trader with Chicago Options Associates; Bezos worked for Wall Street investment firm D E Shaw. Both created institutions which have changed our lives (how we get information and how we shop). Both appear unassailable at present. The difference is that one created a mega-fortune for its founder and one did not.

Software freedom

In contrast to the way the big tech companies protect their intellectual property through copyright and patents, there is the idea of free and open-source software. Free software can be used, copied and distributed in any way at no cost to the user, and open-source means the code is shared so that people can improve the design of the software. This approach offers four essential freedoms:

↳ The freedom to run the program as you wish, for any purpose (Freedom 0).

↳ The freedom to study how the program works and change it so it does your computing as you wish (Freedom 1). Access to the source code is a precondition for this.

↳ The freedom to redistribute copies so you can help others (Freedom 2).

↳ The freedom to distribute copies of your modified versions to others (Freedom 3). By doing this you can give the whole community a chance to benefit from your changes.

This approach is being promoted by Richard Stallman through the Free Software Foundation. Stallman also launched the GNU Project in 1983 to create a computer operating system composed entirely of free software and wrote the GNU General Public License, which is a user licence setting out the code of conduct for sharing free software. Software Freedom Day takes place on 19 September each year and is a celebration of free software and the ideas behind it.

You can demonstrate your support for the idea of free software and help reduce the power (and the income) of the giant tech companies through the software that you choose to use:

Mozilla is a free software community founded in 1998. Its products include the Firefox web browser, Thunderbird email client, Firefox OS mobile operating system, Bugzilla bug tracking system, Gecko layout engine, Pocket 'read-it-later-online' service and others. Mozilla emerged from the tussle between Netscape and Microsoft, which was settled in 2013 after a seven-year court case, resulting in Microsoft paying compensation of $750 million to AOL, which acquired Netscape in 2002 for $4.2 billion. The irony is that Firefox is thriving while Microsoft withdrew its Internet Explorer in 2016.

OpenOffice.org (OOo) is a discontinued open-source software suite which is an analogue of Microsoft Office, except that it is free. It started as an open-source version of StarOffice, which Sun Microsystems acquired in 1999 for its own internal use. Sun open-sourced it in 2000 as a competitor to Microsoft. It decided to discontinue with this and in 2011 it donated the software to the Apache Software Foundation, a non-profit which supports open software projects. There are now several versions, all free to use; the main ones are Apache Open Office and Libre Office, which is used by the UK government's revenue service.

The Linux operating system is an alternative to the Microsoft Windows operating system, which in the early years of personal computing had a near monopoly of non-Apple desktop and later laptop computers. It was developed by and named after Linus Torvalds. In 1991, while at the University of Helsinki, Torvalds decided to create an operating system which could be freely used. This led to the creation of the Linux Kernel, which has become a base for challenging Microsoft's operating systems domination. Brazil, for example, has made Linux its standard offering for encouraging computer literacy and companies including Dell, IBM and Hewlett-Packard offer Linux support to their customers. Linux is now used widely throughout computing and is popular in the netbook market, with many devices shipped with Linux pre-installed.

Linux's greatest success has been with the Android operating system, which is widely used on smartphones, tablets and wearables. This was developed though a consortium sponsored by Google as a challenger to the Apple iPhone operating system.

DO THIS:

Use free software as much as you can. Migrate to the Linux operating system: linux. org. Use Open Office or Libre Office for word processing: openoffice.org and libreoffice.org. Browse the Wikipedia list of free and open-source software to see what is available. Strike a blow for software freedom and save money!

Corruption and kleptocracy

↳

Corruption in today's world

The least and most corrupt countries

Least corrupt countries

1= Denmark and New Zealand 88

3= Finland, Singapore, Sweden and Switzerland 85

7 Norway 84

8 Netherlands 82

9= Luxembourg and Germany 80

11= Australia, Canada, Hong Kong and United Kingdom 77

Most corrupt countries

179= Somalia and South Sudan 12

178 Syria 14

176= Venezuela and Yemen 15

174= Sudan and Equatorial Guinea 16

173 Libya 17

171= DR Congo and Haiti 18

170 North Korea 18

168= Afghanistan and Turkmenistan 19

165= Guinea-Bissau, the Congo and Burundi 19

Transparency International's Corruption Perceptions Index for 2020 ranks 180 countries and territories by their perceived levels of public sector corruption, according to experts and business people. The maximum score is 100. Corruption is most pervasive in countries where big money can flow freely into electoral campaigns and where governments listen only to the voices of wealthy or well-connected individuals. Separately, US News ranked these as the world's most corrupt countries: Colombia (most corrupt), Mexico, Ghana, Myanmar, Guatemala, Saudi Arabia, Brazil, Kenya, Bolivia, Russia.

Campaigning against corruption

'An ethical life is built of integrity, honesty, kindness, decency and belief in truth, justice, honour, respect, compassion, and working together to make life better.'

– Mark Twain

The World Bank ranks corruption as the single greatest obstacle to reducing poverty. It contaminates governance, diverts often much-needed money away from meeting the needs of the poor and it allows regimes to cling onto power, through forming alliances with the military, manipulating electoral processes, changing laws on tenure of office, grooming the next generation and creating a family dynasty. We must believe that it is possible to live in a world without corruption and central to this is exposing corruption in all its forms and ensuring that those in power maintain the highest levels of integrity and ethics.

Transparency International campaigns on corruption in an attempt to stop the abuse of power, bribery and secret deals around the world. They say: 'As a global movement with one vision, we want a world free of corruption.' There are chapters in more than 100 countries and an international secretariat in Berlin.

Corruption is the abuse of entrusted power for private gain and it can be classified into these categories, depending on the amounts of money lost and the sector where it occurs.

Grand corruption: The abuse of high-level power that benefits the few at the expense of the many. It causes serious and widespread harm to citizens and society. It often goes unpunished. The Russian oligarch mafia is an example of this.

Petty corruption: Everyday abuse of entrusted power by public officials in their interactions with ordinary citizens, who often are trying to access basic goods or services in places like hospitals, schools, police departments and other agencies. This is sometimes referred to as 'retail corruption'. India provides a good example of a country where petty corruption is rife.

Political corruption: Manipulation of policies, institutions and rules of procedure in the allocation of resources and financing by political decision makers, who abuse their position to sustain their power, status and wealth. The Mugabe regime in Zimbabwe and his successor Emmerson Mnangagwa (nicknamed 'The Crocodile') with the ZANU-PF party in firm control is an example of this.

State capture: A situation where powerful individuals, institutions, companies or groups within or outside a country use corruption to influence a nation's policies, legal environment and economy to benefit their own private interests. The Gupta family's relationship with the South Africa's Zuma government was often referred to as 'State Capture'.

Corruption can be hard to identify and stamp out for many reasons, and not just because of the power that has often been amassed by the perpetrators. Corruption can be carried out in myriad ways using complex systems and mechanisms. If you want to know more, there is a glossary of terms of the many forms that it can take on the website of Transparency International: transparency.org/en/corruptionary.

Kleptocracy tours

The term 'kleptocracy' describes a government where those in power are looting state resources for their own private benefit. This leads to the impoverishment of the many while creating enormous wealth for the few. Often it is connected to the ownership of or licence to exploit particular natural resources, privatisations of state assets at prices that are far too low, the grant of operating licences for such things as power supply and telecoms, or the diversion of aid budgets for private gain. It can also involve commissions levied on contracts or requirements to use a particular suppler or contractor. It can involve the outright theft of shares and businesses. Money laundering and use of tax havens, buying luxury properties in the capitals of the world, and endowing educational and cultural institutions are all part of the world of kleptocracy.

Kleptocracy has been around from the times when everything was controlled by kings and emperors. But in our more democratic era, where we are seeking a world that is fair to all, kleptocracy is a major barrier to progress.

Oliver Bullough is the author of *Moneyland: Why Thieves and Crooks Now Rule the World and How to Take It Back.* He founded ClampK – the Committee for Legislation Against Moneylaundering in Properties by Kleptocrats – with the mission of 'Exposing corruption, theft and exploitation wherever we can!' He has organised a number of 'Kleptocracy Tours' to raise public awareness, taking participants to visit properties in London and elsewhere purchased and owned by kleptocrats, often with black money. This is similar to the Hollywood 'Homes of the Stars' tours but in this case visiting the 'Stars of Corruption'.

Read this: The Associates: Handling Business for the Kleptocrats, with Liberia, Mali, Mozambique, Zambia, Kenya, Nigeria all featured in ZAMmagazine.com. ZAM is a Netherlands-based online magazine and runs the ZAM Kleptocracy Project.

Integritas360 is an Australia-based consultancy
which seeks to remove corruption from
international development aid by providing
advice, training and anti-corruption certification
to the charity, non-profit, government and
international development sectors.

Presidents with more than $1 billion in estimated personal assets:

Vladimir Putin, President, Russian Federation	2000–present	(see below)
Muammar Gaddafi, Leader, Libya	1969–2011	up to $200 billion
Ismail Omar Guelleh, President, Djibouti	1999–present	$79.2 billion
Hosni Mubarak, President, Egypt	1981–2011	$70 billion
Ali Abdullah Saleh, President, Yemen	1990–2012	$32–60 billion
Muhamed Suharto, President, Indonesia	1967–1998	$15–35 billion
Jose Dos Santos, President, Angola	1979–2017	$20 billion
Zine Ben Ali, President, Tunisia	1987–2011	up to $17 billion
Ferdinand Marcos, President Philippines	1965–1986	$5–10 billion
Mobutu Sese Seko, President Zaire (DR Congo)	1965–1997	$4–5 billion
Sani Abacha, President, Nigeria	1993–1998	$2–5 billion
Yoweri Museveni, President, Uganda	1986–present	$4 billion
Bashar al-Assad, President, Syria	2000–present	$1.5 billion
Robert Mugabe, President, Zimbabwe	1980–2017	$1 billion+
Slobodan Milosevic, President Serbia	1989–2000	$1 billion

The wealth of dictators is hard to estimate. These figures are mostly guestimates obtained from various sources but are probably correct within an order of magnitude. Official figures from Russia claim Putin is worth approximately $150,000; Stanislav Belkovsky, Russian government adviser, has estimated that it is in fact around $70 billion. Bill Browder, CEO and co-founder of the Hermitage Fund, a hedge fund operating in Russia, who fell out with the regime, claims that Putin's personal wealth is as much as $200 billion, which would make him just about the richest person in the world.

Viktor Yanukovych, president of Ukraine from 2010, fled into exile in Russia in 2014 following public protest over his aligning Ukraine too closely with Russia. Although Yanukovych does not appear on this list, he was seen as extremely corrupt. The Mezhyhirya Residence, which he built for himself, has now become a museum displaying his luxurious lifestyle. The 140-hectare estate on the banks of the Dnieper river has a yacht pier, a garage filled with luxury cars, equestrian facilities, a shooting range, a tennis court, a golf course, hunting grounds, an ostrich farm, dog kennels, fountains, man-made lakes, a helicopter pad and a small church (where he could confess his sins). At the time of his ousting, he was building another palace in Crimea.

Two princes

Niccolo Machiavelli wrote *The Prince* in 1513, as a handbook for rulers on the use of power. Here are two quotes: 'Never attempt to win by force what can be won by deception.' 'It is much safer to be feared than loved because … love is preserved by the link of obligation which, owing to the baseness of men, is broken at every opportunity for their advantage; but fear preserves you by a dread of punishment which never fails.'

Antoine de Saint Exupery wrote *The Little Prince* in 1941, a fable which lays bare the human condition. On the question of wealth, the Little Prince asks a king who is counting the stars: 'And what do you do with [the 50,622,731] stars?' 'Nothing. I own them.' 'And what good does it do you to own the stars?' 'It does me the good of making me rich.' 'And what good does it do you to be rich?' 'It makes it possible for me to buy more stars, if any are discovered.'

Global Witness

Many of the world's worst environmental and human rights abuses are driven by the exploitation of natural resources and corruption in the global political and economic system. Global Witness campaigns to end this. Founded in 1993, it explores the links between competition for natural resources and corruption. Its first campaign was to shut down the Khmer Rouge's illegal logging industry; it has also examined blood diamonds (which are diamonds illegally mined and sold to fund conflict) and worked to create greater transparency over oil, gas and mining revenues.

Its investigations focus on who is stealing the money, where they are hiding it and how they are spending it.

Global Witness works in 23 countries, which include Afghanistan, Angola, Azerbaijan, Cambodia, Cameroon, Central African Republic, China, the Congo, DR Congo, Equatorial Guinea, Guyana, Honduras, Laos, Libya, Malaysia, Myanmar, Nigeria, Papua New Guinea, Peru, South Sudan, Turkmenistan, Ukraine and Zimbabwe, investigating conflict diamonds, responsible minerals and mining, oil and gas, corruption and money laundering, forests, land deals, and protecting environmental activists.

Retail corruption in India

Karnataka is usually highlighted as India's most corrupt state, and Bangalore (now known as Bengaluru) is its capital. There used to be a website called Bangalore.com which posted the going rate for bribes in the city, so that citizens could know how much they had to pay to get something done, whether to obtain a drinks licence for a hotel, register a birth, get citizenship papers or pay for a traffic violation. Unofficially, there was a price for everything. The bureaucrats and the police knew this price, and citizens needed to know so they could come prepared and offer the right amount.

The Bangalore.com website no longer exists but one well-informed individual circulated some of the current going rates in a blog, which ranged from 100 rupees for a motorbike traffic violation to around 1,500 rupees for a passport application and up to 500,000 rupees for permission to convert a property (approximately 75 rupees are the equivalent of a US dollar). The blogger advised people to be aware of bribe levels so that they were not paying over the odds. Even bribery can be transparent!

I Paid a Bribe

ipaidabribe.com is a website which collects information from members of the public as a way of tackling corruption. It has aggregated nearly 200,000 reports of bribes being paid in India in 1,081 cities to a total of 37.25 billion rupees ($484 million). The average bribe reported on this website was 190,000 rupees ($2,467). Examples include a cyclist having to pay 2,000 rupees ($30) for a police report required by his insurance company after his bike had been stolen; a small business paying 10,000 rupees ($150) just for the privilege of registering to pay service tax; and a Jaipur resident alleging that he was being 'blackmailed' by the income tax department to pay a bribe or a heavy tax bill would be fabricated for him instead.

The police were seen to be the most corrupt arm of the government, extorting money from members of the public who they are supposed to be protecting. The next three most corrupt departments were Stamps and Registration, Municipal Services and Transport. Bengaluru was reported as being the most corrupt city in India with 24,217 cases reported, greater than the next four worst cities combined: Mumbai, Pune, New Delhi and Ahmedabad.

The website asks for three types of report:

↳ 'I paid a bribe' – why the bribe was paid, to whom and when.

↳ 'I did not pay a bribe' – what you did instead, why you did it and the outcome.

↳ 'I met an honest official' – reporting officials who did not ask for a bribe or who refused to take a bribe when offered.

It also provides advice on accessing official services and methods of redress if things go wrong.

Honouring the honest

A lack of integrity leads to corruption, inequality and insecurity. Addressing this is a global challenge. Citizens often feel helpless when the only way to get something done is to offer a bribe. The culture of bribery and corruption needs to be challenged. One way is to empower citizens to stand up to corruption and give them the tools to do this. The other is to try to change the culture so that bribes are not asked for or expected. One way of encouraging this is by celebrating champions of integrity. The Integrity Icon is a way of doing this, as it aims to develop a next generation of responsible and honest leaders.

The Integrity Icon is a global campaign by Accountability Lab to honour honest officials. Local volunteers travel across their countries hosting public forums, generating a national discourse on the need for public officials to have integrity and seeking nominations for awards. The nominees are then narrowed down by panels of independent experts in Liberia, Mali, Mexico, South Africa, Sri Lanka, Nepal, Nigeria and Mexico to a final five, from which the awards are decided. Accountability Lab also has a Pakistan office.

DO THIS:

Meet some of the Integrity Icons, such as Eric Joboe, a Liberian police officer; Oyeronke Suebat, in charge of a Nigerian blood bank; and Ruth Abay, a paediatric doctor working in Philadelphia, and listen to them tell their stories and explain what integrity means to them: integrityicon.org/icons/.

Can we end world poverty?

39

Poverty in the world today

Numbers of people living in extreme poverty

1 India 141.28 million

2 Nigeria 78.77 million

3 DR Congo 61.62 million

4 Tanzania 27.68 million

5 Ethiopia 21.9 million

6 Madagascar 20.65 million

7 Mozambique 18.92 million

8 Uganda 16.83 million

9 Kenya 16.43 million

10 Angola 16.36 million

11 Yemen 15.95 million

12 Malawi 12.58 million

13 South Africa 11.52 million

14 Bangladesh 10.79 million

15 Somalia 10.60 million

16 Zambia 10.45 million

17 Brazil 9.73 million

18 Pakistan 9.29 million

19 Burundi 9.17 million

20 Niger 9.16 million

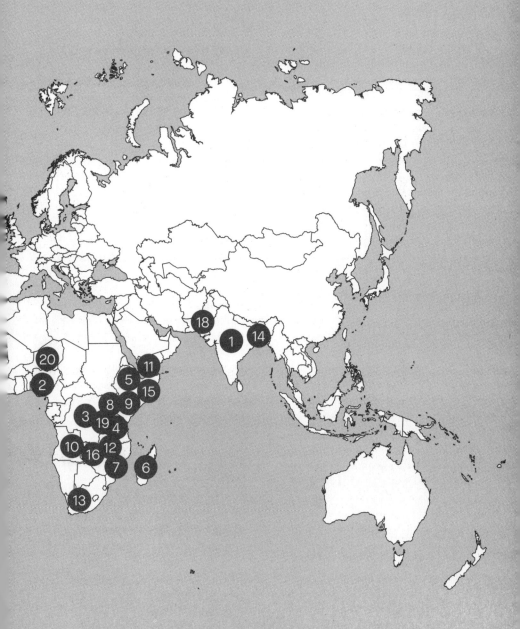

The figures on the previous page are for 2019 (apart from India, 2017). The World Bank defines extreme poverty as living on less than $1.90 per day. In September 2021, a total of 713,850,000 people were living in extreme poverty according to the World Poverty Clock. This includes 635 million living in rural areas – 17.2 per cent of the world's rural population. The UN's Sustainable Development Goal 1 is to eradicate extreme poverty everywhere by 2030. The target rate to do this would be 2.4 people per second escaping poverty; the actual rate is well below this – 0.9 people per second. Venezuela, Suriname and most of East and West Africa are not on track. Browse Our World in Data for more facts and information.

Ending world poverty

According to the United Nations, the decline in extreme poverty in the world continues but is slowing. Many people living in extreme poverty still face serious challenges, including: corrupt or non-functioning governments; a lack of spending on key services including education, health and maternal welfare; few opportunities for formal employment; high birth rate, which means that economies have to expand just to stand still; and a complete absence of resilience in the face of a disaster or a pandemic.

↳ There has been progress but it has not been fast enough. The share of the world population living in extreme poverty declined to 10 per cent in 2015, down from 16 per cent in 2010 and 36 per cent in 1990. Projections suggest that 250 million people will still be living in extreme poverty in 2030.

↳ Even where people have a job, 8 per cent of those in work and their families are still living in extreme poverty. In sub-Saharan Africa, the figure is 38 per cent.

↳ Social protection systems can help prevent and reduce poverty and provide a safety net for the vulnerable. But it is not a reality for a large majority of the world's population. In 2016, 55 per cent (4 billion people) were not covered by any form of social protection. In sub-Saharan Africa, 87 per cent receive no protection from the state.

↳ Worldwide, only 22 per cent of unemployed persons receive unemployment cash benefits; only 28 per cent with severe disabilities receive disability cash benefits; only 35 per cent of children worldwide enjoy effective access to social protection; and only 41 per cent of women giving birth receive maternity cash benefits.

The 0.7 per cent target

In 1970, a target of 0.7 per cent gross national income for official development assistance was first agreed for OECD countries and this has been repeatedly stated as the agreed target. In 2005, the 15 countries which were members of the European Union at the time agreed to reach this target by 2015.

To qualify as official development assistance, a contribution must contain three elements:

↳ Be undertaken by the official sector (that is, a government or government agency)

↳ With promotion of economic development and welfare as the main objective

↳ At concessional financial terms (that is, with favourable loan terms)

It does not include private donations.

According to the OECD, the aid donors who have reached or exceeded the 0.7 per cent target in 2020 were:

Sweden	1.18 per cent
Norway	1.16 per cent
Luxembourg	1.11 per cent
Denmark	0.73 per cent
Germany	0.73 per cent

The UK just about achieved its 0.70 per cent in 2020, but in 2021 it reduced its commitment to 0.5 per cent due to its own internal financial pressures. The largest aid givers are USA at $37 billion, but that represents only 0.17 per cent of GNI, and China at $27.9 billion, which is still only 0.35 per cent of GNI. The aid contributions of other major economies are Netherlands, 0.59 per cent; France, 0.53 per cent; Canada and Japan, both 0.31 per cent. The European Union gives 50 billion euros in international development aid in addition to contributions made by its member states.

Aid takes different forms. Some is linked to social requirements, such as gender equality or advocacy; some is linked to trade, especially Chinese aid, where Chinese companies have been prime contractors for building infrastructure (for more on this read *The Dragon's Gift* by Deborah Brautigam).

Aid versus remittances

Development aid has become increasingly less important as remittances home from family members migrating or living overseas have increased. Remittances transfer three times as much money as compared with development aid, and the amount is growing faster. In 2018, over 200 million migrant workers sent $529 billion back home to developing countries and around one in nine people globally are supported by funds sent home by migrant workers. On average, migrants are sending around 15 per cent of their earnings back home, about half going to rural areas where the poorest live. This is providing a powerful reason for migration by people from poorer nations seeking what is often low-paid work in richer nations.

International money transfers can be costly, with remittance fees and currency conversion losses amounting to around 7 per cent of what is being sent. Sustainable Development Goal 10 includes a commitment to reducing transfer costs to less than 3 per cent. 16 June has been recognised by the United Nations as the International Day of Family Remittances.

Dropping the debt

The Jewish and Christian bible sets out that there should be a 'jubilee year' after seven cycles of seven years when debts should be forgiven. Based on this idea, the Jubilee Debt Campaign advocated for poor country debt to be forgiven to mark the millennium in the year 2000. At the G8 Summit in 2005, the rich nations and international institutions agreed to forgive the debt of highly indebted countries in recognition that it would never be repaid and as an alternative to continued rescheduling.

Since then, though, the debt burden on poor countries has not gone away. Interest rates may be lower but the amount owing is substantial. The total external debt of low- and middle-income countries amounts to $55 trillion, which includes all forms of debt (consumer, business and government).

One issue is that poor people are being robbed by corrupt and kleptocratic elites, where much of the borrowed money is 'lost' in commissions or fraud, or to projects which never show any economic benefit, such as the $2 billion lent to two companies and backed by the government of Mozambique for a tuna fishing fleet accompanied by naval protection which

generated no meaningful revenue, and where 25 per cent of the funds remain unaccounted for. A large proportion of this country's government revenue is being spent on servicing its debt with little left over to provide health, education and other basic services.

Another issue is 'vulture funds'. Hedge funds buy up distressed securities where there is a high expectation of default, and which are seen as worthless. The hedge fund then uses the courts to extract money from the borrowers to settle the debt which they now own. It has bought the 'worthless' debt as an investment, and it wants to maximise its return.

The Jubilee Debt Campaign continues to fight for a just solution to poor countries' indebtedness.

The Sustainable Development Goals

The 2030 Agenda for Sustainable Development was adopted by all United Nations member states in 2015. It provides a blueprint for peace and prosperity for people and the planet, and followed on from the seven Millennium Development Goals agreed for 2000–2015, which were not achieved. The 2030 Agenda includes 17 Sustainable Development Goals (known as the SDGs). These include 169 agreed targets to be met by the year 2030. They are an urgent call for action by all countries – the developed world, which has the resources, and the developing nations, where action is most needed – to join together in partnership to create a world where everybody will be able to achieve a decent standard of life.

In one sense, the goals and targets are just a fanciful wish list for what everyone would like to see happen without any roadmap for how this might be achieved. In another sense, the ambition to create solutions to world poverty is admirable, should be agreed and backed by everyone, and we should all be doing our very best to provide a better, healthier and happier life for everyone on the planet. The world has the resources to be able to do this. But an unwillingness to share resources across the planet more equitably and the urgency that is needed probably mean that the SDG targets will not be achieved, just like what happened with the Millennium Development Goals from 2000 to 2015.

The 17 SDGs are:

1   No poverty

2   End hunger

3   Good health and wellbeing

4   Quality education

5   Gender equality

6   Clean water and sanitation

7   Affordable and clean energy

8   Decent work and economic growth

9   Industry, innovation and infrastructure

10   Reduced inequalities

11   Sustainable cities and communities

12   Responsible consumption and production

13   Climate action

14   Life below water

15   Life on land

16   Peace, justice and strong institutions

17   Partnerships for the goals

Each goal has multiple targets, as well as indicators for measuring progress towards achieving the target. For example, with 'no poverty', there are five targets:

1.1   To eradicate extreme poverty for all people everywhere. Extreme poverty is currently measured as people living on less than $1.90 a day. We have already seen that extreme poverty is being reduced but not nearly fast enough.

1.2   To reduce by at least half the proportion of men, women and children of all ages living in poverty in all its dimensions, according to national definitions. Not just eliminating extreme poverty but trying to lift everybody out of poverty.

1.3   To implement nationally appropriate social protection systems and measures for all, providing a floor to provide a degree of security for everybody, ensuring that there is substantial coverage for the poor and the vulnerable. This includes children, unemployed persons, older persons, persons with disabilities, pregnant women, newborns, work-injury victims.

1.4 To ensure that all men and women, in particular the poor and the vulnerable, have equal rights to economic resources, as well as access to basic services, and ownership and control over land and other forms of property, inheritance, natural resources, appropriate new technology and financial services, including microfinance. The main targets for this are access to basic services and security of land tenure.

1.5 To build the resilience of the poor and those in vulnerable situations and reduce their exposure and vulnerability to climate-related extreme events and other economic, social and environmental shocks and disasters. This relates mostly to natural disasters but the Covid–19 crisis has brought this into a sharper perspective.

You can track progress against the SDGs at sdg-tracker.org.

Solutions that work

'Nearly every problem has been solved by someone, somewhere. The challenge of the 21st century is to find what works and scale it up.'

– President Bill Clinton

Looking at the 17 SDGs and 169 targets, there are solutions that work, whether it is providing access to affordable medicines for basic health needed in poor areas, early years nutrition, secondary education creating skills and opportunities for future life, local energy generated from sustainable sources, more efficient food growing or clean water and sanitation. There are solutions to these and other problems working in practice. Our big challenge is not to invent more and more new solutions (although continuous innovation is important) but to give greater priority towards developing ways of scaling up what has proved to work, and then to find ways of paying for the scaling up.

The Poverty Action Lab at MIT led by Esther Duflo seeks to prove what works through randomised control trials. For example, she found that handing out free mosquito nets was better than charging for them and that 90 per cent of those who received a free net were using it as required. The recipients of free nets were also more prepared to pay for nets next time round than those who had originally had to purchase them. There are many ways in which you might try to enhance school attendance and raise academic attainment, including giving free school uniforms, awarding scholarships on merit or to girls, providing loans based on need, installing toilets, recruiting and retaining better teachers, providing books and creating libraries … all are possible and practical approaches. There will be advocates for each course of action. The only way of finding out what really works and what is most cost-effective is through a properly designed trial, testing out each solution with its different variants. This is what the Poverty Action Lab does. In the case of education, providing free school meals and de-worming children have proved to be the most effective.

Spring Impact, led by Dan Berelowitz, was created as an international consultancy based in London and San Francisco to encourage the spread of ideas that work. Their Social Replication Toolkit suggests a range of different options from growing your organisation to franchising and licensing others to use your methods. The toolkit can be downloaded free from their website. It suggests that you first try to answer these ten questions:

1   Understanding the problem: Is there a good understanding of the problem and how it could be solved?

2   Evaluating the impact: Is there a reasonable level of proof that the solution has significant social impact?

3   Developing a sustainable business model: Is there evidence demonstrating a sustainable business model such that revenue can be earned or generated to cover costs with a reasonable degree of confidence?

4   Setting out the working processes: Are the processes for delivery of the project in place and documented as a starting point for replication (this is sometimes referred to as the 'business in a box')?

5   Leadership in place: Is there a clear project owner who has the relevant skills to take the project to scale?

6   A market for the solution: Is the problem or need widespread with the need not being adequately met elsewhere and by others? Will the scaling up of the solution make a significant impact on the problem?

7   Cultural issues: Is there evidence that the venture can be made to work in other cultures and settings, and a recognition that adaptation may be required?

8   Support for scaling up: Do all the stakeholders in the project fully support the opportunity for replication? Have they been consulted on how this should be approached?

9   Brand and vision: Are the organisation's vison and values clearly documented and agreed? Will these be maintained as the solution is spread?

10 Human resources: Do the right people and organisations exist who are willing, qualified and able to become partners in replicating the project in other geographies?

'Social entrepreneurs are not content just to give a fish or teach how to fish. They will not rest until they have revolutionized the fishing industry.'

– Bill Drayton, founder Ashoka: Innovators for the Public

DO THIS:

Most of us in the West are in the fortunate position of being able to give to help others or achieve change, even if that is only a small amount. How about tithing – keeping 90 per cent of your income for yourself and giving away 10 per cent? This is a 'gold standard' for philanthropy in many religious traditions – Christian, Muslim, Jewish. Or if this is too much for you, then save up your spare change. Each night, put your coins in a box – this is your 'charity pot'. You will find that the amount soon adds up and you won't even notice it.

Toby Ord, a philosopher at Oxford University, founded Giving What We Can in 2009, inviting people to pledge 10 per cent of their income to support the most cost-effective charities. They now have over 1,000 members who will contribute over £270 million to charity over their lifetime: givingwhatwecan.org.

Business
doing better

40

Leaders in corporate social responsibility – the most admired businesses

1 Ben & Jerry's, ice cream
(Unilever, Netherlands)

2 Bosch, engineering and electricals
(Germany)

3 Chobani, yogurt
(USA)

4 Danone, foods and dairy
(France)

5 Google/Alphabet, computer services
(USA)

6 Grundfos, water pumps
(Denmark)

7 Havaianas, clothes and shoes
(Brazil)

8 IKEA, furniture
(Netherlands/Sweden)

9 Intel, computer chips
(USA)

10 Lavazza, coffee
(Italy)

11 Lego, toys
(Denmark)

12 Microsoft, software
(USA)

13 Natura, cosmetics
(Brazil)

14 Novo Nordisk, pharmaceuticals
(Denmark)

15 Patagonia, outdoor wear
(USA)

16 Sony, electricals
(Japan)

17 Tata, automotive
(India)

18 The Walt Disney Company, media
(USA)

19 ZTE, telecommunications
(China)

This is a list of some of the most admired companies around the world for their corporate social responsibility (CSR) policies (assembled from various sources). Included are B Corps, companies which have adopted a business structure which requires a not-just-for-profit approach to running a business, and businesses which are owned partly or wholly by charitable foundations. This is not a definitive list of the best. Many other companies have lively and successful CSR programmes that are worth exploring. But take a look at the very different approaches to CSR by the companies listed here.

Good and evil

'Don't be evil' was the motto first used by Google in 2004. It succinctly expressed what it saw as its corporate mission. Paul Buchheit, the creator of Gmail, said that they 'wanted something that, once you put it in there, would be hard to take out'. Following Google's corporate restructuring and the creation of Alphabet in 2015, which became the overall holding company for the Google businesses, Alphabet substituted 'Do the right thing' as its new motto. The original was retained in Google's code of conduct, but in 2018 this was taken from the preface and relegated to being its final sentence.

Both these mottos are important. A company should always be looking to be doing the right thing. Knowingly doing the wrong thing is contrary to any definition of good business practice. But before even starting to think about doing right, a company should look at all the bad things it is doing and address these as a matter of urgency. Here are some ways in which companies are doing harm:

Selling harmful products

Many products cause actual harm to their customers or society.

↳ 'Big Tobacco' companies make money from selling what they know to be a lethal product. They might wish to explore healthier options, such as e-cigarettes, or even develop new, beneficial products for their market.

↳ Coca-Cola and Pepsico sell products that directly contribute to obesity and diabetes, two leading health issues of our time. Pepsico purchased Gatorade, energy drinks for those taking exercise and who actually need a sugar boost; Coca-Cola developed Cola Life, a greener alternative made with natural ingredients. The Cola Wars could have resulted in a race to create and dominate a healthier drinks market.

↳ The pharmaceutical company Pfizer was selling drugs to be given as lethal injections to execute death row prisoners, until public pressure forced it to stop.

↳ Weapons manufacturers make guns, bombs and missiles that kill people, whether through warfare or gangland killings or terrorism. In 1976, workers at Lucas Aerospace in the UK felt that instead of making lethal weapons, their company should be developing products more useful to humanity. They came up with an alternative plan for the company. The board rejected this outright and sacked Mike Cooley, a leader of this initiative ... who went on to win a Right Livelihood Award for 'promoting the theory and practice of human-centred, socially useful production'.

Harming the environment

Companies can reduce the damage they cause to the environment, whether through extraction or by discharging waste, or by releasing toxins into the atmosphere, or through over-use of water or by using harmful chemicals in the manufacturing process.

↳ The Volkswagen scandal in 2015, when the company was caught knowingly using false emissions figures for its diesel-engine vehicles, damaged both sales and the brand. Diesel emissions contribute towards pollution in cities, and to respiratory disease and death.

↳ Bajaj Auto is one of India's leading automotive companies, owned by a family well known for its philanthropy. But its products, two-wheeler scooters and motorbikes and three-wheeler autorickshaws, have been major contributors to air pollution in India's cities. The company could become a world leader in developing small, cheap, zero-emissions vehicles for getting around cities … which must be the future for urban mobility.

↳ Big oil, and especially ExxonMobil, became entrenched deniers of human-made global warming, delaying the introduction of policies and subsidies to transition to a green economy, which could create the best future for this business sector.

Harmful employment

Companies can stop exposing their workers to dangerous work in dangerous buildings. The Rana Plaza was an unsafe textile factory making clothing for many leading Western brands in a badly constructed building in Dhaka. It collapsed in 2013, resulting in 1,134

deaths. The garment industry is acutely aware that its contractors or sub-contractors who are doing the actual manufacturing of their products are often not providing safe working environments for their workers. But most international brands now recognise that they need to take overall responsibility.

Tech doing bad

Slate.com asked a wide range of journalists, academics and professionals to rank tech companies on the basis of the evil they were doing. The main concerns were data harvesting, surveillance, misinformation, algorithmic bias and opportunities for fraud. These are their top 5 for 2020: 1. Amazon; 2. Meta/Facebook; 3. Alphabet/Google; 4. Palantir Technologies; 5. Uber.

Greenwashing

Once the issue of doing evil has been addressed, next comes the opportunity for using corporate social responsibility more effectively. Typically, CSR involves a company devoting a small percentage of its profits to doing good in the local communities where it operates, encouraging employee volunteering, being a social leader through addressing industry-connected social issues (such as alcohol companies and teenage drinking), and helping build the company's corporate image.

Coca-Cola is one of the world's most recognised brands. Their most famous advertising campaign, released in 1971, was based on an adaptation of the New Seekers' song 'I'd Like to Teach the World to Sing (In Perfect Harmony)', associating love, enjoyment and universal togetherness with their product and those who drink it. On a sunny hilltop in Italy, the company assembled young people from all over the world to sing the song – in perfect harmony of course – ending with the slogan 'It's the real thing'.

Alongside their huge advertising budget, Coca-Cola has a carefully constructed CSR programme. Here are two of their initiatives in China:

↳ They worked with WWF China to bring dolphins back to the Yangtze river.

↳ They teamed up with the One Foundation to bring water into any disaster area within 24 hours (as China is an active earthquake zone). This involves fundraising by children in schools to support the programme and create awareness of earthquakes and what can be done for the victims.

Both these initiatives align closely with a company which sells bottled water; both link the company with respected and influential organisations; both generate good publicity. But they are hardly world-changing and neither addresses the negative impacts of the company's products on health and the environment.

The best companies try to use their CSR expenditure really creatively, but for too

many companies, the main aim is to massage their corporate image as socially and environmentally responsible businesses with good publicity as the primary outcome. The other issue is that only tiny amounts of money are involved. In many countries, the norm is 0.5 per cent of annual profits (in the UK) or 1 per cent (in the USA). Most of the money is spent in the country and city where the business has its headquarters. In India and South Africa, companies are required by law to spend 2 per cent of their profits on CSR, which still leaves 98 per cent for the shareholders. But it is not just a question of how much the company is spending, rather whether there is an ethos of social and environmental responsibility underlying how the company conducts its business.

The Japan Business Federation's Charter of Corporate Behaviour advocates these commitments from business:

1   To develop and provide socially beneficial and safe goods and services for consumers.

2   To engage in fair, transparent and free competition.

3   In addition to communicating with shareholders, to disclose corporate information actively and fairly.

4   To respect diversity, character and personality of employees and ensure a safe and comfortable working environment.

5   To proactively initiate measures in acknowledgement of environmental issues.

6   To actively engage in community involvement activities.

7   To resolutely confront antisocial forces and organisations.

8   In line with the globalisation of business activities, to contribute toward the development of the local economy and society.

The International Organization for Standardization created ISO 26000 in 2010 as an international standard providing guidelines for social responsibility. It advocates seven key principles for socially responsible behaviour: accountability, transparency, ethical behaviour, respect for stakeholder interests (stakeholders being individuals or groups affected by or having the ability to impact the company's actions) and respect for rule of law, international norms of behaviour and human rights. Every company should consider these seven core subjects: governance, human rights, labour practices, environment, fair operating practices, consumer issues and community engagement.

B Corps

Should a business be just about making money and creating wealth for its shareholders, while ignoring everybody and everything else? Or could the business seek to benefit a wider group of stakeholders – not just shareholders, but customers, employees, the local communities where it operates and, of course, the environment, which is important for everybody. And if a business adopts this 'not-just-for-profit approach', could it end up making even more profit for its shareholders?

This is the idea behind the B Corp, the 'B' standing for 'benefit' and 'better way of doing things'. The B Corp movement started in 2006, when the founders of a leisurewear company sold their business and then all their carefully constructed social responsibility was dismantled by the new owner. The founders said to themselves, 'Never again; let's create a way of embedding a wider mission into how a company operates.' Today, over 3,000 companies around the world have been certified as B Corps. These include a number of large international companies, such as Danone for its operations in the USA; Unilever for some of its brands including Ben & Jerry's; Natura (which now includes The Body Shop); and Patagonia. And the number of B Corps is growing month by month.

This is the B Corp 'Declaration of Inter-Dependence':

'We envision a global economy that uses business as a force for good. This economy is comprised of a new type of corporation – the B Corporation – which is purpose-driven and creates benefit for all stakeholders, not just shareholders. As B Corporations and leaders of this emerging economy, we believe:

↳ That we must be the change we seek in the world.

↳ That all business ought to be conducted as if people and place mattered.

↳ That, through their products, practices, and profits, businesses should aspire to do no harm and benefit all.

↳ To do so requires that we act with the understanding that we are each dependent upon another and thus responsible for each other and future generations.

A business wanting to register as a B Corp is examined across five dimensions of its operations:

↳ Employees of the company: how staff are treated and compensated.

↳ The environment: how environmental issues can become a central factor for the business.

↳ The local communities where the company operates: how the business can contribute to the local community and its needs.

↳ The impact of the business on its customers and the public: how the positive impacts of the business can be maximised and the negative impacts minimised.

↳ The governance and the transparency of the business in all its dealings, including how the company is managed, what information it makes public and how it informs all its stakeholders.'

If the applicant company is able to score 80 out of a possible 200 points on the questions it is asked, while also providing evidence to support its answers, it can become registered as a B Corp. Its status will be re-examined every two years, and for many this encourages continual improvement. These are quotes from three business leaders:

'Today's business books say businesses exist to maximise profit for the shareholders. I think that's the dumbest idea I've ever heard in my life.'

– Hamdi Ulukaya, founder of US yogurt manufacturer Chobani

'Capitalism, which has been responsible for the growth and prosperity that has done so much to enhance our lives, is a damaged ideology and needs to be reinvented for the twenty-first century.'

– Paul Polman, former chairman of Unilever

'We do not consider the purpose of this company to be returning money to shareholders. There is a broader purpose.'

– Emmanuel Faber, former CEO of Danone

Business for good

There is an even bigger idea – that a business can provide solutions to social issues through the products and services it creates as a part of its core business. Rather than applying a percentage of profits towards doing good, companies can harness the might of their business, including capital, technologies, research, supply chains, logistics, contacts and their brand, with the aim of seeing a return on their investment while creating a positive social or environmental impact. They could be bringing clean water and better health to everybody in the world, providing quality education at all levels, improving the lives of disabled people and much more. Big companies are probably much better placed to do this than under-resourced charities and in pursuing this 'business for good' approach, the company could find that it is also 'good for business', increasing profits, extending markets, fostering innovation. Here are some examples:

↳ Vodafone and its Kenyan associate Safaricom developed the M-Pesa mobile payment system, which brought banking to the poorest and has transformed the lives of poor people and the economy in Kenya, far beyond the capacity of any development programme – and all well before the introduction of mobile payments by Apple, Google and WeChat. This is now being expanded beyond East Africa. M-Pesa has not only changed the world, it operates as a profitable business.

↳ Amway produces and markets nutritional supplements through its Nutrilite brand. In China, it is working in partnership with government to address the major problem of child malnutrition, which can lead to stunted growth and poor brain development, as nutrition in the child's first five years is critical to its future wellbeing. Amway distributes for free a chewy supplement to all under-fives in two districts of Sichuan Province. This modest CSR initiative is funded largely by sales agents and by customers though a buy-one-give-one promotion. But with ambition, Amway could scale up the provision of free nutritional supplements across the world so that no under-five was handicapped for life though poor brain development. The challenge would be to find a way of paying for this.

↳ The Healthstore Foundation has created a network of child and family wellness shops across Kenya, which are run as successful franchised small businesses. They provide medication for the 12 most common health problems, together representing over 99 per cent of people's health needs. The 'business for good' opportunity would be to spread the availability of medicines and basic health advice to everybody in Africa, to provide access to affordable medicines using this proven model. A Big Pharma company has the resources to do this, which smaller non-profits just do not have.

DO THIS:

Use your spending power to encourage better business practice. Buy preferentially from better companies. Take a look at the B Corp movement and see if any of the companies sell goods or services that interest you: bcorporation.net.

In the beginning …

There was just darkness, water and the great god Mbombo …

Mbombo had a very bad stomach ache. He vomited and his vomit created the sun, the moon and the stars. Heat from the sun evaporated the water covering the Earth, creating clouds, and dry hills rose up from the water. Mbombo vomited again. This time his vomit created nine animals: a leopard and another leopard-like animal, an eagle, a crocodile, a fish, a tortoise, a white heron, a scarab and a goat. His vomit also created many men; one was Loko Yima. The nine animals went on to create all the creatures in the world. The heron created the flying birds, the crocodile the creeping snakes, the goat the horned animals, the scarab all insects and the tortoise all fish.

Three of Mbombo's sons then set out to finish creation. Nyonye Ngana vomited white ants but then he died. The ants burrowed into the ground to find the soil to bury him and in doing this, the Earth's surface became no longer barren. Chonganda created the first plant, which was the starting point for all the trees, grasses and flowers. Chedi Bumba made one last bird, the kite. Mbombo showed his people how to make fire. Once his creation had been completed and the world was peaceful, Mbombo delivered it up to mankind and retreated to the heavens. Loko Yima was instructed to serve as 'god upon the earth'.

This is the creation story of the Kuba people of central Africa. Cultures around the world have produced their own creation stories and many are quite similar to the Kuba story. This is how the Judaeo-Christian version starts:

In the beginning ... God created the heaven and the earth. And the earth was without form, and void; and darkness was upon the face of the deep. And the spirit of God moved upon the face of the waters. And God said, let there be light: and there was light ... [and after seven days] ... thus the heavens and the earth were finished ... and on the seventh day God ended his work.

The first man was Adam ... and out of the ground the Lord God formed every beast of the field and every fowl of the air; and brought them unto Adam. He also created Eve and gave them a paradise to live in, the Garden of Eden. The date of this creation has been precisely calculated as being 6pm on 22 October 4004BC. And this Earth that had been created was placed firmly at the centre of the universe.

Then along came the Polish astronomer Nicolaus Copernicus, who had been studying the sky with his naked eye (telescopes had not been invented then). In 1514, he circulated a handwritten manuscript which stated:

↳ There is no one centre in the universe.

↳ The Earth's centre is not the centre of the universe.

↳ The centre of the universe is near the Sun.

↳ The distance from the Earth to the Sun is imperceptible compared with the distance to the stars.

This was the beginning of modern astronomy, although Aristarchus of Samos had placed the sun at the centre of the known universe more than 2,200 years earlier. In the ensuing centuries, and just by looking at the stars, we have come to discover the true history of the universe and our place within it. This is the timeline:

↳

The history of the universe

13.8 billion years ago: The Big Bang, which was the starting point for all of our universe.

12.6 billion years ago: The formation of our galaxy, the Milky Way.

4.6 billion years ago: The formation of the Sun as the centre of our solar system.

4.5 billion years ago: The formation of our solar system, including the planets, orbiting around the Sun.

2.15 billion years ago: The first evidence of photosynthesis – plants growing by taking in carbon dioxide.

2.4 billion years ago: The 'great oxidation event', when oxygen started to build up in the atmosphere.

3.8 billion years ago: The emergence of life on Earth, starting with bacteria and archaea.

4.4 billion years ago: The formation of the Earth's water and atmosphere.

1.5 billion years ago: The division of reproductive living matter into three groups, which would evolve as plants, fungi and animals.

900 million years ago: The emergence of multicellular life.

500 million years ago: The first vertebrates appear and arrive on land.

465 million years ago: Plants arrive on land.

2.1 million years ago: The earliest human, Homo habilis.

4.2 million years ago: The earliest hominid.

25 million years ago: The earliest apes.

36 million years ago: The earliest primates.

1.5 million years ago: Homo erectus appears in Africa.

300,000 years ago: Homo sapiens appears in Africa.

90,000 years ago: Homo sapiens sapiens, the first modern man, appears.

11,000 years ago: Earliest human settlements are seen.

7,000 years ago: The human population reaches 5 million.

7,000 years ago: Domestication of animals (in Iran).

9,500 years ago: Cultivation of grains (in Mesopotamia, today's Iraq).

Humans have been on our planet for a tiny fraction of its existence. But during that time, we have become masters of our world. We are undoubtedly top species, and we are able to dominate all other species. We have shaped the physical world to our needs. In 2020, it was estimated that the weight of all human-made materials (which includes buildings, roads and other structures) reached 1.1 trillion tonnes, which for the first time exceeded the mass of all living things on our planet (which includes humans, animals, plants and bacteria). We are beginning to refer to this current period as 'the Anthropocene', a new geological epoch which is replacing 'the Holocene', which began 12,000 years ago and was a period when life flourished. This could be the epoch where humans are able to create 'the best of all possible worlds'. Or we could be rushing headlong towards our own extinction as a species. Our planet has seen five mass exinctions so far:

1   The Ordovician-Silurian Extinction, 444 million years ago, when 86 per cent of species were lost.

2   The Late Devonian Extinction, 375 million years ago, when 75 per cent of species were lost.

3   The Permian-Triassic Extinction, 251 million years ago, when 96 per cent of species were lost. This is known as 'the great dying', nearly ending life on Earth.

4   The Triassic-Jurassic Extinction, 200 million years ago, when 80 per cent of species were lost.

5   The Cretaceous-Paleogene Extinction, 66 million years ago, when 76 per cent of all species were lost. This ended the reign of the dinosaurs as the world's top creatures.

The likely cause for the first four of these five mass extinctions was a sudden change in the delicate balance of CO_2 levels in the atmosphere, which has a direct impact on the Earth's temperature through what is commonly referred to as the Greenhouse Effect. The fifth and last extinction was caused by an unfortunate encounter with a huge asteroid. The Chicxulub asteroid hitting the Earth had a diameter of between 11 and 81 kilometres and its crater is still visible in Mexico.

Many people now fear that we are on the brink of the sixth mass extinction, the Anthropocene Extinction, which will be caused again by rising CO_2 levels in the atmosphere, but this time the runaway warming will have been caused by human activity rather than through natural processes.

As the world's temperature rises, crop yields will fall and crops will fail. If it rises above body heat, then our bodies' natural cooling process of sweating will cease to work. The raised temperature will cause heat exhaustion, heat stroke and then death. In September 2019, Paris saw record temperatures reaching as high as 42.6°C, causing nearly 1,500 deaths. Is this a forewarning of things to come if we don't urgently address global warming? Its impact could be catastrophic for the future of human life on our planet.

... And in the end

Our universe started with The Big Bang 13.8 billion years ago. Even if humans self-destruct, life on our planet will continue. But for how long? And when it will all end?

There are several theories for how the universe will continue or end:

The Steady State Theory. As the galaxies move apart, new galaxies would form from matter that was being continually created in space. According to this theory, the universe would not have a beginning and would not have an end. It would be in a 'steady state'. This theory, proposed in 1948, has since been disproved by cosmologists.

The Big Crunch. The universe is expanding and if it has sufficient mass, then gravitational attraction between the galaxies will halt and reverse the expansion. The universe will start to contract and then implode in on itself, so creating a Big Crunch, when all matter is sucked back into a finite point.

The Big Bounce. Once the Big Crunch has taken place, there will be another Big Bang, leading to the start of a new universe 'bouncing' into existence.

Disappearance into nothingness. If the gravitational forces are not strong enough, then the universe will keep on expanding for ever. Over time, the stars will burn themselves out and the universe will become emptier and emptier. It will get colder and colder, and things will eventually end ... in nothingness.

Cosmologists have come up with other hypothetical possibilities. Vacuum decay might occur when a bubble pops up somewhere in the universe, inside which the laws of physics are wildly different and particles interact in fundamentally different ways. This bubble then expands at the speed of light, spreading eventually across the entire universe. This new universe will certainly not be hospitable for human existence.

The Big Rip has the universe expanding at an ever-increasing rate, such that the size of the observable universe is shrinking. At some point, the universe will become too big for the fundamental forces to apply across its entirety. At that point, the universe will be 'ripped apart' and all distances will become infinite.

Whatever happens, and we will never know what will happen, the universe will be there for billions more years. But what about the future of our Sun in the universe, the star around which we are orbiting that gives us the heat and energy that sustains life on our planet? And what about the future of our Earth?

Astronomers estimate that the Sun still has 7 to 8 billion years of its life left. But in about 5 billion years, it will run out of hydrogen. Gravitational forces will then compress the core, enabling the rest of the Sun's matter to expand. The Sun will turn into a red giant so large that it will grow to reach the inner planets, including Earth. It will envelop us in its massive heat and that will be the end of our planet. The time until this happens is over half a million times the span of time that humans have lived on Earth. Humans will be gone by then, as the 'Goldilocks conditions' which enable life (not too hot, not too cold, just right) will have long disappeared.

Then what about our future on our planet? This is much more problematic. There are all sorts of scenarios which threaten our existence. Many books have been written setting out some of the ways that human life might cease to exist. Joel Levy, in his book *The Doomsday Book: Scenarios for the End of the World*, sets out 28 possible ways in which this could happen. He analyses each in relation to three factors: the likelihood of it happening; its impact, the damage it would cause and whether there are ways of mitigating this; and the 'fear factor' – how frightened we feel about it.

These are some of the possibilities he identifies:

↳ Climate change, which in the past has led to four of the five mass extinctions.

↳ Cataclysms, such as an asteroid impact, which led to the fifth mass extinction, a super-volcano or a mega-tsunami.

↳ Ecocide, including poisoning the planet with toxins, water running out, famine and acid seas.

↳ War and terrorism, where humanity kills itself.

↳ A global pandemic, more virulent than Covid-19.

↳ Technology gone wrong, from AI and nanotechnology out of control to a global pandemic and a physics experiment gone wrong.

Joel Levy concludes by saying this: 'Most authors writing on the topic of doomsday seek to end on a positive note, offering at least a glimmer of hope that through a combination of grassroots activism and visionary statesmanship the worst may be avoided and society will find a way out of the mire. I wish I could be so optimistic. Neither history nor current trends suggest that solutions will be found to global problems until it is too late. I look to the future with a wary eye.'

But here is something a bit more optimistic. Although the threat of a comet or asteroid hitting the Earth is real and an impact by a body larger than 1km in diameter would disturb our climate sufficiently for food production across the world to cease for a year or even longer, resulting in starvation, loss of life and civil disorder on an unimaginable scale, we may be able to prevent this happening. The Spacewatch project based at the University of Arizona has detected approximately 1,000 Earth-approaching asteroids larger than 1km in diameter. Identifying them and charting their orbits provides us with sufficient warning and time to prepare spacecraft missions to deflect the path of any potential impactor away from us.

When I started writing this book in early 2020, the Doomdsay Clock had just been advanced 20 seconds, from 2 minutes to midnight to 100 seconds to midnight. The Bulletin of the Atomic Scientists created the Doomsday Clock in 1947 with the time to midnight signifying the extent of man-made threats to humanity and the planet. At the time, nuclear war was the main threat, but today there are others, especially climate change. The decision to change the time is made once a year. On 23 January 2020, the Bulletin included the following passage in its Doomsday Clock statement to citizens and leaders of the world:

'Humanity continues to face two simultaneous existential dangers – nuclear war and climate change – that are compounded by a threat multiplier, cyber-enabled information warfare, that undercuts society's ability to respond. The international security situation is dire, not just because these threats exist, but because world leaders have allowed the international political infrastructure for managing them to erode ...

Faced with this daunting threat landscape and a new willingness of political leaders to reject the negotiations and institutions that can protect civilization over the long term, the Bulletin of the Atomic Scientists Science and Security Board today moves the Doomsday Clock 20 seconds closer to midnight – closer to apocalypse than ever ...

Given the inaction and in too many cases counterproductive actions of international leaders, [we] are compelled to declare a state of emergency that requires the immediate, focused, and unrelenting attention of the entire world. It is 100 seconds to midnight. The Clock continues to tick. Immediate action is required.'

You can read the full statement at thebulletin. org. Take a look at the Doomsday Clock and check out the current time: thebulletin.org/ doomsday-clock/.

In 2009, film-maker Franny Armstrong released her crowdfunded film about global warming, premiering in London's Leicester Square at the world's largest solar-powered film showing. She called her film *The Age of Stupid* because we knew all the facts about global warming, we had plenty of practical ways in which we might address the problem, but despite all of this, we were too stupid to do anything. Her big question was, 'Why didn't we stop climate change when we had the chance?'

The film is set in 2055, in a world ravaged by catastrophic climate change; London is flooded, Sydney is burning, Las Vegas has been swallowed up by desert, the Amazon rainforest has burned up, snow has vanished from the Alps, nuclear war has laid waste to India. An unnamed archivist is entrusted with the safekeeping of humanity's surviving store of art and knowledge. Alone in his vast repository off the coast of the largely ice-free Arctic, he reviews archival footage trying to discern where it all went wrong. You can download *The Age of Stupid* for free at spannerfilms.net.

Can we put back the Doomsday Clock? If we can't, then what? Are you a pessimist, feeling that nothing can be done? That it is all too late and that the problems are just too huge? Or are you an optimist? That we have the capacity to make a better future for everyone on our planet?

Yes we will

In 2008, a young US senator and presidential hopeful called Barack Obama was swept to power with the slogan 'Yes We Can'. The question to all of us today is not 'Can we do something?' – we know that we can and this book has shown all sorts of people trying to find solutions to many of the world's problems. The question is 'Will we do something?' The answer to this question must surely be 'Yes We Will'. Change has to start somewhere and we should not leave it to government and to 'other people'. Change can start with each one of us. 'Be the change that you wish to see in the world,' as Gandhi said. 'If you think you are too small to make a difference, try sleeping with a mosquito,' as the Dalai Lama once said.

Greta Tintin Eleonora Ernman Thunberg, a 15-year-old Swedish schoolgirl, was certainly not big – either in age or in size. But she felt that climate change was just too important an issue to ignore. She thought that there was no point in having an education if our world was to have no future. So she went on strike. On Fridays from August 2018, instead of going to school, she sat outside the Swedish Parliament with a placard that read Skolstrejk for Klimatet – school strike for the climate. Small, on her own, advocating something that she felt passionate about. She was 'discovered', her action was publicised; she was invited to speak by the United Nations and the World Economic Forum and all over the world. She even travelled to the UN Climate Action Summit in New York by sailing boat.

At this summit she said, 'My message is that we'll be watching you. This is all wrong. I shouldn't be up here. I should be back in school on the other side of the ocean. Yet you all come to us young people for hope. How dare you. You have stolen my dreams and my childhood with your empty words. Yet I am one of the lucky ones. People are suffering.' You can listen to Greta's speech on YouTube.

Greta has inspired hundreds of thousands of young people to action. Fridays for Future, the idea of taking Fridays off school for climate action, has spread around the world. Here are some of Greta's most incisive quotes:

'The eyes of all future generations are upon you. And if you choose to fail us, I say we will never forgive you.'

– UN Climate Summit, New York, September 2019

'We showed that we are united
and that we, young people, are
unstoppable.'

– UN Youth Climate Summit, New York,
September 2019

'We are striking because we have done
our homework, and they have not.'

– Climate protest, Hamburg, March 2019

'Since our leaders are behaving like
children, we will have to take the
responsibility they should have taken
long ago.'

– COP24, Katiwice, December 2018

'I want you to act as if the house is on
fire, because it is.'

– World Economic Forum, Davos, January 2019

WATCH THIS: Do it like Greta:
climateactionsnow.org/do-it-like-greta.

Here is another young person addressing a global
need. Ryan Hreljac was just six years old in 1998,
when, one day, he was sitting in his grade one
primary school class in a town just outside Toronto
in Canada listening to his teacher who was
explaining how some people in the world were
sick and some even dying because they didn't
have clean water. Some had to walk for hours
each day to fetch the water they needed for their
families, and all too often it was dirty water.

Ryan knew that all he had to do was to take
ten steps out of his classroom to get fresh,
clean drinking water from the drinking fountain,
and he could have as much as he wanted.
Reflecting on this, he decided that he just had
to do something.

When he got home, he asked his parents to
give him $70, which he thought was a huge
sum and would be just about enough to build
a well in Africa. At first, they told him that they
couldn't as they did not have the money to
spare. But Ryan persisted (this is known as
'pester power'). After a few days, his parents
came to a decision. They told him that they
wouldn't give him the money but that he could
do extra chores and earn it.

Ryan worked for four months to earn his $70,
by tidying his room, doing the washing up,
clearing leaves from the lawn, helping his
dad wash the car and lots of other things. He
then took his $70 in a cardboard box to the
offices of WaterCan, the Canadian NGO which
addresses water issues in the world, and he
asked a member of staff if they could use
his $70 to build a well in Africa. They told him
that the money was not nearly enough, as
building a well would actually cost $2,000. 'No
matter,' Ryan said, 'I'll just go home and earn
it' – which, with the help of his parents and the
involvement of his school and other children,
he managed to do.

Ryan's passion to bring water to Africa led to
the setting up of the Ryan's Well Foundation
in 2001. Since then, Ryan has funded nearly

1,200 clean water projects which have improved the lives of nearly 900,000 people. Not bad for a boy of six!

It is not just Greta and Ryan, it is all of us. We can all do something that will make a difference in little ways and in bigger ways. We can switch off the lights when we leave a room and turn the washing machine temperature down to 30 degrees. We can have meat-free Mondays or even go vegan. We can travel less. We can go zero-waste. We can stop buying from environment-destroying businesses. By doing something, however little, we will also be showing that change is possible and inspiring others to do their bit.

We can also press our governments to act. Some people call the climate crisis an emergency, some use the word extinction. If the UK government can in one week announce £650 billion in grants and loans for tackling the coronavirus crisis, then why not some similar reaction to climate change, which is going to cause death and disruption far worse than any pandemic? Climate change may not seem so immediate as a virus spreading around the world but its impact will be much more devastating.

We have reached a crunch point on many issues which will determine the quality of life for us and for future generations. Not just climate change but also air pollution, plastic pollution, water shortage, loss of fertility, habitat destruction ... We have to do something. Sometimes what we do will fail; sometimes it will not be big enough to make

any real difference. But our biggest failure would be to sit and do nothing. That is the stupidity that Franny Armstrong was referring to in her film *The Age of Stupid*.

We should also be using our creativity. Ideas are often a good starting point for trying to find solutions, and competitions and challenges are a good way of seeking these out. In 2021, the Royal Foundation launched the Earthshot Prize to challenge innovators to come up with practical solutions for some of the planet's most pressing environmental problems. There are five categories, listed here with one of the short-listed entries to illustrate the breadth of creative thinking and ambition of citizens, scientists and even governments to do something:

↳ Protect and restore nature: the government of Costa Rica pays its citizens to protect trees, which has doubled the forested area of the country. This idea could be applied much more widely.

↳ Clean our air: teenager Vinisha Umashankar created Iron Max, a solar-powered ironing cart which avoids using charcoal; a modern approach for a traditional occupation.

↳ Revive our oceans: Sam Teicher and Gator Halpern founded Coral Vita, which grows resilient coral on land which is then replanted in the seas to restore damaged reefs.

↳ Build a waste-free world: the WOTA BOX is a home unit for wastewater treatment. It was designed by Yosuke Maeda and is 50

times as efficient as traditional wastewater
collection and treatment.

↳ Fix our climate: Pacific island-born
Vaitea Cowan, now working in Germany,
co-founded Enapter, which uses water
electrolysis to generate hydrogen
from renewable energy at times when
renewables are generating a surplus. One of
her ambitions is to make Polynesia entirely
energy self-sufficient.

I want to end with three quotations:

'Ever tried. Ever failed. No matter. Try again. Fail again. Fail better.'

– Samuel Beckett, the Irish playwright and Nobel prize winner

I have a lithograph portrait of Beckett with this quotation in my study and it is
a principle to which I adhere and which I advocate. The biggest failure is to do
nothing. Do something. Try to make it a success. But if it isn't, then learn from
what you have done and try again. Eventually you will succeed.

**'I would like to invite you to go on a journey together, a journey
of transformation and of action, made not so much of words but
rather of concrete and pressing actions … we have to imagine
new solutions and commit to carrying them out.'**

– Pope Francis, TED Talk, 2020

**'Get out of your chair, step out into life … There is no Tomorrow,
There is only Now.'**

– Alan Cooke, award-winning Irish bard

And if things don't work out

If things don't work out, we can always prepare for catastrophe. Whether it's a solar flare that knocks out the power grid for weeks and months, or a wildfire that engulfs your community, or a nuclear world war, or a meteor strike which creates the next Ice Age, we can be prepared. There is a growing 'Prepper Movement' of people who are planning their escape to somewhere safe, which could be an underground bunker or some other safe space which they have stocked with supplies of food and water to keep going until it is safe to emerge. They will have a 'bug-out bag' with everything needed to get from where they are to their place of safety. This will enable them to leave instantly when danger looms. They will have planned their route, and maybe buried food and drink and fuel along the way. Preppers want to be prepared right now because if they wait, it will already be too late. Find out more about prepping and read these books: *Bunker: Building for the End Times* by Bradley Garrett and *Notes from an Apocalypse: A Personal Journey to the End of the World and Back* by Mark O'Connell.

If prepping doesn't provide you with the answer, then you have another option. You could escape to Mars. Its scenery is stunning. The travel guide will tell you that it has mountains higher than Everest and canyons deeper than the Grand Canyon. It might once have been (and indeed still may be) a life-bearing planet. It's a new world, ripe for exploration and discovery.

So when our planet Earth has become uninhabitable, perhaps Mars is an escape option – at least, for those who can afford to get there. It will require technological innovation on a huge scale to enable us to travel into space and to set up home on another planet. The journey to Mars would take between 150 and 300 days and will not be without its dangers – exposure to cosmic and other radiation, prolonged weightlessness on the journey, the chance that things might go wrong. NASA has been doing all sorts of concept design, experimentation and feasibility studies, and Elon Musk's SpaceX programme has publicly announced a vision to begin the colonisation of Mars and to develop the transport infrastructure needed to get there.

READ THIS:
Packing for Mars: The Curious Science of Life in The Void by Mary Roach, 2011.

WATCH THIS:
A completely different film with the same title by Thierry Robert, 2018, on YouTube.

JOIN THIS:
The Mars Society describes itself as 'the world's largest and most influential space advocacy organisation dedicated to the human exploration and settlement of the planet Mars'. It was founded in 1998. Or you could just stay on Earth and try your very best to make things work out!

Acknowledgements

This book was researched and written in a 'window of opportunity' provided by the Covid-19 lockdown, when it became my 'big project' undertaken in the first 16 weeks to keep myself sane and active, at a time when much of my other work was inevitably having to take a back seat. I don't want to thank the world for giving me this opportunity, but for all of us this crisis could be a time to reflect on how we might do things differently and better as we emerge from it. The cities where we live have become less polluted, our CO_2 emissions are down, we are wasting less, we are more engaged with our children's and grandchildren's education, we are more neighbourly. The global economy is faltering and we know that we need more resilience and to give much more attention to those who have been losing out. Now should be a time for us to find ways of living and being which are better for the planet and better for all our futures.

I would like to thank Nat Jenkins for reading the first draft of the manuscript and providing me with his reflections on the issues together with his ideas and examples, many of which appear in the final text.

I also need to thank Tim Berners-Lee for giving us the internet, Jimmy Wales for giving us Wikipedia, Max Roser for giving us Our World in Data, and my thanks too for all the other information sources that I have accessed, including Worldometers, World Bank Open Data and other sources which bring together statistics on many world problems. Information on its own is not enough. It needs to lead to understanding, and that understanding needs to lead to action. Small actions by all of us are just as important as big ideas and big solutions.

I would like to thank the team from September for believing in me, and for doing the hard work of turning my manuscript into a book: Hannah MacDonald, publisher; Charlotte Cole, editorial director; Liz Marvin, copyeditor; and Emily Sear, designer.

Finally, like all authors, I should thank my immediate family. My wife, Dame Hilary Blume, who does amazing work in encouraging philanthropy through 'Good Gifts' and in getting the world knitting through 'Knit for Peace', and my children, Toby, Joby and Poppy, who, in their different ways, have each absorbed the values of social justice and the importance of engagement, and to their children for their futures for the world that they will inherit from my generation.

About the author

Michael Norton is a social entrepreneur who creates projects that provide innovative approaches to solving problems in society and the world. His smallest project – developing a self-help group for homeless people – was founded with a £2,000 innovation grant from Crisis in 1995. This started with a Wednesday afternoon club for homeless people to work together on projects that were important to them. This led to the creation of Groundswell, a national federation of homeless self-help groups. His largest project was the creation of UnLtd, the UK foundation for social entrepreneurs, which was set up with a £100 million legacy fund from the UK lottery, which makes awards to individuals with ideas. He has created street children's banks and village libraries in Asia, helped develop an international network of crisis helplines for children in need, developed projects which promote financial literacy for young people, mental wellbeing of adolescents, collecting and cooking surplus food, environmental awareness and action, community engagement and philanthropy for young people and much more. He is a professor at the China Global Philanthropy Institute in Shenzhen, winner of the 2014 UK Charity Award for lifetime achievement and was awarded an OBE in 1998 for services to the voluntary sector.

His books include *365 Ways to Change the World*, offering small ideas every day to encourage people to address many of the world's big issues, *The Everyday Activist* and *Click2Change*.